PADRE PIO
THE STIGMATIST

Photo courtesy of Our Lady of Grace Capuchin Friary,
San Giovanni Rotondo, Italy

Padre Pio
1887 – 1968

PADRE PIO
THE STIGMATIST

by
Rev. Charles Mortimer Carty

TAN BOOKS AND PUBLISHERS, INC.
Rockford, Illinois 61105

Imprimatur: ✠John Gregory Murray
                Archbishop of St. Paul

Copyright © 1963 by Radio Replies Press, St. Paul, Minnesota.

Copyright © 1973 by TAN Books and Publishers, Inc. Retypeset and republished by TAN Books and Publishers, Inc. in 1989. (41st printing).

Library of Congress Catalog Card No.: 88-51884

ISBN: 0-89555-355-4

The 120 photographs used in this book are inserted with the permission of the copyright owner. For copies of pictures, address Signor Frederico Abresch, San Giovanni Rotondo, Foggia, Italy.

Printed and bound in the United States of America.

TAN BOOKS AND PUBLISHERS, INC.
P.O. Box 424
Rockford, Illinois 61105

1989

"It would be easier for the earth to carry on without the sun than without the Holy Mass."

—Padre Pio

CONTENTS

Publisher's Preface

Twenty-five years after the first publication of Father Charles Carty's *Padre Pio—The Stigmatist* in 1963, this book is still probably the best edition in English on this saintly and renowned friar. TAN took over publication of the book in 1971 at the 26th printing; we are now in the 41st printing. This latest edition has been retypeset to change the book over from present tense, as it was in the original, to past tense, since Padre Pio is now deceased, having gone to his eternal reward on September 23, 1968. In every other respect it is verbatim—complete and unabridged—as Fr. Carty wrote it.

I have always felt that God was pleased with this book. For, as one of the first titles that TAN published, it was immediately very successful, and it has remained very popular over the years, despite other biographies of Padre Pio having been issued.

We are pleased, therefore, to reissue this gem, trusting that the provocative rendition of Father Carty will inspire the Faithful with the firm conviction that saints are living even in our present day, and that we have recently witnessed the passing of a saint equal to the greatest. Perhaps many of us will live to see Padre Pio canonized, though we leave that possibility in God's hands. At this time we wish simply to present again to the reading public Father Carty's *Padre Pio—The Stigmatist*, because it is difficult to imagine that any book could better convey the spirit and inspiration of this holy man—a saintly priest who was and is one of God's greatest gifts to the Church in the 20th century.

Thomas A. Nelson
Publisher
December 28, 1988

Preface to the Tenth Edition

During the month of July, 1952, I had for the second time the opportunity and privilege of visiting Padre Pio and his brethren at the Capuchin Monastery of Madonna delle Grazie at San Giovanni Rotondo, Foggia, Italy. Although I had heard very much about Padre Pio from my dogma professor, Monsignor Bonardi, at the Archbishop's Seminary in Florence, Italy during my fourth year of theology in 1923, I never had the privilege of seeing Padre Pio celebrate Mass until my first visit to San Giovanni in April of 1950. It was then and there, after that Mass which spellbound Catholics and non-Catholics alike, that I made up my mind to publish the first English book on this first priest to be stigmatized. I wanted to acquaint my fellow Americans with his existence and his extraordinary works and accomplishments in winning souls by the thousands back to God through his hours of labor in the confessional. As St. John Vianney is called the great confessor of France, so today Padre Pio is widely known throughout the world as the great confessor of Italy.

Before going to San Giovanni in 1952 I visited Fragneto l'Abate, where most of the Italian colony of St. Paul, Minnesota, came from. This town is but three miles away from the town of Pietrelcina, where Padre Pio was born in 1887. After preaching at both Sunday Masses to the people of Fragneto l'Abate I went over to Pietrelcina to photograph the room in which Padre Pio was born, the church where he was baptized, the favorite nook where he studied and prayed near his birthplace, the people associated with him in childhood and the various and numerous individuals who confirmed many of the points brought out in this book. All these places and persons were pointed out to me by Michael Forgione, the only living brother of Padre Pio, and by Padre Alberto, the Father Guardian of the new Capuchin Monastery at Pietrelcina. I stood on the spot where Padre Pio as a young seminarian prophesied the future erection of a monastery. The details about this prophecy I obtained from the archives of the monastery and from the Father Guardian, Padre Alberto.

Pietrelcina, a little town in the province of Benevento, has a population of about 5,000 and is mighty proud of being the birthplace of the first stigmatized priest. The town, which is preeminently devoted to agriculture, is about six miles from Benevento by railroad. There are two churches in Pietrelcina. The Mother or Parish Church was recently renovated and beautified through donations from the Italian immigrants of Pietrelcina who for the most part are now living in New York City and Jamaica, Long Island. There is also the little church of St. Ann where Padre Pio as a child, a cleric, and a young priest, passed many long hours of both day and night in prayer and meditation. When Padre Pio was still a seminarian he often passed long periods at Pietrelcina for reasons of health. He assiduously frequented the church and assisted devoutly at Mass and sacred devotions. Amongst the seminarians from the town he, the humble brother, was the most esteemed and beloved by the pastor, his own cousin Don Salvatore Pannullo, for his extraordinary kindness and humility. One evening, whilst the young seminarian was out for a walk with Archpriest Pannullo and with other seminarians along the road which forks one way to Benevento and the other to Pesco Sannita, he suddenly called the attention of everyone and exclaimed out loud, "What a beautiful odor of incense and what beautiful chanting of Friars. Someday there will arise a monastery on that spot," indicating with his finger the exact spot where the monastery and the church would be built. It was a prophecy. Whilst his companions laughed it off, Archpriest Pannullo exclaimed: "If it is the desire of Heaven, it would be the greatest fortune for Pietrelcina."

In 1922 the prophecy became a reality. Miss Mary McAlpin Pyle of New York, a former Presbyterian, became a Catholic as a result of watching Padre Pio say Mass. After her conversion, she lived in her villa within the shadows of the monastery where Padre Pio had lived after 1917. She was the beloved spiritual child of Padre Pio, to whom she confessed every Wednesday in the garb of a Franciscan Tertiary which she always wore. With the enthusiasm of the people, this great soul spent her entire fortune to bring about the fulfillment of that prophecy and the great heart's desire of Padre Pio. She gave her heart and her capital to build that monastery and church to bring about the reality of the odor of incense and the chanting of friars.

His Eminence Cardinal Luigi Lavitrano blessed the first stone, and the monastery was finished in 1926.

In 1928 the cornerstone of the church was laid with this inscription:

"The year of Our Lord 1928, the 24th of May, his Eminence Luigi Lavitrano most worthy Archbishop of Benevento placed this stone cut from the quarry of this countryside, the first of the Church dedicated to the Holy Family, to St. Francis of Assisi, by the faithful of Pietrelcina in the presence of the commission presided over by the Major Doctor Rodigo Crafa. Receive, O Lord, the petitions, the prayers and the acts of love of this Thy people, who today in the holiness of the liturgy consecrate it to the Divine Family, under the intercession of Thy Levite, Francis of Assisi."

The work was suspended when only a few feet of the walls of the church were built. Work was resumed in 1949, and in two years the present artistic Romanesque church was finished to resound to the chanting and psalmody of the friars who now occupy that monastery, united with the choirs of Heaven.

English speaking visitors to Padre Pio could always be the recipients of Miss Mary Pyle's gracious hospitality and her treasury of knowledge on Padre Pio events. Most of her time was spent as host to the American and English visitors, and in particular to the boys in the military services who flocked there by the hundreds. Miss Pyle, who spent all her capital on this monastery, accepted donations to complete the equipment of this church at Padre Pio's birthplace. Miss Pyle purchased for the Capuchins the one-room house in which Padre Pio was born, for a future chapel, and also the house of two rooms which Padre Pio's father was able to buy with his first earnings as a laborer at Jamaica, L.I., in 1898.

On June 30, 1952, I arrived at this hallowed town of San Giovanni Rotondo to study the events recently connected with Padre Pio and to have the privilege of being embraced by him on three occasions in the Franciscan and European custom of cheek to cheek. I was present at several of his Masses to study the changing expressions of his face in his prolonged minutes of either contemplation or ecstasy. I marveled at his wit in recreation and rejoiced at his human gruffness as he shouted, with his booming voice, commands to the noisy congregation to keep silence and to kneel for the prayers at the beginning of Mass.

In conclusion I am very grateful to Miss Mary Pyle and to the secretaries of Padre Pio for their kind and gracious hospitality and for their account of various happenings brought out in this twenty-fifth edition on Padre Pio the Stigmatist.

AUTHOR'S DECLARATION

With regard to the special revelations that have been made to the saints, belief in them is not required by the Church even when she approves them. By this approbation she only intends to declare that nothing is to be found in them contrary to faith or morals, and that they can be accepted without danger and even with advantage. Whatever the author of this book mentions as a revelation does not demand consent of the reader as involving an obligation of revealed truth.

Benedict XIV is very clear on this subject. "What is to be said of those private revelations which the Apostolic See has approved of, those of the Blessed

Hildegard (which were approved in part by Eugene III), of St. Bridget (by Boniface IX), and of St. Catherine of Siena (by Gregory XI)? We have already said that those revelations, although approved of, ought not and cannot, receive from us any assent as embracing Catholic faith, but only human credence, in keeping with the rules of prudence, according to which the aforesaid revelations are probable and may be piously believed."

When the Church approves revelations, they are merely received as probable and not as indubitable. They are to be used as is customary in deciding questions of history, natural philosophy, or theology, which are matters of controversy between the doctors. It is quite permissible to differ with these revelations, even when approved, if we are relying upon solid reasons, and especially if the contrary doctrine is proved by unimpeachable documents and definite experience.

In presenting this volume the author declares his sincere submission to the decree of Urban VIII, the Canons of the Church, and the decrees of the Holy See.

To the prodigious facts narrated in this book with normal historical criticism, in view of human testimony, he attributes a purely human credence.

REV. CHARLES MORTIMER CARTY

Introduction
by Barbara Ward

Those who read this book will obtain some idea of the spiritual power and impressiveness of PADRE PIO'S personality, but I am certain that those who have had the grace of meeting him face to face will also carry away a most vivid memory of his downright common sense and intensely practical attitude towards life. Now the chief fact about life in the south of Italy and indeed about the lives of nine-tenths of the people who came to PADRE PIO for comfort is unrelieved poverty. This in its turn is the root of so many neglected diseases, lifelong ill health, cripplings, blindness, infirmities and miseries—all the tragic load that had to be born by "Brother Ass," the weight of suffering which, day after day, was the spectacle upon which PADRE PIO had to look from the moment he entered the church at dawn until the last penitents went on their way.

PADRE PIO was the last man in the world to let his friends forget that Our Lord not only preached to souls but also healed bodies and promised Heaven to those who feed the hungry and clothe the naked. If people are sick, they need medical care. If there is to be medical care, there must be doctors and hospitals. If PADRE PIO'S work was to be done to the full, the hospital needed to be in San Giovanni Rotondo, where sick pilgrims streamed in and nursed. Medical services even for the local people were quite inadequate. This was the common sense of the situation as PADRE PIO saw it, and from his friends he expected the common sense reaction of practical support for his project. That those who sent their gifts for the completion and steady operation of the hospital also played some part in a great venture of the spirit goes without saying. This book is evidence enough of blessings and graces and joys without number. But these are the uncovenanted mercies. What each one who felt friendship for PADRE PIO can do is share in his realism and help forward, by practical help, the completion of his most practical and charitable plan.

BARBARA WARD

PADRE PIO
THE STIGMATIST

CHAPTER I

His Life

Francesco Forgione, known later to the world as Padre Pio, was born on the 25th of May, 1887, in the village of Pietrelcina near Benevento. His parents, Orazio Forgione and Maria Giuseppa De Nunzio were extremely poor, of peasant stock. There were eight children, three of whom had died in infancy; one brother, Michele, and one sister, Grazia, or Sister Pia, in religion. In order to support his family, Orazio Forgione made two trips to the United States, where he worked as a laborer in Jamaica, Long Island.

We have little information about his childhood. Francesco was a quiet and deeply religious boy; he could never tolerate blasphemy and when he heard the name of God, Our Lord or the Blessed Virgin taken in vain he would run off and hide weeping, and kneel down in some corner to pray. As he grew older he avoided games and arguments with his classmates and was shy and retiring. He says of himself that from childhood he was *"un macherone senza sale,"* or a noodle without salt—in other words, a colorless character.

Zi' Orazio, Uncle Orazio, as Padre Pio's father was known to his neighbors, used to tell how one day as he was watching his older boy Michele working in the fields under the hot Italian sun, he turned to Francesco and said, "I am never going to let you see the sun!" When the child asked him what he meant by such a statement he said: "I am going to have you study to become a monk." Francesco protested that there was not enough money to make this possible, but his father answered that he would go to New York and earn what was needed. This in fact is what he did, and we have the good man to thank for his powers of observation and his courage.

The teacher who was at first chosen for little Francesco was not a success, and when we consider the character of the small pupil, it is easy to understand. What seems strange to us is that his parents should have even attempted the experiment. Dom Domenico Tizzani had been relieved of his duties as a parish priest because he had ignored his vows of celibacy. Francesco's mind seemed closed to all knowledge, in spite of Don Domenico's efforts to the contrary. The little boy was in the habit of serving Mass every morning in the parish church before going to his class. This annoyed the ex-priest, who complained that he was wasting his time—and he finally went to Francesco's mother and told her that her child had better go to work in the fields as he had no brains for book learning, and they were wasting their money and his time. When Francesco was told this, the usually gentle and silent lad flared up in great indignation: "My head is no good? You mean that his head is no good! He is living in sin in his own house!" Francesco was only seven at the time, but his horror of sin was so great that he could detect its presence, innocent as he was, and that presence seemed to paralyze his faculties.

Francesco was taken away from his books and back to the farmhouse, two miles from town. There he moped and mourned, seeing his dream of a religious life shattered.

Zi' Orazio was away while this was going on. He was working as a day laborer in New York, trying to make it possible for his Francesco to be educated for the priesthood. He must have had some inkling of the difficulties in the situation, although it seems doubtful that either he or his wife were equipped to carry on any detailed correspondence. In any case he became worried by the fact that Francesco was studying with a man whose life was anything but a good example to his pupil, and for this very reason the authorities might refuse him admission in the school. He wrote home telling his wife to remove Francesco from Don Domenico and find him a more suitable teacher.

The choice fell upon Maestro Caccavo, about whom we know little beyond the fact that he was not a priest, and that he owed money to Don Domenico. He first refused to take the child, fearing reprisals from that quarter, but he was finally persuaded by threats and entreaties. Padre Pio's mother, Maria Giuseppa, was not easily discouraged, and enlisted the help of Maestro Caccavo's brother-in-law, who responded effectively with the pronouncement that all connections between the two houses would cease and that his wife, Caccavo's sister, would never speak to him again unless he took Francesco as a pupil. This simple method resolved the situation, and Francesco went back to his books. Maestro Caccavo may not have been deeply learned, but a few months later he told Maria Giuseppa that Francesco was making such strides that *he* would soon be teaching *him*.

A consoling sequel to this whole episode is that Dom Domenico later repented of his sins and died shriven and anointed in the arms of his former pupil, Padre Pio di Pietrelcina.

Francesco made rapid progress in his studies and soon passed the examinations required by the Capuchin Friars to enter their school. He was much beloved of both schoolmates and teachers. His great goodness and simplicity were free of any trace of priggishness. The Superior told someone one day that "This child seems to observe the rules better than we do!" Whenever the other boys wanted to obtain some favor they always turned to Francesco to negotiate the deal. On one occasion the school had been given a two-day leave. This was not long enough for some of the boys who lived far away and who would have to spend most of the free time in traveling to and from home. They appealed to Francesco, whose home was nearby and who therefore did not share their problem; he must ask the Superior for an extension of time. The boy was unusually shy and disliked the job assigned to him, but he also hated to disappoint his friends, so he plucked up his courage and went to the Superior to ask for the extra day. The Superior looked surprised and then said: "Ah, yes, I understand, you are asking for your friends. Well, give them the good news, their vacation has been extended."

In 1902, Francesco Forgione entered the Capuchin Monastery at Morcone, in the province of Benevento, to begin his year of novitiate. The community life, with its prescribed fasts and rigorous discipline, must have been a strain on the delicate constitution of

Francesco, for when his parents saw him at the end of a year they were so shocked by his emaciated appearance and his pale face that they thought that their son was being starved to death, and begged the Father Director to let them take him home. He assured Zi' Orazio and Maria Giuseppa that their boy was getting plenty to eat; that what he probably needed was a change of air. He was sent to S. Elia in Panisi, where he stayed for four years.

In spite of the change of air, Fra Pio's health did not improve. He was subject to frequent bouts of very high fever, which would disappear as suddenly as they came. For long periods of time he could retain no food, and it is said that he once subsisted for twenty-one days on no other nourishment but the sacred Host, while at the same time his faithful observance of the rules of community life was in no way impaired. He spent many hours in prayer, and so great was his respect for his sacred duties that he was often seen reading his textbooks on his knees.

His life of prayer and penance was interfered with by other than physical obstacles such as fevers and nausea; he was tormented by vicious attacks by evil spirits, as though the powers of darkness were putting up a desperate fight to destroy this little monk who was going to prove to be so powerful an adversary. Pio told no one but his confessor of these visitations, but many stories have since been given to the public and they remind us of the terrifying experiences that were so frequent in the life of St. John Vianney, the Curé d'Ars. He, too, was a great warrior before the Lord, and was accountable for the salvation of thousands of souls.

Fra Pio's cell was often visited in his absence, and he would find everything in dire confusion, books torn, blankets strewn on the floor, and ink spattered all over the walls. This was not all, however, for he often found himself surrounded by hideous monsters who jeered insults at him and challenged him to do battle. Sometimes the demons came disguised as monks. One of these appeared as his old confessor, Padre Agostino, who exhorted him to give up his life of asceticism and penance, assuring him that God did not approve of his way of life. Fra Pio was shocked and bewildered by the tirade, but had the presence of mind to order the monk to cry out with him: *"Viva Gesu!"* It had the immediate effect of causing the apparition to vanish, leaving no trace behind but a sulfurous stench.

At another time, on a hot summer's night, Fra Pio could not sleep. He heard someone walking up and down in the cell next to his, and thinking that it was Fra Anastasio, who was also being kept awake by the heat, he went to the window to exchange a few words of sympathy about the weather—but what was his horror and amazement at seeing a monstrous black dog sitting on the neighboring windowsill, staring at him with wild ferocious eyes! Pio had no time to cry out before the creature gave a tremendous leap and vanished over the housetop. The next day he found out that Fra Anastasio had been previously moved to another cell, and that his room had been empty that night.

Fra Pio's health, which must have been very poor indeed, began at last to cause some concern to his superiors. They had him examined by a doctor who declared him to be tubercular. This did not interfere with his chosen vocation, however, and he was ordained to the priesthood on August 10th, 1910, in the Cathedral of Benevento. On the following day he said his first Mass at Pietrelcina, and on Sunday, August 14th he sang his first Solemn High Mass in the Church of St. Mary of the Angels where he had received the Sacrament of Baptism twenty-three years earlier.

One fact must have caused real disappointment to the young priest; his father had been forced to leave his family once again in search of a livelihood, and had left for America almost on the eve of the great day. It is good to know that Zi' Orazio was able to celebrate the event with his fellow immigrants in Jamaica, and that he was able to enjoy some of the honors that were being showered upon his son.

Padre Pio was stationed at Foggia after his ordination. His health gave him increasing trouble and from time to time he was sent home for a rest. It is during one of these visits that he underwent some mystical experience that marked him as a victim, a living witness of the Passion of Christ. We only know where the scene was laid; for, of the drama that culminated three years later in the chapel stalls of San Giovanni Rotondo, Padre Pio told no one but his confessor.

It happened on a hot summer day, in the beginning of September, 1915. Padre Pio had built himself a little hut in the back of his father's garden to shelter himself from the sun and give him a place where he could study and pray in peace. It is not difficult to reconstruct the scene; Bellini painted one like it which hangs on the walls of the Frick Gallery in New York. St. Francis of Assisi is depicted as a thin young man, standing with outstretched hands and gazing into the blue Italian sky. He stands in front of a rather flimsy erection of saplings and leafy branches like a hastily constructed summer house. A book and a crucifix are the only furnishings. There is a little hilltown in the distance; a man is ploughing a neighboring field, and a bird is singing in the tree over his head. The landscape is peaceful and smiling, and the quiet pace of rural life is following the rhythm of the day. Only in the face of St. Francis is there a blaze of white light. Was he transported like St. Paul to the Seventh Heaven and did he hear those mysterious words that no man can understand? We do not know, but we do know that he bore the wounds of that encounter for the rest of his life.

Padre Pio had been praying all morning. It was noon now, and a drowsy peace had settled on the garden. The country noises had given way to the stillness of midday, when people eat and rest from their labors. Maria Giuseppa's chickens were crooning a sort of lullaby in the farmyard. The silence was suddenly broken by the familiar strident call that dinner was ready. Maria Giuseppa had brought her men in from the fields with that far carrying note for many years. Pio, trained by years of obedience, left his retreat and hurried to the house. His mother stood at the kitchen door, watching for him. As he came across the garden she saw that he was waving his hands in the air as though they had been stung by bees. "Are you playing the guitar, Francesco?" she called out to him. "No," he answered with a smile, "but I have stinging pains in my hands." And he let it go at that. It was the 20th of September, 1915, and the parish was commemorating the Stigmata of St. Francis of Assisi.

Italy became involved in the First World War, and Padre Pio was called up for military duty. He was given a uniform of twice his size and placed in the medical corps. Although military life must have been distasteful to him, he made no complaint and performed whatever duties were assigned to him. His tubercular condition became apparent, however, and he was sent home to rest for a few weeks. He returned to duty at the military hospital at Naples, but was again sent home, this time for a six months' furlough. It is not perfectly clear just what happened at the end of these six months. Padre Pio was transferred by his superiors to San Giovanni Rotondo. The authorities, seeing that he did not return to them after the expiration of his sickleave, sent out tracers. There seems to have resulted a sort of Mozartian farce of confused identities.

The emissary of the army was sent to Pietrelcina to look for a certain Francesco Forgione, a deserter. He could find no trace of him, and no one seemed willing or able to help him. After combing the neighborhood he came across one of Padre Pio's sisters, who told him that the missing man was her brother, and was at San Giovanni Rotondo. A new set of inquiries were sent off in that direction, but with equal lack of success. No one there had ever heard of Francesco Forgione. The weary messenger finally visited the monastery, and there repeated his question. This time he was rewarded; Francesco Forgione was there, only he was now known as Padre Pio. The final scene in the little drama may well be the result of one of the many practical jokes that the angels seemed to play for Padre Pio to get him out of difficulties. He was brought before the captain of the district and roundly accused of deserting from the army. Padre Pio produced his furlough papers, which clearly stated that he was to go home for six months and *await instructions.* "My instructions did not come to me until today." He did return to the army, but after one month he was given a final discharge "for reasons of health." He was offered a pension, which he refused, saying that he had done nothing to earn it.

Padre Pio was now settled for good in San Giovanni Rotondo, the isolated monastery from whence his influence would before long be felt in every corner of the globe. Succeeding civilizations have woven a close pattern over the Italian Peninsula and it is impossible to study any part of it without finding traces of fallen empires and pagan cults of great antiquity whose temples and monuments were gradually adapted as Christian churches. San Giovanni Rotondo is no exception to this. It was originally the site of a temple to the god Janus, the Roman deity whose two faces gazed at the same time on the past and on the future. The name *"Rotondo"* reminds us that the temple was circular. It was succeeded by a church dedicated to St. John. The little town is situated in the very barren district overlooking the Adriatic known as the Gargano Peninsula; its highest peak is Monte Calvo. From earliest times it has been the site of pilgrimages, for like Mount Carmel in the Holy Land, its barren beauty seemed to offer a refuge from the market-places of the world, and men went there to breathe the purer air of the spirit and commune with God. There is a cave on the eastern slope of the mountain where the ancients believed that the god Apollo had done battle with a mythical monster representing the forces of evil. It was considered even in those remote times as a holy and mysterious spot. Christian tradition tells us that the Archangel Michael routed the devil in that same cave, and later appeared to some shepherds demanding that a church be erected in his honor to commemorate the event. It became, and still is, immensely popular as a shrine; and the feast of the Apparition of St. Michael on May 8th is celebrated all over the Catholic world.

When Padre Pio first came to San Giovanni Rotondo, he found a very poor and primitive mountain village that was reached by a rough road traveled mostly on foot or on mule-back. It was a steep climb, as it lay halfway up Monte Gargano, at a height of about 1,800 feet above sea level; Foggia and Manfredonia were the nearest cities and lay fourteen and twenty-five miles away, respectively. A mile and a half above San Giovanni, the little Capuchin Friary of Santa Maria delle Grazie clung to the rocky hillside. The church still is a small, square building, lacking any kind of a facade. The door is not even in the middle of the wall, and the bell that surmounts the whole is the only indication of its ecclesiastical nature. The two-story convent with its row of tiny windows clings to one side of it as if for protection. A stone well in the courtyard provided the water supply for the needs of the community. As we are told by an inscription over the narrow door, the church which had been previously dedicated to Our Lady of Grace was rebuilt in the year of Our Lord 1616. St. Camillus of Lellis made his novitiate here.

Padre Pio settled down to a life of prayer and obscurity and spent about a year in this peaceful pursuit. The Capuchin Fathers celebrated the feast of the Stigmata of St. Francis on the 17th of September in that year of 1918 as they had for centuries. It happened to fall on a Wednesday; the following Friday, the 20th, Padre Pio was in the choir alone making his thanksgiving after Mass. When a piercing cry rent the silence of the chapel, one of the monks, Padre Leone, ran to the choir. He found Padre Pio lying on the floor unconscious, bleeding profusely from five deep wounds in his hands, in his feet and in his side.

He was carefully lifted by his brethren and removed to his cell, where he soon regained consciousness, begging the monks to respect his secret.

Some secrets are too hard to keep, or else they are not meant to be kept; at any rate this one was not, and the news spread swiftly all over that wild region, where there were scarcely any roads and where telephones must have been almost unknown. People came flocking in droves to see "The Saint," and to kneel before him in the confessional.

The Church is consistently distrustful of such outward manifestations, which are often and rightly branded as hysteria. The Father Provincial of the Capuchins of Foggia had the wounds photographed and sent the photographs to the Vatican for the record and for instructions, and invited Dr. Luigi Romanelli of Barletta to pass on the medical aspects of the case. There followed for the next few years what must have been the equivalent of a prolonged martyrdom for Padre Pio. Besides the constant pain he suffered from his wounds, he was repeatedly subjected to the most persistent and trying medical investigations, as well as to every variety of attempted cure. Nothing, however, changed the character of the wounds. They never closed, they never stopped bleeding, neither did they ever become infected, whether they were covered with unguents and air-tight bandages or the dark woolen socks and mittens that he wore for many years. Volumes have been written on the subject with the most detailed medical reports, the clearest of which, by Dr. Festa of Rome, has been reproduced in the back of this volume. The authorities finally decreed that the poor man was to be left in peace, and that no more cures could be attempted and no more examinations made. What all can see is that he could not close his hands, that it was difficult for him to tie a knot when vesting for Mass, and that walking was painful; he came down the altar steps backward when distributing Communion to save his wounded feet.

Padre Pio never talked about himself and was never known to complain; but on being asked by some foolish person if his wounds hurt, he replied lightly: "Do you think that the Lord gave them to me for a decoration?"

The Church, being well versed in mass psychology, silenced Padre Pio everywhere but in the confessional, which was for years his only battleground. He could not write letters and he could not preach, but although this may seem to some a harsh and unnecessary restriction, no one can fail to observe the miraculous abundance of his harvest of souls; his faithful obedience to the commands of his superiors repaid him a hundredfold. Without these lines being drawn there would have undoubtedly occurred a sort of mob canonization during his lifetime, and the good man himself must have been the first to appreciate the protection to his humility and his privacy. A very few of his writings exist from the days before the ban, and a selection from them will be found in this volume.

During one of the many physical examinations, the doctors declared his lungs to be absolutely free of any sign of tuberculosis. We only know that this cure must have taken place in the same year that he received the stigmata.

CHAPTER II

His Work

Padre Pio lost the frail appearance of his youth. He became a stocky, vigorous man of middle height. His hair and beard were mostly gray, but his eyes were penetrating and bright with the fire and strength of an apostle's. He had the quick wit and the homely speech of a man of the soil; his expressions were often earthy, but his meaning was clear and his manner always frank and direct. His powers of endurance were phenomenal, for he sat in the confessional for long hours every day, giving his most meticulous attention to the endless problems of conscience and tales of infidelities to the laws of God, without any perfunctory or routine handling of his penitents. He never failed to go to the heart of the matter, and his powers of observation—as well as his knowledge of hidden truths—could only be described as miraculous.

Excepting for the stigmata, which caused him to suffer real pain and impede his motion, Padre Pio was a healthy man. He was operated on for a hernia in 1929, and refused all anaesthetic. We have the account of this by the same Dr. Festa of Rome, who had also made the original examination of the stigmata. His report will be found at the end of the book.

Padre Pio arose at 3:30 every morning, and at five he said Mass. In the early days the little square before the chapel of Santa Maria delle Grazie was almost always full of people by two in the morning. They waited for hours in the most inclement weather for the doors to open so that they might get a good place near the altar for Mass, and then push their way to the confessional ahead of the others. The women were heard in the morning and the men in the afternoon. In the last few years of his life the confusion was put to an end.

Those who desired to go to confession to Padre Pio had to be able to speak Latin or Italian, and they had to register their names. When my secretary, who spoke Italian, registered for confession she learned that her ticket number would be called in ten days. This gives you an idea how many confessions Padre Pio heard each day. Appointments for confession could not be made by a third person or by telegram in order to avoid a delayed stay at San Giovanni Rotondo. One priest was allowed to register for every five laymen.

Padre Pio's parish embraced the whole world, for his influence reached across both hemispheres. People came to him as much for advice and correction as for the support he gave them. His loving kindness and compassion made him the most comforting of friends.

We have many accounts of Padre Pio's Mass, which was the great daily occasion at San Giovanni Rotondo. At the moment when Padre Pio made the Sign of the Cross at the foot of the altar of St. Francis of Assisi, his face was transfigured. He was no longer the simple smiling priest who celebrated the Divine Sacrifice, but he was the man of God, chosen to give testimony of His existence, chosen to collaborate with Jesus in the continued martyrdom of the five wounds of the Passion; it might almost be said that he died mystically in each Mass that he said. The people who crowded about him were all deeply affected and unaware of the passage of time as they remained in silent prayer for the hour and 10 minutes that it took before he left the altar. He made a prolonged thanksgiving and then took a glass of water as his breakfast before going to the sacristy to hear the confessions of the men.

At noon he took his only meal of the day. He drank wine, sometimes three tumblers at a time. He did not take milk because it was only served at breakfast with the coffee. He ate meat sometimes, but preferred vegetables, fish and cheese. He had to be careful of his diet, as he had been subject to attacks of indigestion since his student days. His midday meal was never a heavy one.

On very warm days, as he worked before his desk, he drank big glasses of water or sometimes a little coffee or anise. In the evenings while he read or studied he sipped a bottle of beer which at a certain hour was brought to his cell. Generally, before midnight this bottle was finished; but it was difficult to estimate how much he took and how much was consumed by other persons who visited him, to whom he always willingly offered a portion. For some time beer, which seemed to be his preferred drink, was replaced by substitutes such as water with a little sugar and lemon juice. We must marvel that with only 300 or 400 calories of food and with only three or four hours rest at night, he could endure the arduous task of hearing confessions and conversing with hundreds day after day, year after year. He did not eat enough food to make up, in a natural manner, the amount of blood which he lost each day from his wounds. He did not participate in the recitation of the Divine Office with the community because it was too difficult for him to stand so long on account of the wounds in his feet.

One day Padre Pio spoke at the dinner table about the time he was sick with stomach trouble for eight days. He took nothing but a little water during the whole illness. He had weighed himself shortly before. Father Guardian told him to weigh himself after he got up from his eight days' fast. He had gained in the meantime! Then Padre Pio laughed heartily and added: "I think I'll have to eat more to reduce!" Evidently he considered the entire incident as an amusing anecdote.

Besides being a man of God, Padre Pio had a vigorous humor; his conversation was full of fun, and even his quick and sometimes caustic comments in the confessional can never be forgotten. When his friends speak of him they cannot help smiling in affectionate reminiscence of how much he made them laugh. Humor is an indescribable gift; it brings light into the most drab surroundings, it fills everyone with a sense of well-being, a feeling that after all, things cannot be so bad, one can still laugh! Padre Pio's quips are impossible to translate since they were expressed in the homely vernacular and were often a play on words. He was never unkind, but he often brought people up with a round turn when he neatly pointed out to them the folly of their ways or the confusion of their thinking.

Padre Pio, who sought only God and souls and

Upper left: The winsome smile of Padre Pio.
Upper right: 1935.
Lower left: 1940.
Lower right: 1959.

Upper left: A G.I. letter.
Upper right: Before Mass.
Lower left: Humorous petition.
Lower right: Sense of humor.

Upper left and right and lower left and right: Last blessing.
When all can see his exposed stigmata.

Upper left: Church entrance.
Upper right: His father.
Lower left: His mother.
Lower right: Casa Sollievo (Hospital).

preferred the hidden monastic life, was sought by the whole world—literally—by correspondence. In 1963 he received an average of 600 letters a day, about three-fourths of them from Italy. Sometimes the number ran up to 700 or 800. Besides this, he got 50 to 80 telegrams daily.

Where did the letters come from? From every country in Europe, except from behind the Iron Curtain, and even from there some slipped through occasionally from Poland, Hungary, Yugoslavia and Czechoslovakia; from all countries of North, Central and South America; from Canada to the southernmost tip of South America, Africa, Egypt, Eritrea, Tunisia, Nigeria, Uganda, Kenya, Libia, Cerenaica, Gold Coast, South Africa, from the Orient, Australia, New Zealand, India, Pakistan, Ceylon, Solomon Islands and the Seychelles.

It is evident that Padre Pio could not read all these letters; there were too many, and he had too little time after the many hours in the confessional, his Divine Office and other spiritual exercises. Nor could the secretaries translate them or speak to him about them, except in very unusual cases. He had been forbidden to write letters since 1923. Besides, writing was painful for him because of the wound in his hand. He prayed for all who recommended themselves to him. Besides his private prayers and mementos at Mass, the community prayed a perpetual novena to the Sacred Heart for the same intentions, as part of night prayers. Padre Pio led in these prayers.

When the secretaries, therefore, answered the letters, it was an acknowledgment of the petitions and an assurance of these prayers. There were secretaries for the following languages: Italian, English, French, German, Hungarian, Latin, Spanish and Portuguese.

When the letters, besides requests for prayers, also asked for advice or counsel, the secretaries proposed the questions to Padre Pio. But one had to be reasonable. Padre Pio did not wish that questions any confessor could answer be proposed to him. One was to seek the ordinary ways God has given man for spiritual guidance. To other questions such as: Am I in the state of grace? Padre Pio said that if persons had faith in the efficacy of the Sacrament of Penance, they should not put such a question. Or: Am I pleasing to God? Am I on the right path? To questions of what vocation one should choose his usual answer was: "I will pray. As regards their vocation they should consult their Father Confessor."

A very evident truth which some questioners did not seem to realize is that Padre Pio was not omniscient; only God knows all things. Nor was he a fortune-teller. His mission from God, as it seems, was particularly to save souls through his prayers, sufferings and guidance in the confessional.

The healing of the sick, the conversion of sinners, the return of the unfaithful, the gift of scrutinizing and of bilocation, were not the only signs of divine predilection granted with so much largess to our Padre. He possessed the gift of invisibility. It is said that he made the Holy Hour every evening in the House of Loreto, but who saw him? A lay brother, Fra Daniele, asked him one day: "Padre Pio, were you ever in Loreto?" "No." "But, Father, people have seen you there!" "Oh, that is something different." He was not at Loreto as one ordinarily understands it, making a trip to the Holy Shrine. But bilocation is something different. It was surely his most singular gift of all, to pervade the atmosphere of a room—whether he was present or absent—with the perfume about which we shall speak in the following chapter.

Padre Pio sometimes understood people when they spoke a language he did not study. He knew only Italian and Latin, and very little French. He consistently refused to hear confessions except in Italian or Latin. It is not true, therefore, as del Fante reported, that he possessed the apostolic gift of tongues. Those who could confess only in English, German, etc. were sent to other monks by Padre Pio.

The privilege of seeing in creatures and in things that which is hidden was manifested in him from the beginning of his monastic life. In the act of hearing confessions, which took up so much of his time and energies, God aided him by disclosing to his eyes the status of the souls of the penitents and by permitting him to reveal part or even all that he discerned.

This discernment permitted him to solve in a few minutes a task that would normally require a long time, and such a faculty was confirmed by the accuracy of his statements. How could he otherwise tell a penitent the exact number of times he missed Mass on Sundays and Holydays? How could he solve a hundred problems that were proposed to him, without that supernatural aid? How could he answer questions not yet formulated? How could he disclose what is contained in letters without opening them? Whence came the faculty to destroy other letters because they did not merit an answer?

Why he did not answer certain requests in spite

of his good will, he explained himself: "The Lord makes me remember only whom and what He wishes. He in fact, the Lord, often presents to me persons whom I have never seen nor spoken to, save to pray for their favors, which are always heard. On the contrary, however, when the Lord does not wish to hear me He makes me forget to pray for those persons who had every good and firm intention. My forgetfulness is sometimes extended to those more needful things, such as eating, drinking, etc. I thank Providence that He has not allowed me to forget things belonging to my state."

Before anyone spoke, Pio knew whether a caller came with sincerity or pretense, whether he presented himself with the proper disposition or simple curiosity.

A doctor entered the Sacristy and left it without conferring with Pio.

"Where is he?" Pio asked those present, and they answered, "He left." "He will soon return," said Padre Pio with assurance. He returned, and Pio said to the doctor immediately:

"You carry your own condemnation in your pocket; you are a delinquent—read the letter in your pocket." It was the recommendation of a friend that Padre Pio convert the doctor. The doctor read the letter, grew pale, and then, kneeling at the feet of Padre Pio, he asked and obtained pardon.

Even the reading of thoughts at a distance was easy for our Capuchin, and numerous facts prove it. Two sisters obtained, with difficulty, permission from their father to visit Padre Pio, but with the prohibition of kissing the gloved hands which came in contact with so many lips, because the father thought it would bring infection. The girls promised obedience, but when they saw Padre Pio enter the church and the people press forward to kiss his hand, they could not resist the temptation to do the same. He looked at them, smiled and withdrew his hand, saying, "How about the promise?"

Let us consider this prophetic power. If God conceded to His servant the faculty of seeing in the past and in the present, it is clear that He could concede to him the power to see the future. The proofs are innumerable, multiplied above all during the last world war. Every inhabitant of San Giovanni had examples to tell. With all this, Padre Pio sought to keep himself through humility in obscurity and let all believe that he knew nothing. When questioned, he often gave sibylline replies that were clarified in time.

He assured the people of San Giovanni that their town would not be bombed. During the war the Americans had an airbase at Bari, about 75 miles from San Giovanni. There were still Germans in the neighborhood, and the American officer in charge at Bari heard they had a munitions dump in or near San Giovanni Rotondo. So he called his officers, planned a raid and said he would lead in the first plane. He was a Protestant. When they neared San Giovanni Rotondo, he saw high in the air, ahead of his plane, a monk with arms outstretched as if to ward off his coming. The general was stupefied. He ordered the formation to return to base and drop the bombs in an open field where they would do no harm to their landing planes. When he returned to the base and was asked how things had gone, he related what he had seen. An Italian officer told him there was a monk

at San Giovanni Rotondo, whom the people considered a saint. Probably he was the one the officer saw
in the heavens. The officer determined to find out.
He and another officer went to San Giovanni, and
together they went to the sacristy with other laymen
to watch as the fathers came down for Mass. He immediately recognized Padre Pio as the one he had
seen high in the air in front of his plane.

Every time that Padre Pio promised the cure of
a grave illness or other graces in desperate cases, and
when he predicted the sex of an unborn child, was
it not the prophetic spirit that he manifested?

His reticence in some cases was often suggested
by the desire of not making one suffer, and if he was
silent to certain demands it was because God did not
consent to speak to him. In the autumn of 1940, he
predicted that Genoa would be bombed.

One of his spiritual sons asked, "Padre, will they
bomb Genoa?"

With a nod of his head he affirmed that they would
bomb Genoa.

"I am afraid," said his penitent. "Your fear will avail
nothing. Genoa will be bombed." All at once Pio grew
pale, and looking afar his eyes glistened with tears.

"Oh, how they will bomb the poor city. So many
homes, buildings and churches will crumble." Then
he turned and cheerily consoled him saying, "Be calm,
your house will not be touched."

That prediction did not remain a secret. When the
bombs rained down pitilessly on the great city, among
the mass of ruins the only house that remained standing was the one whose preservation had been
predicted. Someone shook his head and said: "Padre

Pio foretold this!"

It was just at the beginning of the war when Padre Pio announced that Italy would be the first nation to seek an armistice, and sadly added, "It is not the war that frightens me, but the postwar."

Dr. Sanguinetti,* who was the director of Pio's hospital project, visited him every evening and from these daily visits he found out much about Padre Pio. He told how one evening in January, 1936, he and two other laymen were in Padre Pio's room. Suddenly Padre Pio knelt down and asked them to pray "for a soul that is soon to appear before the tribunal of God." They all knelt down, and after they arose again Padre Pio asked them, "Do you know for whom you prayed?" They said, "No, except for your intention." He told them, "It was for the King of England." Then the doctor said, "But, Padre Pio, just today I read in the paper that the king has only a slight attack of influenza, and that his condition is not serious." Padre Pio answered, "It is as I say." At that time a young Capuchin, P. Aurelio, was writing the life of one of their fathers who had died having a reputation for sanctity, P. Raffaelle da S. Elia in Pianisi. The morning after the above incident, Dr. Sanguinetti met P. Aurelio in front of the church. P. Aurelio told the doctor he had had a queer experience the night before. While he was writing, he heard a knock at the door, about midnight. When he opened, Padre Pio stood there and said: "Let us pray for a soul, which at this moment is to appear before the tribunal of God, the King of England." The two fathers prayed together for a while and then Padre Pio returned to

*Dr. Sanguinetti died from a heart attack, Sept. 7, 1954.

his room. When the newspapers came that afternoon they announced that the king had died precisely at the time that Padre Pio had been in P. Aurelio's room.

A widow with many children asked Padre Pio whether she should marry again, as there was a man who wanted to marry her. Padre Pio said, "Up to the present you have cried with one eye, but if you marry again you will cry with both eyes."

Unfortunately for this poor woman she did not follow Father's advice and had much to suffer from her new husband; she was even put into prison on his account although she herself was a very good woman.

A mother of five children came with a group of other visitors from Bologna to see Padre Pio. She asked him to accept her as one of his spiritual children and he consented, but owing to the length of the journey and the expense, five years passed before she was again able to visit Padre Pio. In those five years, however, she daily called upon Padre Pio saying, "Padre Pio watch over my children, protect and bless them."

When she did manage to return to San Giovanni Rotondo she went to confession to Padre Pio. When she finished her confession she said, "Padre, please, please watch over my children and protect them." He answered her rather abruptly, "And how many times are you going to ask me the same thing?" With surprise she answered, "This is the first time I ever asked you, Father." And Padre Pio replied, "You have been saying this to me every day now for over five years."

A young woman came from Benevento to ask a grace for her husband who had become totally blind. Having heard that Padre Pio had cured many people, this woman had hoped for a cure. She asked Padre Pio, who told her that her husband's only hope for salvation was to stay blind since his blindness was a punishment which Our Lord had sent upon him for beating his father.

The poor woman could hardly believe this. When she returned to Benevento she told her husband what Padre Pio had revealed to her. At first the husband denied it but later admitted that when he was sixteen years of age he had severely beaten his father with an iron rod.

A Dominican Father found the sisters in a convent at Pompeii divided into two groups. One group was for Padre Pio and the other group, who knew little about him, did not have much faith in him. The Dominican, to settle his doubts, decided to visit Padre Pio in civilian dress.

When he arrived at San Giovanni Rotondo he found Padre Pio hearing the men's confessions in the sacristy. All the time Padre Pio was hearing one man's confession he kept staring at the Dominican priest garbed in civilian clothes. The Dominican felt somewhat embarrassed and changed positions; but Padre Pio's penetrating eyes kept following him and finally he beckoned the Dominican, who felt there must be some mistake since he never met Padre Pio and surely Padre Pio did not know him. Thinking that Padre Pio was beckoning some other man, the Dominican did not move until one of the men informed him that Padre Pio wanted to speak with him. Surprised, he went over to Padre Pio, who whispered, "Go and put on your habit, then come back and I'll hear your confession." The Dominican answered, "It is unnecessary

Padre, I came in order to find out something and I have found out what I wanted to know."

It is surprising that the name of Padre Pio has given rise to the most fantastic legends and completely spurious accounts of his life and deeds. He was credited with innumerable false prophecies, and unauthorized books and pamphlets have been circulated about him in Europe and the United States.

Here are some points to remember when hearing any such assertions:

1) Fr. Pio never made prophecies concerning world events. He may have predicted something as the bombing of Genoa.

2) He never published or had others publish revelations.

3) When asked his opinion of visions and visionaries he always answered: "This is not my affair. It is up to the Bishop, the Ecclesiastical authority to decide such matters."

4) When the Church had made a decision, as in the case of Heroldsbach and Necedah, Wis., Fr. Pio when asked about these cases said very emphatically: "People must obey their Bishops."

5) Letters supposed to have been written by him after 1924 are automatically spurious, by the very fact that Fr. Pio scrupulously and reverently obeyed his superiors who forbade him to write after that year.

6) The only thing that was ever written for publication by him before 1924 was a meditation which was published with ecclesiastical approval for the first time in March of 1952 under the title, *"Agonia di Gesu nell' Orto di Getsemani."* This publication of Padre Pio, *"Agony of Jesus,"* is published in pamphlet form

by TAN Books and Publishers, Inc., P.O. Box 424, Rockford, IL, 61105, U.S.A. for $1.00 per copy. Padre Pio's first cousin, Padre Ezechia Cardone, O.F.M. published during the Marian year a *"Meditation Prayer on Mary Immaculate"* which was written by Padre Pio before 1924. This has also been published in English by TAN Books and Publishers, Inc., P.O. Box 424, Rockford, IL 61105, U.S.A. for .75 per copy.

CHAPTER III

His Perfume Odor

The phenomenon of perfume, a singular gift of the servant of God, has made many of the incredulous laugh, just as the stigmata have caused numerous discussions and publications, but here also science has had to admit its failure. No chemical preparation applied to the wounds for the purpose of disinfecting, and still less tincture of iodine and carbolic acid, can produce the pleasing and peculiar perfumed odor which emanated from the blood of the wounds as Drs. Festa and Romanelli have confirmed; and further still, they testify that the blood does not become corrupt, as it normally should if it were not an extranatural phenomenon.

The perfume was not constant. The opinion of those close to Padre Pio is that whenever anyone noticed the perfume it was a sign that God bestowed some grace through the intercession of Padre Pio.

The perfume which emanated from Padre Pio was especially the odor of violets, lilies, roses, incense, or even fresh tobacco. It was sometimes persistent, as Dr. Festa, who died Sept. 24, 1940, testified, "I can affirm that on my first visit I took from his side a small cloth stained with blood which I brought back with me to Rome for a microscopic examination. I personally, being entirely deprived of the sense of smell, did not notice any special emanation. But a distinguished official and other persons with me in the automobile on our return to Rome from San Giovanni, not knowing that I brought with me that piece of cloth enclosed in a case, despite the strong ventilation due to the speed of the automobile, smelled the fragrance very distinctly and assured me that it precisely corresponded to the perfume which emanates from the person of Padre Pio.

"In Rome, in the succeeding days and for a long time after, the same cloth conserved in a cabinet in my study filled the room with perfume—so much so that many patients who came to consult me spontaneously asked me for an explanation of its origin."

The three-year-old son of a writer, Mr. Carlo Pedriali, of Genoa, happened to be in the sacristy waiting with his father for Padre Pio to come out of the cloister at 4:45 for his morning Mass. As soon as he entered, the little lad pulled his dad's sleeve and cried out, "Daddy, where is this smell coming from?"

St. Martin de Porres' body frequently gave off the odor of perfume. When his grave was opened after 25 years of burial the same fragrance came from his body, and the surgeons, examining his flesh, found congealed blood.

The objections proposed by the skeptics melted before the vast experience of those who visited Padre Pio for years and at the confirmation of very many persons of indisputable reliability. It would be absurd to think of a phenomenon of suggestion, since suggestion does not create perceptible odors at a distance and contemporaneously by persons of diverse sensibility. It is not an illusion; how can it be an illusion if it reached great distances? It was reported in distant lands and across wide oceans.

Padre Pio's message of perfume always had a positive value; it testified to his spiritual presence. Sometimes it served as a warning of approaching danger, sometimes as an appeal against sin and temptation; but more often it came as a message of comfort to some soul in distress. It was not always an answer to a cry for help, for it came as a surprise to many, like the sound of a friendly voice in the dark. Sometimes it came in a manner impetuous and sudden like a strong sea breeze, and vanished as quickly as it came. At other times it lingered and persisted for a while. It also clung to objects that Padre Pio had touched.

Often persons smelled his perfume before going to him or after leaving him. Some had smelled it while travelling in an auto or train.

In May, 1950, a seminarian from the state of Washington, James Bulmann, came to see Padre Pio and had the joy of serving his Mass. Later in the day he told a Father that while he was answering the prayers at the foot of the altar, he noticed a beautiful perfume he never had smelled before. He had come with little knowledge of Padre Pio and had not known of this phenomenon. The Father to whom he related this smiled and congratulated him. He explained to the seminarian that this is generally a sign that God, through Padre Pio, has bestowed some particular grace.

Among the various supernatural gifts of Padre Pio I give precedence to the gift of perfume. This we find in his cures, in his conversions, in the discernment of souls, in prophecies, in short, in every one of his supernatural acts. The perfume is an announcement or the confirmation that he has heard our prayer or request.

Many saints have had this gift, both before and after death, but Padre Pio seemed to be able to project it at will and used it as a means of communication.

Dr. del Fante wrote: "On the 28th of February, 1931, I was coming home with my family after a visit to my parents. As it was Saturday, and thinking that the next day I could have a rest, I decided to write and work until three in the morning. Before going away I had left this particular piece of work unfinished, so now I started where I had left off, but omitted to bless myself, as is my custom. I was suddenly aware of a delicate scent, which I did not at first recognize. Padre Pio's different odors do not have the quality of commercial perfume; they resemble each other but are not the same. This was the smell of incense. I called my wife and my children, who had already gone to bed; they all came down, including the maid, Maria Rocca. Every one of them smelt incense excepting my Flora. In order not to influence them I asked them to tell me what they could smell. My wife and my oldest daughter as well as the maid said at once that it was incense; my little boy could not exactly describe it. I was most particular in not suggesting the word incense to any of them, being anxious not to give them any lead.

"Padre Pio was telling me that I had not held to my bargain with him to make the Sign of the Cross and say a prayer before starting to work. The scent remained in my room for a while, and I was made very happy by it, feeling that I had Padre Pio near me.

"There are innumerable accounts of this kind, and it would be very worthwhile to make a study of each particular case, since each one reveals the manner in which Padre Pio follows souls, and how he guides, counsels and comforts, using this divine gift. Many of these souls are suffering from various trials, and there are those who are begging for his powerful intercession with God. There are mothers with sick children, fathers asking help in financial difficulties, people who want him to guide, support, and help them. He makes them aware of his perfume to warn them not to be afraid, but to hope, to pray and to behave well. He warns them not to return to the wrong road but to steer always toward the right goal. Their spirits become serene and their hearts are filled with hope because they no longer are alone, but feel that they are sustained by a supernatural strength. Many people have been assured of their prayers being answered through the Father's perfume, and each time the scent suggests the favor that he has asked for.

"As I have said, the perfume is indescribable. It has all the varieties of ordinary odors, but it also has elements that are new and different and hitherto unknown. Sometimes it is more distinct than others, sometimes it reminds one of roses, violets or lilies, or in fact of any sweet-smelling flower. At other times it is like incense or carbolic acid, and again it is like some very fine oriental tobacco. This is the first kind of odor that is noticed particularly by recent converts, and it is what I smelled the first time that I went to see him."

"One of the qualities of mysticism is the power to transform the body according to the aspirations of the spirit. In other words, if the spirit has a different rhythm to that of the body, the latter will become more agile, more flexible, healthier and more accessible to external influences and therefore more tranquil within. This transformation of the physical life often reveals itself through a characteristic odor that emanates from the body. Thomas à Kempis tells us that the room occupied by St. Lydwine was filled by a delicious perfume, and that he too, like Father Sepas with St. Teresa of Jesus, thought at first that she used perfume. The perfume that surrounded St. Lydwine became more intense after she had received Our Lord or after one of the visits of her guardian angel; also after one of her visions had transported her to Heaven. This perfume also affected the sense of taste, for it left in the mouth an impression that one had been chewing cinnamon. The hand that had been held by her guardian angel was more scented than the other."

Dr. Romanelli of Barletta was the first doctor to be called in to see Padre Pio. About the perfume, he reported as follows: "In June, 1919, on my first visit to Padre Pio, I noticed a peculiar scent, so much so that I said to Fr. Valenzano who was with me at the time, that I thought it very unsuitable for a friar to use perfume. For the next two days, either when talking to the Father or just sitting in his cell, I did not notice anything. Before leaving, however, as I was going up the staircase, I had a whiff of the same odor, but only for a moment, as it soon disappeared. I have consulted several learned scientists in order to learn their opinion on the perfume of the blood. They have all declared that it is impossible for blood to give out a sweet odor, but the blood that drips from the stigmata of Padre Pio has a characteristic one, which even those who have no sense of smell can detect. Besides which, when the blood is coagulated, or dried on some garment that he has worn, it still retains its perfume. This is contrary to all natural properties of blood, and yet many have and still do experience it."

In order to dispel the doubts of those who may think that it all came from suggestion, I will explain that whereas light and sound are caused by vibration, perfume is a true emanation of organic particles that start from the source of the odor, and produce a characteristic and specific effect when they come in contact with the mucus membrane of the nostrils. Some people have said that when kissing the hands of Padre Pio, instead of smelling roses and lilies, they have smelt some acid, or even iodine. I must hasten to say that for many years, the Father used none of these chemicals, which were ordered for him in 1919, in order to heal the lesions. This healing has never taken place. Chemistry also teaches us that caustic substances destroy odors, therefore if out of humility or obedience, in order to hide his own perfume, he used any of these lotions, they would destroy all the other smells; whereas actually some recognized the perfume of roses, some of lilies or violets, and still others could only smell carbolic acid. All of which proves that almost every case differs.

If we smelled the Father's perfume when far away from him, it simply meant that he was near us.

From a Capuchin Father I received a letter on the 10th of November, 1946, and I give you the following extract: "I am going to tell you a wonderful story: Last year in the month of November, as Visitor for the Congregations of the Third Order, I went to visit the Congregation of Palazzo Adriano, consisting only of women. I was most anxious to organize one for men, so I recruited more than 20 from the local Catholic Action group, to enroll them as tertiaries. I had no scapulars, so I went next door to the house of a tertiary who was a seamstress, and asked her to make them up for me. The conversation turned to Padre Pio, and I said to her parents that I had on me a relic of the Father, a bit of linen that had touched the wound in his side, and when I showed it to her mother, she cried out with joy: 'I smell a wonderful perfume that goes down from my nostrils to my throat and refreshes my whole body!' Seeing this, I turned to the daughter and asked her to give me the scissors, so that I could cut off a little piece of the relic. While the daughter was on the stairs, on her way to the first floor to fetch the scissors, she noticed a strong smell of flowers of every kind. 'What a lovely smell on the stairs!' she called out, 'It smells like Heaven!' She brought me the scissors, and I cut a piece from the relic. She then told me that she had prepared a letter to send to Padre Pio and would I please write a word of introduction on the blank page? I took the letter, and on the empty page I started to write: 'Dearest Padre Pio...' when suddenly from the letter there came a strong odor of scented soap! To all three of us the Father had shown himself in a different manner.

"On the 21st of January, I had finished my visit to the Franciscan Third Order of Porto Empedocle. I was in the sacristy, and about to take my leave from the sister of the group. I showed them my little piece of relic, and all of them smelt a most extraordinary odor, which seemed to grow stronger all the time.

The sisters were all enjoying the perfume when in came the sacristan. He touched the little piece of cloth and cried out: 'Why this is the same odor that I noticed yesterday when I was delivering a letter from Padre Pio to a neighbor!'

"I later went to lunch with the Archpriest. In his house was his paralyzed sister, who was seated in a chair; I handed her my relic, that she knew nothing about, and asked her if it had a smell, of what did it remind her; 'Of violets?' . . . 'No, of roses,' she answered. Padre Pio was in the room, and satisfied with the visits of inspection, that had really borne fruit.

"One of our tertiaries, Signorina Alfonsina Parisi, received a small piece of this same relic from me. She had a pain in her leg. That evening, she placed the relic on the spot where it hurt her. The next morning the pain was gone. While she was working in the kitchen, she said to herself: 'My leg does not hurt me any more; perhaps Padre Pio has cured it!' In her heart she was expecting an answer, and she did smell an extraordinary perfume of flowers. It was the Father who was making his presence known.

A Sicilian Priest."

I quote from a letter of Dr. Luigi Bellotti, architect, and president of "Domus Nostra" of Venice:

"Venice, July 16, 1946

"Dearest Friend and Brother, Dr. Alberto del Fante,

"I received your very kind letter of the 15th inst. and thank you warmly for the return of my letter of requests to our beloved Padre Pio. Even if he can not materially answer me, as I well understand, I know that he will help me with his divine influence.

"Some time ago, early in the morning as I was dozing, I received a very clear impression of Padre Pio; I seemed to be transported to San Giovanni Rotondo, and was assisting at his Mass. I then followed him into the sacristy and we talked together. I seemed at this time to see something like a picture of his past life, and at the end, I kissed his hands. At other times I have seen him, and smelt his perfume, of roses, or oriental tobacco, or some other similar scent. I think of him always, and especially at night when I say my prayers before retiring.

"From the time when I first got to know him through your splendid biographies I not only believed in him implicitly, but even loved him, as I love the great Saints. I always have sung his praises to my friends, and associates, urging them to recommend themselves to him. In fact, many of my friends who were able to do so have been to see him. I have longed to meet him in person, but this favor has always been denied to me, for the reasons that I have frequently made known to you.

"With a brotherly embrace, I remain always your most affectionate,

Prof. Luigi Bellotti."

★   ★   ★

I received this letter, which I quote in part, from Signora Bice Crespi, a pharmacist in Ligi near Urbino, on the 3rd of November, 1948:

"My three days at San Giovanni Rotondo are quite unforgettable. I had returned to the church some time before, but I went there, without quite knowing why I did so, last June. You had written to me urging me to go, after my letter to you which told you of my having noticed the perfume of the Father several times; you had even answered immediately, telling me how he must have protected me through some of the most difficult times of my life.

"On the 15th of June I assisted for the first time at Padre Pio's Mass. I have waited before analyzing my impressions, in order to let myself be carried along by my daily life and its many occupations, the pharmacy, my family, etc. I can only conscientiously assert one fact: I did not experience a moment of merely temporary exaltation, but the re-awakening and ever increasing growth of a faith that had at best been superficial and easily shaken.

"Has this not been a great grace for me? I have plenty of troubles, both physical and mental, and how could I have managed to overcome them, if I could not do as I do now, take refuge in Faith? I am able to receive comfort from it which makes life beautiful, and I am no longer afraid as I once was of the day when I will have to render an account of the actions of my whole life.

"The news of my trip to San Giovanni Rotondo quickly spread abroad, as always happens in small places. There has been a steady stream of people coming to the pharmacy, wanting to know all about it. I immediately procured your other books that are now in circulation, in order that little by little everyone may know about Padre Pio. Some people have gone to see him already, and soon there will be others. Some day I hope to go back there myself.

Bice Crespi Di Ligi."

A letter from Signora Annita Righini, widow of Mr. Manini, of Leguigno di Casina, Reggio Emilia, which I received in October, 1948:

"Leguigno, October 25, 1948

"Dear Mr. Alberto del Fante,

"I have at last found a moment in which to write you of a matter that I am most anxious that you should know about.

"Last summer, during the holidays, I went to San Giovanni Rotondo to speak to Padre Pio. I left in the morning of the 29th of July, with a young woman teacher from my village, and a colleague from the Commune of Casina. We did not have to change between Reggio Emilia and Foggia, so we had a most agreeable journey.

"On the 30th of July we reached San Giovanni Rotondo at ten thirty, and by eleven o'clock we were already in church. I went in first, so great was my desire to see the Reverend Father; and in fact I saw him at once, as he was in the women's confessional.

"I cannot describe to you my joy, which was all the greater because I had the impression that he was expecting me; he pulled the curtain of the confessional aside for a moment, and looked at me. I was covered with confusion and lowered my eyes.

"At noon, when the two other teachers and I were having our lunch together, we compared our impressions of the morning and found that we had experienced the same emotion; we had all felt that Padre Pio had been expecting us and was giving us a welcome. We all felt sure that the reason for this was the fact that we had each of us, the night before leaving, sent our Guardian Angels on ahead of us to warn the Father of our visit. We could not have made a better journey; Padre Pio had really protected us and was expecting us.

"We stayed at San Giovanni until the 4th of August. The schoolmaster went to confession on the afternoon of our arrival; the young teacher only succeeded in getting there on the day before we left, and because a kind little old lady gave up her place. As for me, in spite of my great desire, and all the energy I had employed, I never succeeded at all. The crowds of women at the confessional were at that time so great, that although both of us got up at two in the morning in order to be the first to get to the church, we always found many others who had been there all night. (This no longer takes place as all must register.) For five mornings I did this, that is, I got up at two o'clock, but all to no avail. The Portiuncula indulgence happened on one of those days, so in view of the fact that I could not go to confession to Padre Pio, in order to gain the indulgence, I went to another priest for confession, and received Holy Communion from Padre Pio himself. In this way I was able to see the stigmata from nearby.

"The Father to whom I went to confession urged me to go home, and not to insist upon going to confession to Padre Pio, assuring me that he well realized all my needs, and the effort I had made to get to him. I gave my little girl's clothes and her photograph to be blessed, and Brother Gerard in returning them to me said that Padre Pio had expressed great hopes of her recovery. This gave me much happiness and filled me with hope.

"Still hoping to go to confession to Padre Pio, I stayed another two days in San Giovanni, but seeing that it was simply not possible, I decided to go back with my colleagues. I had sent my child's clothes and her photograph once again to Padre Pio by the schoolmaster in order to have them blessed, and also to know if the Father would take us both as his spiritual children. He told me that the Father had said: 'Yes, I accept them, I do.' And then added: 'It is not my fault if the mother was not able to get to confession. There is too much of a crowd.'

"I left San Giovanni not entirely satisfied. I was glad to have received the messages about my little girl, that we were the Father's spiritual daughters and that I had received Holy Communion several times from him, being present at his Mass and the ecstasy at the time of the Elevation. My only disappointment was that I had not been able to talk to him. On the express train from Foggia to Naples, six of Padre Pio's spiritual children found themselves in the same compartment, that is to say, we three from the Commune of Casina, a lawyer from Catania who joined us, and a young lady and a colonel from Messina, all of them coming from San Giovanni Rotondo, although we were meeting for the first time.

"The conversation naturally fell on the subject of Padre Pio, and everyone was very pleased with his trip. The young lady from Messina, on the way from San Giovanni to Foggia, had smelt Padre Pio's perfume, especially in those spots where the road is the most dangerous; all the others had noticed it too, but I did not. Everyone was happy excepting me. I was humiliated, and complained loudly saying that it had been I who had instigated the whole expedition, it was I who had persuaded the other two to come to the Father, and whereas they had succeeded in talking to him, I had not. The young lady from Messina reassured me: 'Signora, don't complain: you'll see that you will receive greater blessings than we!' In that moment a wave of perfume enveloped me. I asked the others if they had noticed it, and they all said no. In a little while they did all smell it, but after it had faded away from them, I continued to enjoy it until after we passed Benevento. They all congratulated me saying: 'You see, Padre Pio is not letting you down, cheer up! Your little girl will get well.' The kind words banished my sadness, and sweet hope took hold of me.

"At Naples the colonel and the young lady took the train for Reggio di Calabria, and the rest of us spent the night, going the next morning to Pompeii. I have nothing to tell you of the rest of the journey.

"Upon reaching home, I found my child much as usual, although my sister said that she had slept well at night, a most unusual thing, because every time that I had been forced to leave her, she had not closed an eye and had been very restless. Padre Pio had heard me, because at San Giovanni I had mentally prayed to the Father to keep my little girl calm.

"In my village I keep up a real apostolate. One day I met a lady from a neighboring town who asked me about my trip to San Giovanni Rotondo. She is a very good Catholic, but did not in the least believe in Padre Pio. She even felt a real aversion when she heard his name mentioned. I did my best to make her understand that Padre Pio is a man sent from God, that he has many spiritual gifts, besides having the stigmata just like Our Lord and St. Francis of Assisi. I then persuaded her to read del Fante's books. She took them out of mere curiosity, but she did read them.

"About three weeks later, I had a chance to see her and she greeted me with the news that not only did she believe in Padre Pio, but she was enthusiastic about him. I answered: 'You see? I told you so!' The woman said: 'It was not on account of the books that you gave me, but because I had a dream. Listen: I dreamed that I was in bed, that I was in a sort of drowsy state; I had my hands crossed on my breast. You know that, between ourselves, I have always been rather vain, and use makeup as well as nail polish. As I was saying, I was lying with my hands crossed, and suddenly I saw Padre Pio coming towards me. He took one of my hands, and said: 'Painted fingernails are not becoming to a woman who is devoted to Our Lord.' Then he seemed to rub my fingernails up and down, as though he were trying to clean them. I woke up and felt very upset. I looked at my fingernails, and they were still covered with enamel. I tried to go to sleep again but could not. I lit the light and got up to find something with which to clean my nails. Remember that in order to remove enamel you must have to have the right detergent, and that you have to rub very hard to take it all off. Well, I took from my dresser a pair of nail scissors to scrape it off. I did not need to scrape, because every time that the scissors came near the polish, it seemed to jump off as by magic. I understood then that Padre Pio had touched my heart as well as my fingernails. I am a real enthusiast and as soon as my health permits, I will go to Padre Pio. You may be sure, Signora Manini, that Signora____(she does not wish me to give her name) will never again paint her fingernails!'

"I have as a matter of fact seen her several times lately, and her nails were 'natural.'

"All this I can assure you came about through Padre Pio.

Annita Righini."

A letter from the most Reverend Mother Caterina
Cuzzaniti, Superior of the College of Santa
Maria di Bagheria, (Palermo).

On the 13th of April, 1949, I received a very long letter from the Very Reverend Mother Caterina Cuzzaniti, which I quote in part:

"Bagheria, April 13, 1949

". . .Many people from here who are either suffering from ill health or some other trouble, have written and sent telegrams to the Very Rev. Padre Pio, besides contributing to the hospital. I myself have written several times, and assure you that I have smelt the odor of incense. I will tell you how it came about.

"On the evening of the 18th of November, 1948, shortly before retiring, we had been talking, as often happens nowadays, about the conversions brought about by the Very Rev. Padre Pio. With rather a feeling of disappointment I was saying that I had not had any answer to a letter that I had sent to him. I had sent a second one by hand through someone who was going to San Giovanni Rotondo, and who had placed it directly in the Father's hands. Although I had not received any answer to this one either, I was sure that my prayers had been answered, and I had obtained what I had asked for in the second letter.

"Having retired, I awoke at about 4:30 (I consulted my watch). I put out the light, but no sooner had I placed my head on the pillow, than I was struck by a sweet and most unusual perfume, which at first I could not define, but which became stronger and stronger. It was a delicate and most aromatic kind of incense, but there was something different about it, something beautiful, that cannot be described in words. I remained with my head glued to the pillow, breathing this most delicious scent and aware of being surrounded by some element of the supernatural. I felt as though I were in church, and was much perturbed by the thought that Padre Pio had deigned to give an assurance that my prayers had been answered, to me who was so far away, and above all so unworthy! I thought at once of the favor that I had asked him to obtain from God, but little by little a light began to dawn in my brain that was actually intoxicated by the persistent perfume.

"I thought of my conversation with the other sisters before retiring, relating to the letters I had written to the Rev. Father, and how sure I was that in spite of receiving no answer I had enjoyed the benefit of his precious prayers and blessings. Putting all this together, I came to the conclusion that through this perfume the good Father had given me the proof that he had granted my request as expressed in the

letter I had sent him in August, 1948, and that had
been placed in his saintly hands.

"At this thought my emotion was increased to the
point of tears. I could do nothing but pray and give
thanks. I felt myself in the presence of God, as though
in a church. I also felt that the Father was in the
room, and in those precious moments I recommended
to him all the intentions that were nearest to my heart:
my own poor soul, and several people who were
suffering whom I had recommended to the Father
for relief and comfort.

"When at last the perfume began to fade away, I
still retained in my nostrils that indescribable scent.
I heard the parish clock strike; it was 5:45. One hour
and a half had passed. I could not close an eye, and
only at dawn did I get some sleep.

"In the meantime a great peace and tranquility have
remained within me, and I feel like a child in its
mother's arms. I am also aware of a sweet odor of
incense which speaks to me of God, of goodness and
mercy, and lifts up my soul to Heaven in an unceasing hymn of thanksgiving to my Creator for having
given us mortals the good fortune to have in our midst
so holy a priest endowed with such heavenly gifts.

"I feel protected by the Father, as well as all my
dear ones, and my community too.

"Now I will tell you of a miracle obtained by the
uncle of one of our Sisters. This same Sister told me
about it, having heard it from her uncle on a visit
to her home.

"Mr. Antonio Olivieri, from Misilmeri (Palermo)
when 69 years old was afflicted with a serious heart
condition which made it impossible for him to work

in the fields, as he was unable to take sufficient nourishment. Although he was an atheist, he wanted to go to Padre Pio together with a group of his neighbors. When he stood before the church where Padre Pio is to be found, he said to himself: 'How can I introduce myself to this holy priest if I don't put myself in a state of grace by a good confession?' Already God was working in his soul.

"He made a good and sincere confession to the first priest that he met. Later as he was talking with his friends, he told them that he had not been to confession since his marriage, and that he had taken in the priest with a bad and insincere confession. He heard Padre Pio's Mass with his friends, and had later the good fortune to come near him and tell him his troubles. The Father placed one hand on his heart and one on his head, then stroking his face, he smiled at him. From that moment he began to feel well. He was able to eat properly and was even able to go back to his work in the fields. He is also full of fervor, and has enrolled in the Congregation of the Holy Souls. He edifies the whole village and admits that although he formerly believed neither in God nor the Blessed Virgin nor the Saints, he now believes in everything, and is most grateful to the holy priest who cured both his soul and his body.

"I have several other graces and miracles to tell you, but not being sure of the dates, I will put off writing about them until another time.

"I can however tell you of the following events that I learned from Mr. Olivieri. While they were in church they heard some very loud screams. It turned out to be a poor girl who was possessed, and who

had a great desire to get into the church, but who
was violently pushed back from the door by an evil
spirit. The people present, who included Mr. Olivieri,
were filled with compassion for her and went to Padre
Pio, to whom they described the condition of the poor
girl, and why it was that she could not get into the
church. The Father then, from where he was, made
the Sign of the Cross in her direction, and immediately she was freed from the evil spirit that tormented
her. She began to cry out: 'I am cured! I am hungry!
Give me something to eat!' She was in fact completely
and immediately cured.

"This same Sister told me another story, this time
about a man who was also from Misilmeri. I do not
know his name, but the Sister saw this with her own
eyes. This man was a great sinner, having committed
many crimes including robberies. His conscience having been awakened, and feeling a strong sense of remorse, he was advised to go to Padre Pio in order
to make a good confession and receive absolution for
his misdeeds. Before he had even begun his confession the Father said to him: 'How heavily the hand
of God rests on your head!' The poor man made a
sincere confession and is now leading a model existence, to the edification of the whole village.

Mother Caterina Cuzzaniti."

Signora Vera Bertolo Bianco, of Veglio Mosso in
the province of Vercelli, wrote me on the 13th of
February, 1950, as follows:

"Many people come to me for news of Padre Pio,
and I am most happy to be able to give them information about our beloved Father.

"Last Saturday there came to our house a certain professor who has a great deal of influence in Biella; he wanted to hear about Padre Pio. To our amazement there came that delicious perfume. It persisted from nine o'clock until eleven, in a most wonderful manner. What a joy that was for my husband and me! The professor was profoundly moved, and promised to go to San Giovanni Rotondo, lucky man!

"From Turin a professor writes me the following on a postcard: A child of seven, being desperately ill in a hospital, recovered and was sent home in eight days completely cured, to the great surprise of all the doctors who declared it to be a true miracle. I shall do my best to obtain the data of this case for your book.

"I have received many other letters confirming favors and graces received through the intercession of the good Father.

"The professor from Biella has just telephoned me to say that the perfume of the other evening accompanied him all the way to his house. . . . How wonderful, and may the Lord be thanked!

"You were right in saying that I have such satisfaction, and I owe it mostly to you!

Vera Bertolo Bianco."

I answered Signoro Bertolo, thanking her and asking her to let me have the documents on the child and the statement of the professor from Biella. On the 17th of February I received the two reports, which I quote:

Report from Dr. Amanzio Duodo, who wrote the following:

"Dear Signor del Fante,

"Although I am convinced that my evidence is of little importance in comparison with the overwhelming amount that comes daily from every corner of the earth—and that confirms what one might call metaphysical virtues of Padre Pio while he is still living—I am happy to add my small voice to the immense chorus of praise that gives glory to God, and to be able perhaps to contribute a faint spark to the great flame that burns so brightly, and shines in the materialistic darkness of our century.

"On the 15th of February, 1950, I was with the Battista Bertolo family of Vallemosso, engaged in agreeable conversation. There were present besides myself all the members of the above-mentioned family, most dear to Padre Pio, who deigns to manifest his presence to them with various and very intense perfumes. A friendly soul who had lately come from a visit to San Giovanni Rotondo was describing to us the great humility of the Father, in spite of all the publicity about his work, when suddenly—and above all, unexpectedly—an intense perfume of violets enveloped us all, lasting about a half hour, although the doors and windows were wide open.

"Later a pungent and strong perfume assailed us, giving us the joy of knowing that Padre Pio was with us in spirit.

"I thanked God with real feeling and committed a sin of envy toward that blessed house!

Faithfully,

Dr. Amanzio Duodo,
Veglio Mosso Picco (Vercelli)."

I also record the letter of Dr. Bianco:

"Vallemosso, February 17, 1950

"I, the undersigned, assert that on the occasion referred to by Dr. Duodo I was present and also smelled
the odor of violets. I must add that on various other
occasions I have repeatedly perceived odors of roses,
violets and carnations, whose source was positively
not artificial.

"I wish also to declare that these observations of
mine elude all scientific explanation, although I have
done my best to rationalize them.

Faithfully,

Dr. Edoardo Bianco."

From Signorina Colombani I received the following letter:

"Allow me to say that as soon as I learned of this
chosen creature of God, I was seized with such a
strong impulse to weep, that on the evening of the
13th of April, which happened to be Wednesday in
Holy Week, I decided to receive Holy Communion
on the following day, that is, on Holy Thursday. Being
very tired and far from a church, I was afraid that
I could not manage it. At midnight I prayed to the
Reverend Padre Pio to help me, and tearfully fell
asleep. At half-past five in the morning, on Holy
Thursday, I dreamed that the Father was blessing me
from the altar. I felt this blessing so deeply that I
awoke with a start.

"I went to church and received Holy Communion, returning immediately home to work. At 9:30,

when I was feeling very exhausted, I suddenly was aware of a most delicious perfume of roses and lilies, so strong that I turned around to see whence it came. There was nothing in my room to cause this, so I thought that the Father had wished to show his approval of my little sacrifice.

"June 1, 1949.

Maria Colombani."

There is much that I could write about Domenico Tognola of Zurich, Switzerland, who has become a most ardent spiritual son of the Father. From a great many letters received from him, I quote this one:

"Zurich, July 30, 1949

"Most esteemed Signor del Fante,

"Forgive me if I bore you, but I cannot remain silent about the many graces that I have obtained from the Rev. Padre Pio.

"First of all I must thank you for sending me your books, which have introduced me to this great priest. He has changed my life and made me contented and happy.

"The first grace that the Father granted me happened on the 11th of last February. My mother being very ill at the time, I heard a voice that was certainly that of the Father, telling me to hurry to her bedside, as she was dying. Leaving immediately, I arrived on time to see my poor mother before she died, although I had to travel a distance of thirty miles.

"I received the second favor on Holy Thursday of this year. That evening before retiring, I noticed an odor of incense, and on Holy Thursday one of roses.

This made me very happy, because I realized that having invoked the Father, he had made himself manifest to me with these odors.

"The third time has for me the most importance; it happened on the 27th of July (1949). In the morning of that day, I awoke smelling a very strong odor of violets. I understood the meaning of this when the postman brought me a letter from my brother whom I had not seen for 32 years; I had thought he was dead.

"Your brother in Christ and in Padre Pio.

Domenico Tognola."
Schrennengasse 21, Zurich, 3. Switzerland.

CHAPTER IV

Bilocation

Bilocation means to be in two places at once; that is to say that one's personality must be divided, if such a thing were possible, so as to be at the same time, say in Padua and Lisbon, as happened to St. Anthony of Padua; or like St. Alphonsus Liguori, who was seen at the funeral of Clement XIV, while at the same time he had not left his parish of St. Agatha of the Goths, where he was bishop. Fr. Tannoia, disciple and biographer of St. Alphonsus, writes that: "On the morning of the 24th of September, 1774, after saying Mass, instead of making his thanksgiving at the foot of the altar, as was his custom, he went into his room and threw himself into his armchair, where he remained without moving, without speaking, and completely unconscious. On the morning of the 25th, he had not changed his position. At about seven o'clock, he rang his bell to say that he wished to say Mass. His servants came running, with other people, too.

"But why all these people?" asked the bishop in a surprised tone of voice. "What has happened?"

"It is a whole day since you spoke or ate or gave a sign of life; and you ask what has happened!"

"That is true," said the Saint, "but don't you know that I have been to see the Pope, who is dead?"

It was later known that the Pope had indeed died

at the very moment referred to by the Saint.

I do not know how this can be done, but history and the Church agree that only the Saints, that is to say the heralds of God, have accomplished these supernatural deeds.

When Divine inspiration breaks the ties that hold the human body enslaved on earth, the spirit rises upward to God, and this permits the body itself to become one with the spirit. The ecclesiastical historians tell how once St. Peter of Alcantara was able to pass over the River Guadana, swollen by recent rains; and how another time when he was engrossed in reading of holy things, without interrupting his study, he passed over a river in a heavy rainstorm.

St. Alma is said to have crossed the Seine dry-shod; and St. Marcarius, St. Bridget, and St. Dominic as well as other saints crossed rivers without getting wet, to say nothing of St. Peter.

At other times the Saints have been carried over from one shore to another, without knowing how it happened. This happened to St. Teresa when she went to found the convent of Talamina.

The Saints have the curious power of commanding the elements. One evening the engineer Todini of Rome remained until late at San Giovanni Rotondo. When he was on the point of leaving Padre Pio, he noticed that there was a downpour of rain. He then asked the Father to allow him to remain in the monastery, but he refused.

"Father, how will I manage to get down to the village without an umbrella? I'll be soaking wet!"

"I'll go with you (in the spirit of course)," answered the Father.

Signor Todini said goodnight to Padre Pio, and left the monastery. Before opening the door that led into the square in front of the church, he could hear the rain splashing on the pavement. He turned up the collar of his coat, and pulled down his hat so that the wind would not blow it away, and opened the door. A violent gust of wind struck him, but what was his surprise to notice as he walked that it was barely sprinkling, a few drops here and there, and no more. When he got to the village, he went into the house where he was lodging.

"How wet you must be!" his hosts called down to him from the head of the stairs, when they heard him come in.

"Why, it was not raining at all!"

"Not raining? Why it seemed like the end of the world!"

He was able to show them his clothes were perfectly dry, to the great surprise of all, including Signor Todini, and no one was able to give any explanation.

I was able to observe that when one recommended a soul to him, his face changed color, and often became luminous. He murmured a prayer, and looked at him carefully. It seemed as though he were leaving us and transporting himself to the person of whom we are speaking, in order to help him. It often happened when speaking to Padre Pio of someone who was far away, that the said person either smelled his perfume, saw him or felt him to be near them.

There have been many saints who have been lifted from the ground during an ecstasy: Ven. Mary of Agreda often rose above the floor when she had received Holy Communion. Dominic of Jesus and

Mary was once rapt in ecstasy in the presence of Philip II, and he was able to move him about by merely blowing on him. St. Agnes of Bohemia, the wife of Frederic II, or of his son as some maintain, was seen by a nun to be raised from the floor to a height of four inches. St. Dominic was seen in the Abbey of Castres suspended in mid-air. The same thing happened to St. Francis Xavier, to St. Albert, and to the pious Conradin in the prison where people of Bologna had placed him because he had too harshly criticized their obstinacy. There are so many others that it is useless to enumerate, like St. Louis, who was wont to remain for three or four days in an ecstasy suspended above the floor.

In all that St. Teresa has written about herself, she gives us but a very faint idea of what bilocation really is, because according to her writings, many saints experienced only the first phases of this supernatural gift, that is of being raised from the ground, which is known as levitation, whereas in the case of Padre Pio, the bilocation was complete. He moved his body about from one place to the other.

One of his forms of bilocation was through the use of his voice. This happened in the case of many of his spiritual children as well as to strangers at any distance from him, bringing news, or giving advice or reproaching them as he so often did in dreams. In this last case, the fortunate one heard his voice clearly and distinctly without seeing him.

★   ★   ★

On the 8th of May, 1926, a dozen people from Bologna were waiting for Padre Pio in the hallway of the monastery of San Giovanni Rotondo. They had come from Monte Saint Angelo, where they had been to visit the magnificent sanctuary with a hundred other pilgrims. Some of the group were already in the church praying. It is well to note that at this time there was no door leading directly from the sacristy to the monastery; therefore the Father had to pass through the church if he wanted to get into the sacristy.

The group waited in vain for a long time, wanting to be the first to speak to him. Another Father told them to their surprise that Padre Pio had been for some time in the church already, hearing confession.

Signor Giuseppe Borri, the Misses Stefanelli of La Quercia (Bologna), Signor Milani of Veggio Grizzana, and Signorina Carolina Giovannini and others went to the church and really did find Padre Pio, who was in the women's confessional. When they asked how he had gotten there, they were told that he had come the usual way.

The twelve visitors from Bologna realized that he could only have gotten there through supernatural means, as they had been waiting for him in the passage for more than three hours.

Now that I am on this subject, I would like to quote del Fante of another case of this kind that happened to an actor. It was told me at San Giovanni Rotondo in February of 1931.

"One day this gentleman arrived from Foggia in a car, together with some ladies of his theatrical company. Their general behavior astonished the good people of the village; on alighting from his car, he asked them:

" 'Where is Padre Pio? I want him to convert me, I want to go to confession!' And leaving his lady friends giggling and highly amused at the whole performance, he went into the church.

"Several spiritual children of the Father's who happened to be there and to whom he turned for information told him that the Father must be in the sacristy, as that was where they had just left him. He went into the sacristy, but could not find him. He was sought for everywhere—in the monastery, in his cell, in the garden, in the recreation room; but it was impossible to find him anywhere.

"Finally, being tired of waiting, he said: 'Well, I think I'll be going. I had wanted to be converted by him!' But he said this with a sarcastic laugh. He got back into his car, and started back toward the village. He had hardly gone three hundred yards, when the people who were there found themselves face to face with Padre Pio.

" 'Father, where have you been? We have hunted for you all over the place!'

" *'I was right here, I passed in front of you three or four times, but neither you nor he noticed me.'* "

The good people of San Giovanni understood, and said nothing.

Speaking of the invisibility of the Saints, it is said that St. Lucianus, when he was passing through the streets of a city, could make himself invisible to anyone by whom he did not wish to be seen. St. Francis of Paola made himself invisible to sixty soldiers sent by the King of Naples to arrest him. They went right by him, but never saw him as he prayed to the Lord to help him.

Violante, the wife of King John of Aragon, wishing at all costs to see the inside of St. Vincent Ferrer's cell, had the door forced open and saw the cell, but not the Saint. On being asked by his superiors where he had been, he told them that he had never left his cell. When the Queen had gone, the Father Superior asked St. Vincent why she had not been able to see him. The Saint answered: "I have never allowed any woman to enter my cell, even the Queen; and God, to punish her for the sin of forcing her entry, is covering her eyes while she is here, so as to prevent her from seeing me." The queen left the monastery immediately, and St. Vincent followed her. When she saw him, she apologized for what she had done, and went away.

At San Martino in Pensilis, a group of devout followers of Padre Pio and members of the Third Order of Saint Francis were in the habit of gathering in the house of one or the other for their Franciscan reunion. Before starting they would all say a little prayer to the Guardian Angels, asking the celestial messengers to go and call Padre Pio, asking him to be present in their midst. Very often, after having prayed to their Guardian Angels, they all noticed the perfume of Padre Pio, and they all reverently knelt down saying: "Padre Pio is with us; he will direct our meeting."

On one of these occasions, the meeting was in the house of the police marshal Trombetta. Giovannino, his five-year-old son, was present. Suddenly the little boy ran to his mother's knee and hid his face, saying: "Mamma, I am afraid, because Padre Pio is here. I see him." "Where, Giovannino, where? Is he still here?"

they all asked. The child clung to his mother, as he peeked out and again hid his face, pointing with his finger to the place where he saw the Padre, saying, "Now he is here, now he is there. He is still with us," and finally, "He is going away now." All eyes followed the direction of the little pointed finger but saw nothing.

Several of those present went to San Giovanni for the purpose of asking Padre Pio if he had really been with them. They told him what had happened, and then said: "Padre, was it really you that Giovannino saw?" "And who else could it have been?" was his abrupt reply. He was always very embarrassed and almost painfully timid when people openly spoke to him about his supernatural faculties, but "fools jump in where angels fear to tread." So these good people, before leaving, wanting a more positive answer, again asked: "But, Padre, were you really present with us at that meeting?" And he replied: "Do you still doubt it?"

★   ★   ★

Mrs. Devoto of Genoa was seriously ill and in danger of losing her leg. A consultation was held, and the doctors decided to amputate the leg. One of her daughters was alone in her room praying that her mother would not have to submit to an operation. She also called upon Padre Pio for help. Suddenly she saw Padre Pio standing in her doorway, looking at her. Her desire to obtain the grace for her mother was so great that she did not stop to wonder how Padre Pio could be in Genoa, instead of San Giovanni Rotondo, hundreds of miles away; nor did she have the slightest doubt that he was actually there in person. Throwing herself on her knees she implored him, "Oh, Father, save my dear mother." He looked at her and said, "Wait for nine days." She wanted to ask him for an explanation; she raised her eyes, but saw only the door of her room—no light, no Padre Pio.

The next day she informed the doctors that they must wait. The doctors tried to convince her in vain. Even the other members of her family, when they saw that the mother was growing worse each day, could not dissuade her from her decision to wait nine days as Padre Pio instructed her.

On the tenth day, when the doctors visited their patient, they were surprised to find the leg completely healed and their patient well on the road to recovery.

Mother, father, sons, daughters, in-laws, and grand-children all came to thank Padre Pio for the grace which had been bestowed upon them, but Padre Pio will never accept thanks and will always say rather gruffly: "Go into the church and thank Our Lord and the Mother of Divine Graces."

*   *   *

Telegrams, telephone transcripts, testifying letters, and many contacted eyewitnesses gave testimony of the foregoing bilocations and that Padre Pio was seen throughout Italy, in Austria, distant Uruguay, and Milwaukee, Wisconsin.

Padre Pio himself admitted, when asked, that he was in Milwaukee, Wisconsin, June 25, 1950, to assist at the death of the father of a Capuchin.

Can you imagine Father Pio, all out of breath, raising himself in the air, and flying over the heads of the congregation, to go out of the sacristy and the church, to enjoy a little fresh air in the esplanade in front of the church? Don Giovanni Miglionico, a former member of Pio's community who had to leave because of heart trouble writes: "On the feast day of St. Anthony (I do not remember the year), Padre Pio was sitting at table with Padre Ludovico, and said these words, 'This morning I felt myself suffocating from the great crowds of men in the sacristy, whilst I was hearing confessions; not being able to stand it any more I began to walk on the heads of the people and I went out on the esplanade for a little fresh air, and no one noticed me.'"

Padre Ludovico told this to us as an example of the great simplicity of Padre Pio, who mentioned this as though it were nothing; though it was, of course, an extraordinary thing.

For the consecration and inauguration of her private chapel in Via Tritone 53 in Rome, the Countess Virginia Sili had addressed several invitations; and among those invited were her cousin Cardinal Gasparri and her brother-in-law Cardinal Sili. The Countess and her most eminent guests were discussing amongst themselves to what Saint they would dedicate the new oratory. A novice ended their discussion when she entered, holding in her hand a reliquary containing a relic of the Holy Cross, and told the following story:

"Last night there appeared to me in flesh and bones Padre Pio, who consigned to me this relic, bidding me to bring it to the Countess in the morning before the consecration of the Chapel."

A few days later the Countess went in person to

San Giovanni Rotondo and obtained from Padre Pio himself the confirmation of the story of the novice.

Without taking a train or an airplane, Padre Pio in the night flew to Rome, and the following morning was already back at San Giovanni Rotondo to celebrate Mass at dawn.

St. Martin De Porres had been seen at Manila in the Philippines, Africa, France, and in five different places at the same time, and when asked to explain this phenomenon he replied, "If Christ multiplied the loaves of bread and fishes, then why cannot He multiply me?" He was seen frequently raised in the air in a state of ecstasy, as was also St. Agnes of Bohemia, Louise Lateau of Belgium, St. Dominic, St. Francis Xavier, and St. Albert.

Signora Concetta Bellarmini of S. Vito Lanciano declared that she was suddenly stricken with a blood infection followed by bronchial pneumonia with a very high fever. She was reduced to such a state that the doctors despaired of ever saving her. The flesh had become yellow from the infection which had spread throughout her body. A relative urged her to direct her prayers to Padre Pio. She prayed to him whom she had never seen, when suddenly in full daylight a stigmatized monk appeared to her, and smiling, blessed her without touching her as he stood in the middle of the room. The woman asked him if his appearance signified the grace of the conversion of her children, or else the grace of her physical cure. The Padre answered, "Sunday morning you will be cured"; then he vanished from the room, leaving an odor of perfume which the servant girl also smelt. After this visit her flesh turned a normal color, the fever ceased, and in a few days her health was completely restored. She went with her brother to San Giovanni Rotondo to see if Padre Pio was the one who appeared to her. When she arrived at the monastery and saw Padre Pio in the church, she turned to her brother and said, "There he is, he is the one."

Signor Arturo Bugarini of Ancona was urged by friends to turn to Padre Pio for the cure of his boy. Whilst he was standing near the bedside of his critically ill son he felt three consecutive taps on his shoulder, whilst a voice said: "I am Padre Pio, I am Padre Pio, I am Padre Pio." At the same time he felt all over his body a wave of heat as if he were next to an intense flame, then all of a sudden it ceased. This visit of Padre Pio restored the health of the son. Father and son visited the monastery to thank Padre Pio for the miraculous cure and the spiritual conversion of the father and all the Bugarini family.

On July 20, 1921, a Monsignor D'Indico of Florence, whom this author met in 1923 when studying theology at the Archbishop's Seminary at Florence, was alone in his study. He felt the sensation of having someone at his back. He turned and saw a monk, who disappeared. He left his room to tell a chaplain what happened. The chaplain thought it was mere hallucination due to his state of anxiety over his sister, who was very ill. He invited him to take a short walk for mental distraction. When they returned they called at the sick room. His sister, who a little before had been in the state of coma, at the same hour when her brother felt the sensation of being in the presence of Padre Pio, told how she had seen a monk enter her room who approached her and said:

"Don't be afraid; tomorrow your fever will disappear, and after a few days there will be no trace of your illness on your body." "But, Padre," she answered, "are you then a saint?" "No, I am a creature who serves the Lord through His mercies."

"Let me kiss your habit, Padre."

"Kiss the sign of the Passion," and he showed his hands transfixed and bleeding.

"Padre, I recommend to you my husband and child."

"Pray, pray that you will be good, and be assured that your child will be under my protection," and blessing her, he vanished.

She immediately got better and in eight days was entirely cured.

Several witnesses testified that they saw Padre Pio at the tomb of St. Pius X, in the crypt of St. Peter's at Rome. He was seen there five times.

One day Padre Pio, speaking about the holy figure of *Papa Sarto*, St. Pius X, said:

"I never met Leo XIII, nor Pius X, but certainly this last one is the most sympathetic of all the Popes that I know from St. Peter down; for he is so simple and humble that he, more than anyone else, resembles Christ through his simplicity and humbleness."

The Bishop of Salto, Uruguay, narrates that a very distinguished prelate confided to him that during the beatification of St. Therese of the Child Jesus, he saw Padre Pio in the Basilica of St. Peter. At the moment he approached to speak to him, Padre Pio vanished.

All know that Padre Pio for many years never left San Giovanni. This report circulated around the Vatican until it reached the ears of Pius XI, who, desiring to learn the truth of it called the priest Don Orione, noted for his sanctity, to find out the reason of this circulated story.

Don Orione replied, "I have seen him myself." "If you tell me that, then I believe it," said Pius XI.

One evening, Dr. Wm. Sanguinetti (faithful friend and personal physician of Padre Pio) told us that he and a few others were in Padre Pio's room, when the doctor opened the following conversation:

Dr.: "Padre Pio, when God sends a saint, for instance like St. Anthony, to another place by bilocation, is that person aware of it?"

Padre Pio: "Yes. One moment he is here, and the next moment he is where God wants him."

Dr.: "But is he really in two places at once?"

Padre Pio: "Yes."

Dr.: "How is this possible?"

Padre Pio: "By a prolongation of his personality."

This explanation, obvious to Padre Pio, may be a problem which we leave to philosophers and theologians to explain.

★   ★   ★

Externally the condition of Padre Pio in ecstasy was, as I noticed, the same as though he were asleep. He awoke from it as if from slumber. The members of his body were numb to all external influences. For example, an extremely bright electric light, the flashing of a camera taking a three-dimensional picture of him in ecstasy at Mass, which under ordinary circumstances would have blinded him, could be done over and over without awakening him or leaving his sight impaired. At the beating of the most powerful kettle drums, his hearing remained passive, like a deaf mute. "During the highest flight of ecstasy, nothing is seen or heard," says St. Theresa.

When Padre Pio was first ordained, everyone at Pietrelcina was edified by his piety at Mass—although some complained about the duration of Padre Pio's Mass to the pastor, Don Salvatore Pandullo. Many times during Mass the young priest would be lost in ecstasy. Undoubtedly he would have continued in this mystical state had not the pastor made a mental command and rung a little bell for the purpose of recalling him to go on with the Mass.

MONSIGNOR DAMIANI OF SALTO, URUGUAY

Msgr. Damiani, Vicar General of the diocese of Salto, Uruguay, South America, was a faithful friend of Padre Pio and came to visit him repeatedly. Upon one such visit in 1929 he said to Padre Pio: "I would like to die here so you could assist me." Padre Pio answered: "No, you will die in Uruguay." "Will you come down there to assist me?" Padre Pio said, "Yes." One forenoon during this visit, the Monsignor had a slight heart attack. He sent for Padre Pio immediately. But, since he was hearing confessions, he did not heed the call. When he came upstairs about noon and went to the room of Msgr. Damiani, the latter chided him in a friendly way: "Padre Pio, why did you not come when I sent for you? I could have died." Padre Pio answered with a smile: "Man of little faith. Did I not tell you that you would die in Uruguay?"

During Holy Week of 1949, Most Rev. Antonio Maria Barbieri, O.F.M. Cap., Archbishop of Montevideo, Uruguay, came with 38 of his diocesan people to pay Padre Pio a visit. When they arrived he asked to see Padre Pio alone first. He went to confession to him and then had a little chat with him. Later, after Padre Pio had gone to the confessional, the Archbishop spoke with the rest of the fathers and related the following:

"In 1942, Bishop Alfredo Viola of Salto celebrated his Silver Sacerdotal Jubilee and at the same time had the laying of the cornerstone of his minor seminary. The Apostolic Delegate and five bishops lodged in the episcopal residence. On the vigil of the Jubilee, about midnight, I was awakened by a knocking at my door. The door was open about a foot. I saw a Capuchin pass by and heard a voice: 'Go to the room of Msgr. Damiani; he is dying.' I arose, put on my cassock, called the other Bishops and some priests, and we went to the room of the Monsignor. On his night table I found a slip of paper written by Msgr. Damiani: 'Padre Pio came.' (The Archbishop had this paper with him.) Now today, when I spoke to Padre Pio after confession a little while ago, I asked him: 'Padre Pio, were you the Capuchin whom I saw in the residence of the Bishop of Salto, the night Msgr. Damiani died?' Padre Pio was embarrassed and did not answer, although he easily could have said no. When I insisted and he still would not answer, I laughed and said: 'I understand.' Padre Pio nodded and answered: 'Yes, you understood.'"

Here we have: first, the promise of Padre Pio to assist the Monsignor at his deathbed, then the Monsignor's written testimony that Padre Pio had come; the testimony of the Archbishop and finally the practical admission of Padre Pio.

One day during the war General Cadorna was in his study absorbed in thought, and he held his head in his hands, thinking of all the young men who, for the love of country, would have to give up their lives; when suddenly he smelt a very strong perfume of roses which was wafted around the room. Raising his venerable head, he was stupefied to see a monk with a seraphic look and with bleeding hands. Passing in front of him, the monk said, "Be calm, they will not do anything harmful to you."

With the disappearance of the monk, the general no longer smelled the perfume. He told a Franciscan about the vision, and when he mentioned the perfume the Franciscan said, "Your excellency, you have seen Padre Pio." Then he told the general all about Padre Pio. The general decided to visit San Giovanni; and when he arrived there incognito, he was immediately approached by two Capuchins who had recognized the general even though he was trying to disguise himself in civilian clothing. They approached him and said, "Your excellency, Padre Pio is waiting for you. He sent us to meet you."

★   ★   ★

Emma Meneghello, a very pious young girl of 14, was afflicted with epilepsy which threw her into fits several times a week. One afternoon while in prayer, Padre Pio appeared to her and placed his hand on the bed sheet, then smiled and vanished. The cured epileptic arose to kiss the place where the Padre had placed his hand, and she noticed a cross of blood left on the sheet. A small square cut of the sheet with the bloodstains is conserved today in a glass picture frame. "Through the intercession of Padre Pio," she wrote, "I have obtained other favors, especially for dying babies."

Mrs. Ersilia Magurno, a woman of great faith, for two months was taking care of her husband, who was stricken with influenza. This illness would not have given alarm were it not that he was also afflicted with a very weak heart. Night and day, helped by a nun, the wife was watching her husband with every possible care, while praying and invoking Padre Pio. He grew worse, and the doctors advised that the last rites be given to him because of the very alarming failure of his heart. One night the wife noticed in the room a strong perfume of flowers. The next morning, however, a worse condition prevailed, and the dying man was approaching his end. A telegram begged Padre Pio's intercession. Two days later Mr. Magurno entered into a state of coma. The wife did not give up hope and sent a second telegram. Finally on the 27th of February, 1947, the sick man, after a day of prolonged crisis, fell asleep. The nun was away, and the wife remained alone to watch him; and at midnight, she noticed that his sleep was more restful than usual. At 7:30 in the morning, noticing that he was awakening, she rushed to his side and said, "How do you feel?" "I am cured, I am well. Padre Pio just left the room; open the window, please, and take my temperature." It was entirely normal.

"Ernesto," asked the astonished wife, anxious to hear and to know. "What are you saying? Have you seen Padre Pio? And what did he tell you?"

"He came together with another monk; he examined my heart and said, 'This fever will go away;

tomorrow you will be cured, and within four days you can get up.' Padre Pio looked around, examined the medicines, read the medical reports and remained in the room all night." To confirm this miracle, a strong odor of violets was observed in the room.

Five months later, on July 27, the couple went to San Giovanni, and Mr. Magurno immediately recognized Padre Pio as the monk who had cured him. Padre Pio received him with fond greetings, and placing his hand on his shoulder said to him: "How much this heart has made you suffer."

We must not think that Padre Pio arrived always unexpectedly at the bedside of the sick, for sometimes he loved to announce the time of his coming. Once a little sick girl told her parents the approximate hour of his arrival, and the parents in their simplicity, not understanding the phenomenon, went to meet him at the railroad station. When they returned to the child disappointed, they found her asleep.

"Padre Pio didn't come," her mother said sadly, as soon as she saw her waking.

"Why, he was here up to now," the child answered.

A young girl who had also been cured of a grave infirmity desired to test the powers of Padre Pio and came to him feigning the infirmity that once afflicted her.

"Go away, child," he said, striking her jokingly on the shoulder, "go away for you are quite cured, and be careful that you never again tempt the mercy of the Lord."

One woman, after long torments caused by a cancer that gave her the most excruciating pains, was promised by Padre Pio that she would be cured if she had faith, much faith. The cure took place. One day from a cross on the wall of her room there came forth an intense odor of violets which flooded the house, to the astonishment of many people who were there. There was no doubt that the miraculous cure had taken place. The woman, paralyzed for a long time, could not only abandon her bed and walk, but was able to go out of the house the next day to church to thank God.

A few days after, however, for greater assurance on the advice of a radiologist, she consented to complete the cure with a new application of radium.

She should have never done it. The pains returned more acute than before. The poor creature was forced to bed and never got up again. The supplications of her husband did not obtain a second cure.

Padre Pio said to him: "You did well to thank God because He gave you a wonderful sign. Since you did not have faith in spite of such a wonderful sign, and so great a grace, you did not know how to bow before this grace and sing the praises of the Lord in His glory. You did not know how to await the progress of the grace already so miraculously accomplished before your eyes; you wanted to complement the miracle with useless and perhaps injurious cures. Why? This humanity has eyes, but does not know how to see."

Padre Pio renewed his prayers, but Jesus, instead of granting a second miracle, called her unto Himself, with a holy death June 14, 1950.

A couple from Genoa visited Padre Pio to tell him that they had no children.

"Bring him to me to be baptized when he is born,"

was his answer. He could always foretell the sex of an unborn child.

The following year the fortunate couple returned with their baby boy, but in the Church of Our Lady of Graces there was no baptismal font, and there was such a crowd in the church that they could not reach Padre Pio. The mother remained in the parish house of San Giovanni Rotondo one mile away, whilst the father went to the monastery to protest that Padre Pio had invited them to come there; otherwise they would not have come. He waited in vain. He returned to the parish house to learn from his wife that even though Padre Pio at the time specified was very preoccupied with the people, he had come and baptized the baby.

In a city of central Italy a teacher and ex-secretary of a Fascist organization was accused of having furnished arms and bombs to the Fascisti, who perpetrated an explosion that killed military and civilians. But the teacher was innocent. Taken by force from her home to be tried and shot, she succeeded in bringing with her a rosary and a photograph of Padre Pio. They conducted her to observe the destruction and to see the spectacle of the dead whose death they attributed to her. They then brought her to the place of execution.

Meanwhile some members of the firing squad entered her home with the pretext of searching for arms. Instead they began stealing money, objects of gold, and clothing, until all of a sudden there thundered a shout, "Enough," so resolutely and imperiously that the soldiers fled, abandoning their loot.

The sister of the condemned girl, watching the

whole scene cringing in a corner, recognized in the shouting of "Enough" the voice of Padre Pio.

The order to aim and fire had been suspended because of the arrival of an interminable column of armored cars, horses, cannon, ambulances and marching troops. The commander of the firing squad remained standing on a car as if hypnotized.

The young teacher could hardly breathe as she reflected that her hour would come when the last soldier passed by. She began to pray to Padre Pio for the grace of seeing God's will in her execution. A gentleman approached her and asked what they had decided to do with her.

"I don't know, I no longer know anything, they are all away, there is only the commander there," as she pointed him out with an expression full of horror.

He was motionless, as if cemented to his post.

"Then consider yourself free and come with me." He brought her in his automobile to her home, where many women were comforting her grief-stricken sister. The condemned girl threw herself into her sister's arms, and then, taking a picture of Padre Pio from the wall, kissed it and pressed it to her heart. In that instant she felt a hand gently patting her cheek.

A few months later the teacher went to San Giovanni to thank her saviour.

"Padre," she said, "my life will not be enough to thank you." He said: "My child, how much your faith caused me to run."

One of his secretaries writes that a lady wrote from Waiakoa, Kula, Mani—one of the Hawaiian Islands. She thanked Padre Pio for visiting the prison on the island of Oahu, where her husband was an inmate.

Her husband had phoned her, gave her Padre Pio's address, and asked her to write. He did not go into details as to what Padre Pio had said or done, but whatever it was, the prisoners were all consoled by the visit. This was clearly another case of bilocation.

Padre Onorato, who was a student in the monastery when Padre Pio was spiritual director, one day saw Padre Pio leaning out of the window saying the formula of absolution. Several days later some people from Marcone came to thank Padre Pio for having assisted a dying man. He had not been out of the monastery, but was there by bilocation, at the time P. Onorato heard him say the formula of absolution.

In August of 1947 at Bolzanet in the Via Madonna della Guardia, after the third apparition and visit by Padre Pio, the Blessed Virgin appeared to twelve-year-old Rosetta Polo Riva, who lived from October 1946 to August 1947 between life and death. She was stricken in the beginning with an obscure malady, with a sore throat and persistent fever, aggravated later on by pleurisy and emphysema which necessitated the extraction of fluids from the lung.

The general condition of the child, already suffering with acute endocarditis with dilation of the aorta, was certainly not favorable for an operation. The medical consultants decided to operate. After the operation, the child was left to die. Her family recommended little Rosetta to Our Lady of the Guard, burning a candle to her every day at her altar.

The child came through the operation and began to get better, so much so that she was able to leave her bed by New Year's of 1948. But she could get up only for a few days, when she became seriously ill again with an attack of pneumonia which was checked with penicillin. She remained in bed till the month of March.

Although on her feet, poor Rosetta was not yet cured, since the condition of her heart was worse and was judged incurable by the doctors. Two or three times a day she fell into such faints that each time the family thought they would lose her.

About the end of July a friend of the family wrote a letter to Padre Pio with these words: "To you, Father, we confide the little heart of our Rosetta that you may present it to the hearts of Jesus and Mary in order that they restore it as she ought to have it at her age."

On August 8 at 2 p.m., Padre Pio appeared in a vision to the child who at that moment was in the downstairs apartment with her godmother.

Rosetta was listening to the radio when she was stricken with a new heart crisis. When she revived from the fainting spell, she saw before her some small white clouds which approached her and fused into one big cloud. This cloud then opened up and she saw the figure of Padre Pio.

"Good afternoon, Rosetta," he said, "don't be afraid, I am Padre Pio from Foggia," he said smiling; "you wrote to me to obtain a cure. Instead of answering the letter, I thought it best to come myself. If you will be good, I shall return tonight at 2 a.m., when your parents will also be here, and I shall bless you all."

The godmother, who saw the little one start back and heard her exclaim as if in ecstasy, "Oh, Padre Pio! Yes, yes, I shall tell it." She hastened to call her parents, who ran to her alarmed and convinced that she was delirious. But with the vanishing of the vision, Rosetta completely revived and told everything.

That night there was no way to make her retire early. She was excited; she wanted to wait up for the coming of Padre Pio, who anticipated his visit by two hours.

"Oh. . .mamma, he is here," announced the child, staring at one place in the room.

"I came ahead of time," said Padre Pio, "to allow you to rest. I did not like to wake you up." Then he took off a glove and showed her his lacerated hand, which was bleeding. He also showed her pictures of babies he cured. "See? This one was blind and is cured, this other one was mute and now speaks. You must tell your mother that she must not cry. I have not come to announce your death, but your cure. I have permission to tell it to you. The Madonna della Guardia will bring you the cure. She will come to you the 28th day of August at 8:15 in the evening. Prepare a beautiful little altar and above it place her picture."

Padre Pio then invited the child to recite with him the Our Father and Hail Mary. The parents and her sisters joined in the prayers, although they saw no one. With his hand still uncovered he blessed all the family.

He disappeared, to reappear on the 28th of August at 8:00 in the evening to point out to the child the window from which she could see the Madonna.

At 8:15 Rosetta began to hear a distant song. She looked anxiously at the ceiling. The singing became more beautiful and distinct as it approached her. It was a chorus of angelic voices that melted her heart and filled her eyes with tears.

Finally there came to the window a great white cloud surrounded by the tiny heads of little angels. The cloud opened, and there appeared the Madonna with a marvelous face under chestnut hair and so resplendent with light that the child could not fix her eyes on her. The Madonna was dressed in red with a blue mantle embroidered with gold stars, and she was holding in her arms the Child Jesus, with blond hair, wrapped in rose-colored swaddling clothes.

The Virgin smiled, with her ineffable smile, greeting the child affectionately. "I am the Madonna della Guardia; be good always, Rosetta, pray very much and I shall help you."

This apparition took place in the apartment of her godmother, and there was there also an old widow who was full of grief over the loss of a son in the war. She was always expecting his return, knowing that he was taken prisoner by the Germans. Rosetta asked the Madonna about him. The Blessed Virgin replied that the young man was in Purgatory, but that he would soon be released; but do not tell the mother now so she can live on in hope. Then she confided to her a secret to be jealously guarded. In good time, if she conducted herself well, the Virgin would return and tell to whom she should reveal the secret. She smiled again, as did the Child Jesus, holding up His three fingers of His right hand. Then the cloud returned to surround them and the vision ended.

Rosetta was still amidst the clouds when Padre Pio reappeared. "I am here again to disturb you. Wasn't the Madonna beautiful?" And he smiled also with a smile that is impossible to express in words. "You feel well," he added, "I cannot remember everything because I have so many, but you must remember all your life what you have seen tonight. When the Blessed Virgin returns, I shall return also."

From August, the little one was completely cured, as testified to by Dr. Sidi Raul Acconer.

Up to this writing the author of this book knows that Rosetta Polo Riva, who has corresponded with me, has not yet been revisited by the Madonna della Guardia. What the secret is and to whom it shall be revealed I do not know.

Upper left: Domine Non Sum Dignus.
Upper right: Holding paten.
Lower left: Blessing the Host.
Lower right: Adoring.

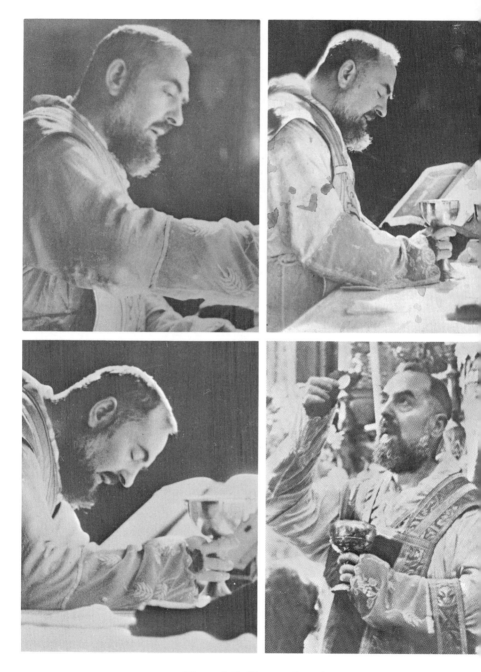

Upper left: Uncovering chalice.
Upper right: Communion.
Lower left: Meditation after receiving the Host.
Lower right: Ecce Agnus Dei.

Upper left: Main altar of Monastery.
Upper right: Opera Tenor Gigli singing "Mamma Mia" for Padre Pio.
Lower left: Buses from everywhere.
Lower right: Monastery garden well, Hospital in background.

Upper left: Birthplace of Padre Pio.
Upper right: Monastery gardens.
Lower left: His brother Michael, father and sister Grazia, now Sr. Pia.
Lower right: Barn at birthplace.

CHAPTER V

Conversions Reported by Alberto del Fante

If I could make known all the names of the persons whom Padre Pio converted, this book would become rather voluminous. I shall touch upon but a few of the most famous conversions. Alberto del Fante, the most prolific writer on Padre Pio, asserts that he is not ashamed to affirm in print: "I was a Mason, I was an atheist, I believed in nothing; Padre Pio has given me life under all aspects; today I pray, today I attend Mass every Sunday; it gives me pleasure when my children, before eating, make the Sign of the Cross to thank God, who gives us 'our daily bread'; today I receive the Blessed Sacrament, and I am happy when God enters my body. Whoever has my courage, will have my happiness. The great and infinite God gives all to all who love Him."

Mr. Luigi De Mercurio, born at Benevento, but living at Pietrelcina, believed in nothing, neither in God, nor Christ, nor even in any of the Saints.

When he married, he did not want holy pictures of any kind in his home, and he even once spat upon a picture of St. Lucy, whom his wife loved and venerated. Many times his wife and the Florios, friends of Pio's parents, advised him to go to Padre Pio, who would change his attitude. "Padre Pio," he always repeated, "will never succeed in changing my mind." One night Padre Pio appeared in a dream to his wife, and advised her to persuade her husband to go to San Giovanni Rotondo.

On June 19, 1925, Mr. De Mercurio, having business to attend to at San Giovanni, met a group of the faithful who were going to see the Padre. He went there for business, but also out of curiosity, and in order to deceive his wife.

The evening of June 19, 1925, he presented himself before Padre Pio, whom he had never seen, and as soon as he faced him, the rebel and the apostate felt forced by a superhuman force to kneel before him and kiss his habit.

He never knew how to explain why he acted in this manner and said, "It seemed to me that two strong hands forced me to kneel, and I was forced even to kiss his habit."

He came down into the town of San Giovanni with the others without telling the Padre who he was.

The morning after, he went to confession to Padre Pio and received the Blessed Sacrament from his stigmatized hands.

His esteem now for the Padre was great, but lingering doubt was still alive in him. He wanted from the Padre a proof that would definitely convince him.

In the evening at dinner his friends said: "Gigino, tomorrow is your name's day, the feast of your patron saint; you must pay for a treat to all of us." "Yes, yes," he answered, "I shall buy you all a drink of anise." "But that is too little!"

"Well then I shall buy a bottle of Strega."

Going to bed, Mr. De Mercurio, persistently thinking of Padre Pio, said to himself: "Padre, I shall believe in you, if tomorrow morning not one of my

companions will extend greetings on my name's day
from the time I get up, to the time I arrive at the
threshold of the monastery. You, Padre, must be the
first to extend the greetings of my feast day." He said,
"You must be the first to extend the greetings,"
because he knew that the Padre did not know his
name.

The morning after, June 21, the Feast of San Luigi,
which is his name's day, Mr. Mercurio was awakened
by his companions.

"Gigino, hurry up, we are late; through your fault
we shall not be able to assist at the Mass of Padre Pio!"

Nobody extended to him the greetings of his day.
No one called him by his proper name, neither in
the house, nor on the road to the monastery one mile
away.

His heart beat more rapidly every time he himself
mentioned "Luigi, Gigino or Gino," since he feared
that someone would recall to him the pledge made
the night before, not through fear of having to pay
for the bottle of Strega, but because his doubt would
have attacked him anew.

"Listen," he was saying to himself, "now they are
saying it; the pledge is broken and I do not believe;
it cannot be that all have forgotten that today is my
name's day; there are twelve of them, it is enough
that at least one remembers, one is sufficient."

Little by little as they approached the monastery
he repeated to himself, "Still 500 yards, then 300, still
100, then yards"; finally he arrived at the doors of
the church without ever hearing a greeting from any
one of the group.

"And now, here is the test," he said, "how can the

Padre extend to me his greetings before anyone else if he does not know my name? Haven't I asked perhaps too much? It is impossible. I have been a blockhead."

Padre Pio, after his Mass, retired to the choir for his thanksgiving. With his friends, Mr. De Mercurio waited for him to come out; a little later, Padre Pio came toward them smiling.

"Luigino, my greetings to you; today is your name's day," said the Padre as soon as he saw him.

Luigi De Mercurio stiffened; he wished to speak, he wished to thank, he wished to smile, but his voice left him and he could not say a word.

The others stood stupefied and were amazed at not having remembered, and they recalled to their friend the promise of the preceding evening.

De Mercurio, having won the argument, knelt before the Padre, kissed again his habit, raised his eyes toward him who knew all, and wept with joy.

Padre Pio looked at him and seemed to be saying, "The voice is silent, but the heart speaks."

"Pardon, pardon, pardon, Padre! You alone know what I have thought. You alone know how much I have desired and feared this moment. I am conquered, I am convinced, I am convinced, I believe, I believe, I believe, I shall love you just as you are loved by all those who approach you, I shall become your spiritual child...You have converted me."

Here we must testify that no one ever told Padre Pio that Mr. De Mercurio was called Luigi.

One family at San Giovanni Rotondo had the nickname of Tampa-Tampa. The family was very poor. Two sons were Capuchin Fathers, and a third son who was the idol of the mother had sought employment in Abyssinia. When the mother learned that her favorite son had died in Abyssinia she could not resign herself. A procession of Our Lady of Sorrows passed her house shortly after she heard about her son's death. The afflicted mother was unable to contain her grief, and instead of humbly asking the help of Our Lady of Sorrows she ran out into the crowded procession and blasphemed in a most scandalous manner against Our Lord and His Mother.

One of her Capuchin sons came home for a day's visit. He was grieved to find his mother poverty-stricken and seriously ill with heart trouble, and above all he was pained to hear about her falling from grace because of her public blasphemies. He went to the monastery and begged Padre Pio to pray for his mother that she might die in God's grace.

One morning the poor old mother dragged herself slowly to the monastery. She was exhausted when she arrived at the church. She confessed at length to Padre Pio, face to face under the arch where he hears the deaf, the crippled or the very aged who are unable to kneel down at the confessional.

The laments and loud sobs of the mother were heard by all in the church as she poured out her woes and sins. Many of those who were in the church knew about what had happened. They undoubtedly thanked the Lord that this soul was returning to grace.

When the long confession was ended, Padre Pio passed through the church to the confessional where numerous penitents were awaiting him. His face was white and his eyes expressed infinite grief, compassion, and love.

Outside the church, the old mother told all that she begged Padre Pio to tell the Lord to call her in death, as she was so tired. She was so exhausted that she could hardly stand up. Fortunately, a car was waiting in front of the church. She was taken home in the car. To her daughter she said: "Put me to bed and call all my children, Padre Pio has pardoned me." These were her last words, for she soon closed her tired eyes forever.

★   ★   ★

Alberto del Fante wrote the following: "Whoever has done evil must do penance—I have done evil by having been a Mason. The penance that I do today and that is for me a real joy is to persuade my former associates to return to the bosom of Mother Church.

"One of these former companions met me one day, and after exchanging greetings and passing the time of day I said to him: 'Buy the newspaper *La Settimana*. In it is published one of my articles.'

"A few days later I met him again. 'You know,' he said, 'I have read your article. Tell me more.' I was delighted, but wishing the dart to sink deeper and having too little time that day, I told him that I would see him about it at some other time.

"The next time I saw him I told him that I was returning to Padre Pio. He asked me to take a picture of St. Francis that he always carried in his pocket. 'Take it,' he said, 'and ask Padre Pio to bless it for me, and tell him that whenever I can I shall visit him.'

"When I met the Padre and pulled out the picture to be blessed, Padre Pio said to me, 'It belongs to a Mason, but a Mason who keeps St. Francis in his pocket has already the spirit of faith.'

"I shall be brief. After my return, Mr. X left for San Giovanni. From there he sent me a card with these words:

"'San Giovanni Rotondo, February 27, 1931

"'I am happy; later by word of mouth I shall explain; I could not take a better step in my life than this. For it I am grateful to you.'"

Such a card Alberto del Fante keeps in his files among the very numerous others that he has received. They are for the most part words of thanks, because after reading the articles and books on Padre Pio by the author del Fante, many have felt the need of going to the Padre.

This convert wrote the following to del Fante:

"Bologna, November 18, 1931

"Dear del Fante:

"It is through gratitude that I send you this letter. It is already one year since I met you one evening on Via Galliera, do you remember? You invited me to read one of your articles written in a weekly newspaper. I bought the paper and read your article. I read it again. I became very disturbed. In it I found reflected my own state of soul.

"I meditated very much over your article. I thought of the many years I had passed in the search of truth and the true light, of the errors when, urged on by the living desire of knowledge, I dedicated myself with all the enthusiasm of my young years, to the study of the materialism of Haeckel, then in great vogue,

from whom, however, I withdrew nauseated, not
being able to admit that, mountains of thought, like
the works of Dante, Leonardo, Michelangelo, etc.,
which defy the centuries, were simply the result of
chemical physical combinations, and the negation of
the soul, which is that which forms our ego, which
is in us and outside of us, because it is not simply
elaboration of material. These concepts were incon-
ceivable to me and in full contrast to my conscience.
I sought out other ways, and finding in the theosophic
teachings something that was satisfying to my spirit,
I dedicated myself to the study of the theories of
Steiner, Besant, etc. The years passed and I found myself with the same doubts, with the same uncertain-
ties, and my restlessness was greater; the crises of my
soul were always more frequent. When in Assisi, Paul
Sabatier spoke to me about St. Francis and explained
to me his preaching, and this return to the Saint of
Assisi made me realize that the path rejected by me
was not the right one, that the light that I was seeking was not the true light. Then I asked myself what
is the right way and where shall I find it?

"Dear Alberto, the Lord has infinite ways. I met
you on my path. You indicated to me the good way,
I listened, I ascended the bitter path of Mount
Gargano, I found the Master, he welcomed me with
joy, because in me he saw a blind man. Smiling he
listened to my doubts, with simplicity of word, but
with immense profundity of thought, he demolished
one by one all the theories with which my mind
was saturated; without having arguments to oppose,
he exposed my soul and showed me the teachings
of the Lord, he reopened the eyes of my soul; I saw

the true Light, it touched my heart, I knew and recognized the true Faith.

"Now I feel truly at peace in my soul. Now I know the true God.

"For this I am grateful to you, I owe you much, I owe all to Padre Pio.

Yours affectionately,
Ferruccio Caponetti."

Ferruccio Caponetti died on October 7, 1944. He died a serene and happy death, after having suffered a long illness with Christian resignation. (Alberto del Fante).

Andrea Bacile, of S. Martino in Pensilis, a peasant farmer, was an atheist who believed in nothing and never approached the Sacraments.

One evening after a quarrel with his wife, he prepared dinner for himself and his children whom he dearly loved; then he went to bed.

He still had the light on when a monk appeared to him in his room. It was Padre Pio, whose photograph he had seen many times.

Instead of being afraid, he said to Padre Pio: "Padre, I wish to make my confession."

"No," answered the monk, and he vanished.

The morning after he made up with his wife and was seized with the desire to go to San Giovanni.

First he went to the cemetery to pray for his deceased relatives, then on foot he went from S. Martino in Pensilis, which is in the province of Campobasso, to San Giovanni, fasting for the entire three days of the journey.

Arriving at the monastery the evening of the third

day he confessed to Padre Pio, who after giving him absolution, said to him:

"And now you can break your fast." Padre Pio, without hearing a word about his fasting, knew that for three days Andrea Bacile was without food.

Bacile returned to his village a changed man. He became a practicing Catholic and a model husband and father, never failing to follow the advice of Padre Pio.

Attorney Festa, cousin of Dr. Festa who wrote the valuable scientific book on Padre Pio, had heard Dr. Festa speak many times about Padre Pio, but from the beginning he believed it to be all exaggeration.

Furthermore the attorney was one of the leaders of Masonry at Superba, near Genoa, and hence had little sympathy for priests and monks.

One day, urged by the desire of seeing this miracle-working monk, he left Genoa for San Giovanni.

Presenting himself at the monastery, and before he had a chance to open his mouth, Padre Pio approached him and said:

"What, you here amongst us? But aren't you a Mason?"

"Yes, Padre," answered the dumbfounded lawyer.

"And what task have you in Masonry?"

"To combat the Church on political matters," he answered.

Padre Pio smiled with pity and tenderness, took his hand and spoke to him kindly about the prodigal son who returned to his father's house, spoke to him about the infinite mercy of the Lord, and of the greatest good he could obtain by approaching the Church which opens her divine mantle and welcomes all those who return to her penitent and converted. One hour after, the attorney from Genoa was at the feet of Padre Pio pleading to make his confession. Full of joy and zeal, the new convert like all other converts, wanted to tell the world of his joy.

Before leaving he asked the Padre what he should do about publicly casting away the insignia of Masonry.

"No," answered Pio, "do nothing now and wait. When the opportunity presents itself, the Lord will notify you."

Attorney Festa returned to Genoa in a happy mood.

He wrote immediately to his cousin, Dr. Festa of Rome, giving him the glad tidings and saying to him: "Thanks, you have opened for me a way which I shall follow. I cannot tell you anything in writing because I cannot write it down. I tell you solely that I return home with a profound peace in my soul, desirous of silence, and that nothing disturbs my spirit."

But as in the case of all his converts, after a brief absence he longed to see Padre Pio again; he seemed to be obsessed by the thought of him until he finally found himself on the train to San Giovanni Rotondo.

Padre Pio wrote on the frontispiece of his Gospel: "Blessed are they who hear the divine word, jealously keep it, and faithfully fulfill it."

Happier than ever, the attorney returned to Genoa.

Religion was beginning to plant its roots.

A few days later he went to Lourdes with a pilgrimage directed by Cardinal Ratti of Milano, who became Pope Pius XI.

When he returned to Genoa, he wrote Dr. Festa

in these words:

"I returned yesterday from Lourdes, the city of miracles and of prayer. I have made a long journey in Franciscan simplicity, in the third class of the train, with the sick, the infirm, and the 'brancardiers.'

"I recalled how St. Francis of Assisi had so much repugnance for lepers, but he ended by serving and loving them. I, who could not bear to look at certain ones of the sick pilgrims, stayed with them a long time to comfort and serve them. I have learned my lesson. I have seen, felt and understood how much suffering there is within human flesh. But I have seen the miracle. How much comfort and how much intimate joy there is to withstand so much illness."

At his return the *Avanti,* the Italian socialist newspaper, published an article with a satirical heading: "A Mason at Lourdes," in which the lawyer was bitterly attacked.

Imagine the hatred of the "brothers of Masonry." Invited by his lodge to justify himself, they showered upon him abuse and threatened him with sanctions.

He instead never lost his tranquility.

As soon as he learned that his old brethren were holding a secret meeting, he joined them.

The same morning he received a letter from Padre Pio, who for four months had not written to him, which concluded with these words:

"Do not blush about Christ and His doctrine; the time has come to bring the fight into the open. The Doctor of every good will give you the strength."

Let us imagine the zeal which possessed Mr. Festa, and curious and strange must have been the looks of his ex-companions, when they in the lodge heard him speak of God and the teachings of Christ with the same ardor as a Lenten preacher.

Today this noble figure is a fervent Franciscan Tertiary, a most eloquent lecturer and a writer of pure Franciscan faith.

His writings, his deeds, and all his actions are turned to that God who loves with divine love.

At his return from San Giovanni Rotondo, the convert attorney was received by Pope Benedict XV. To the Vicar of Christ, the attorney spoke of Padre Pio.

His Holiness said to him: "Padre Pio is truly the Man of God. You must assume the task of making him known. He is not appreciated by all as he merits."

These are the words of a Pontiff, who was an *admirer* of the Padre.

But Pope Benedict XV is not the only one, for more than one Cardinal and Bishop asked the Padre, when they were at the monastery, for the permission to serve his Mass.

One day to Padre Pio's own archbishop, Pope Pius XI said, *"Io non sono stato maldisposto, ma io sono stato malinformato del Padre Pio."* (I have not been badly disposed toward Padre Pio, but I have been badly informed about Padre Pio.).

In May 1926, there came to San Giovanni Rotondo Signor Di Maggio, a lawyer from Palermo, then a young man of about thirty, who was at that time living in Rome. Those who were present at his arrival can bear witness to what I am telling for the glory of God. I must add that this story was told me by one of Signor Di Maggio's very good friends, a young lady who was there at the time, and became his confidant.

The young man was the bearer of a letter from a lawyer, Manguso Canonesi of Buenos Aires. The letter was to serve as an introduction to the above-mentioned young lady, for the young lawyer who was in need of a spiritual guide.

Di Maggio went to the church without speaking to anyone in the village. He sat down next to the altar, near the railing, as though he were in some public place without any religious significance. His behavior was such as to arouse the curiosity of everyone in the church.

A few minutes after he got there, the Father came out to say his Mass. When the young man saw the little priest, he turned around to the people about him and pointed with his hands as though to ask, "Is that Padre Pio?" The lady who told me the story nodded in the affirmative. He was not impressed, and stayed where he was, showing complete indifference.

Padre Pio began his Mass. The lawyer stared at the Father, and as his interest was aroused, he began to shift his position, in order to see better, and to observe him from every side. He even ended by kneeling in front of the high altar, before the Father had finished his Mass.

When Padre Pio returned to the sacristy, Di Maggio did not dare to follow him, being new to such approaches. Instead, he turned to the person who told me about it, and asked if it were possible to speak with the Father, and begged her to lend him her prayer book for a moment, as he wished to go to confession. She told him to wait for the Father, and in the meantime to make his examination of conscience; she did not find out until later that it was many years since he had been to the Sacraments.

Shortly after this he was able to talk to Padre Pio, and not only to go to confession but to Communion also, and later he was again able to pluck up his courage and to talk to him in the sacristy.

When he left the church his face was radiant with joy, and he longed to share this joy with everyone about him. On his way down to San Giovanni and in the village itself, he spoke freely of his wonderful conversion, and of his former life which had been spent away from the church and had been far from exemplary. He had been an intellectual and pleasure-loving, and his absolute freedom from all discipline had led him into many forms of excess. It is therefore easy to see that a tremendous weight of sin was lying on his soul. He told his listeners that a few days previous to all this he had made the decision of studying the drama, as he wanted to go on the stage.

After the visit to Padre Pio, his former life filled him with disgust, and he was determined to reform completely and take up the study of Sacred Scripture. Back in the inn he began at once to write his impressions of his confession and of all that had occurred in his soul since his meeting with the Father. Some thought him to be a journalist who might in his writings do harm to the Father, and were suspicious of him. Others thought he was a crank, an enthusiast and a false convert. This was probably caused by the excessive ardor with which he spoke of Padre Pio, an ardor that was shared by all of his neophytes.

Whereas he had come to San Giovanni Rotondo out of sheer curiosity and had intended to leave at once, not only had he stayed on, but he telegraphed to Rome to a friend, who was also a lawyer, to come and join him immediately. His friend, thinking that he had been in an accident, came at once, but on learning that Di Maggio had only sent for him because he wanted him to be converted also, immediately decided that he was merely excitable, easily influenced and probably mad. However, being also curious, the friend went with Di Maggio to see the Father. One visit was enough to convert him, too, and he thanked not only the Father, but also Di Maggio and the person who told me this tale, and who gave him a rosary and prayer book.

A few days later as Di Maggio was taking his leave of the Father, he said to him: "Father, I am now returning to Rome and the old occasions of sin. What shall I do to keep my promises? Please help me!" The Father answered: "My son—pray, don't ever leave off praying, and be assured that when I have raised a soul, I never let it fall."

Di Maggio went back to Rome, and his conversion was real and sincere, as proved by the letters he wrote later, and by his return to San Giovanni Rotondo before Christmas. He left there on Christmas Eve, as he wanted to be with his family for the Feast. He came back several times to the Father, because many people from Bologna saw him there, in the shadow of that monastery that spread so much grace abroad.

I feel certain that Signor Di Maggio's humility will not be impaired by my account of him, because he

knows that what I write is for the glory of God, and
of him who converts everyone.

★   ★   ★

A trolley car conductor from Rivarolo in Liguria,
whose name I cannot recall, had a child who suffered
from epilepsy. He heard about the case of Signora
Bonardi and asked me to give him the address of the
Father. He appealed to him devoutly, and after a few
months he had the joy of taking his little girl to San
Giovanni Rotondo, completely cured, and was able
to thank the Father and receive his blessing.

Several of my friends, urged on by me, went to
visit the Father, and one of them said to me: "In my
life I have suffered much through injustice and human
wickedness, but I would be happy if the wrongs that
have been done me could be duplicated so that I might
forgive them ten times over; this is the feeling I had
after my visit to Padre Pio."

★   ★   ★

An engineer of Bologna, whose name I have been
asked not to repeat, a few years ago had a dream
in which he saw Padre Pio, of whom he had never
even heard. He dreamed of a friar standing with his
hands crossed on his breast, and the hands were lacerated by the glorious stigmata of Christ. This friar,
who had an angelic appearance, gazed for a long time
into his eyes without changing his position; then after
a while he said: "Happy you who have been able to
endure my gaze!"

The engineer woke up and found himself much
shaken by this most unusual dream. He tried to

remember if he had ever seen such a friar, but he was forced to admit that he had not, for this friar had a charm and a certain quality that was peculiar to him.

It was only after he heard of Padre Pio and the gift that he had to project himself to any distance, even through dreams, that it occurred to him that he was his friar. This idea came to him although he was far removed from the Faith and from the religion of Christ.

After this dream the young engineer began to experience a sensation that he had never felt in his life. It was his conscience that reproached him for the life that he had led and was still leading; it was remorse for not having always done right, for having yielded to pleasure, for having taken no notice of those who suffered and of the humble, in short for having silenced the voice of the soul.

The gaze of the humble friar pursued him like a gadfly everywhere. That look had nothing in it of the Divine, as it was purely human, but it seemed like a reproach, a summons, an invitation to renewal and change to a better life, and a return to the right road.

Eight years went by...

Many years ago in Bologna when an earthquake made its unwelcome appearance, our young engineer, being perhaps badly frightened, and hearing persistent talk about Padre Pio, thought of going to San Giovanni Rotondo to make the acquaintance of this friar, and to make his peace with God. He left Bologna with this in mind, but the train had only covered a few miles when he felt ill and was forced to interrupt

his journey. On his return to his house, being puz-
zled by this strange indisposition, he decided to write
to Padre Pio. He did not know that it was forbidden
to him to answer letters, but he complained to him
that just as he had been inspired to do something
good, he had been prevented by a strange illness which
had prevented him from proceeding with his plans
to visit him.

Another Father answered him—I know his name—
telling him that his time had not yet come, that he
must wait with patience and resignation, that he must
direct all of his actions toward the right goal and that
the great moment would come for him, too, someday. He added that Padre Pio sent him his blessing.

A few months later the engineer referred himself
to certain spiritual children of Padre Pio living in
Bologna for some information, and having received
it, without giving his name, he took the train for San
Giovanni, promising that he would tell them the
results of his journey. A few days after his return from
San Giovanni, his face transfigured with joy, he gave
them his name, and told them of all the emotions
he had experienced.

He had left Bologna feeling very anxious to know
the Father. When he got to San Giovanni Rotondo,
he found in the sacristy of the little church of Our
Lady of Grace the same Father who had answered
his letter. He brought him to the monastery and
promised him that he would have him meet Padre
Pio, who must at that time be either in the choir
or in his cell. Having opened the door of the modest
room that serves as a parlor, the good friar was
amazed to find Padre Pio, standing up with his arms

crossed on his breast, turned toward the door as
though waiting for someone. The Father introduced
the young man, and without saying anything more
went out and closed the door. The engineer was
speechless with amazement, for there was the same
friar that he had already seen in his dream; in the
same position, with the same gaze, and the same stigmatized hands! He was looking at him with the same
expression, but this time it was true. The young man
fell to his knees and broke down in a flood of tears.
"Father," he said, "I have known of you for eight
years!" "And a lot of good it did you! You were taking your time! Change your life, my son!"

Our young friend made a general confession, worthy of his new life. When he left the Father, his heart
was bursting with joy. He went back to Bologna and
told those who had given him advice all about his
conversion. He was at first rather confused, and spoke
of God, of Christ, His Mother, Padre Pio, and Holy
Mother Church. After a while, however, he became
more calm, serene and enlightened. The storm in his
soul had ceased; he was aware that love, the only true
and great love was being reborn in his heart.

Professor G. Felice Checcacci of Genoa is well-
known. He lived for some forty years in the Orient
and had the opportunity to study many religions. On
his return to Italy some years ago, having read about
Padre Pio, he was impelled by the desire to go and
see the Father, and came back full of enthusiasm. His
age, his studies, his many journeys and contacts with
famous people in the world of culture, religion and
the arts, gave an effective guarantee that his judgment was free of prejudice and exaggeration. He was

the author of many popular novels with an oriental background, of several plays, and of hundreds of musical compositions. The professor wrote to del Fante the following letter on July 25, 1940: "Lucky you who can go so often to the Father, what peace of soul you must enjoy! Embrace him humbly for me...I am sending you some notes on the Father; you may use them if you like."

Checcacci wrote as follows:

"Tormented and obsessed by my studies in comparative oriental religions, I finally fell into the heresy of considering Christianity to be a derivation of Brahminism and Buddhism. At this time the booklet of del Fante, "From Doubt to Faith," fell into my hands. I read it all at one sitting, I re-read it, I meditated on it and studied it, and wrote to del Fante, who then sent me his book, *For History*.

"This book made such a profound impression on me that one night I dreamed of Padre Pio, and that he said: 'Come and see me.'

"I did not give any importance to this dream, but three months later I dreamed of Padre Pio again, who said to me this time: 'I waited for you, but you did not come.'

"I would not have paid any more attention to this dream than I had to the others, were it not for the fact that one sleepless night, some time later, I saw, yes actually *saw* Padre Pio enter my bedroom, and coming toward me he said: 'If you cannot come, write.' The impression that this made on me was tremendous and indescribable; I still can feel goose-pimples as I write. I jumped up from my bed, but the vision had disappeared.

"The next morning I wrote to Padre Pio, not asking for material assistance, but for peace of soul. Two days later, in the late afternoon I felt a sudden start and a voice within me saying: 'Go to church and pray.' I must confess that it was over thirty years since I had gone into a church out of devotion. I obeyed, and while I was praying, the inward voice whispered: 'Faith is not to be argued over, either you accept it with your eyes closed, admitting the inadequacy of the human mind to understand its mysteries, or you reject it. There is no middle way. The choice is up to you.'

"From that day I have chosen my road, and I owe to Padre Pio the return to the Faith of my fathers. I was able then to understand both the beauty of Christian charity, and the egoism and the indifference to human suffering of the Asiatic religions that have for their basis mere fatalism and the belief in reincarnation.

"I have just received the following letter which I quote in full, as it deserves that all should read it:

'Dear Signor Fante,

'I hear that you are writing a new book about Padre Pio, and that you welcome impressions and experiences from people who have been to him.

'I am of German origin, but speak Italian fairly well. I feel, however, somewhat embarrassed at having to write in that language, especially about Padre Pio. There is so much that is exalted and stupendous to say about him, that I am not always able to find adequate words to express my thoughts.

'I do not wish to make a complete account of all

that has happened to me, because I would have to write an entire volume; but among all my experiences I shall choose one, that is the story of my conversion, which I hold to be the greatest miracle of all.

'When in November of 1928, I went for the first time to Padre Pio, I had been only recently converted from Lutheranism to Catholicism; I had done this for purely social reasons. I had no faith, at least today I can see that I was merely under the illusion of having one. Having grown up in a completely anti-Catholic family, and being imbued with prejudice against all dogma that a most hurried course of instruction was not able to eradicate, I was nonetheless fascinated by the occult and the mysterious.

'I found a friend who introduced me to spiritualism. I soon grew weary, however of these inconclusive messages from beyond the tomb, and I threw myself with ardor into the field of occultism and magic of every description. I made the acquaintance of a gentleman who with a mysterious air, declared himself the possessor of the only truth: "Theosophy". I soon became his disciple, and on my bed table there began to grow an accumulation of books with the most attractive and intriguing titles. I was able to roll on my tongue with assurance such words as *reincarnation, logos, brahma, maja,* awaiting always that certain something both great and new that must surely come.

'I do not really know why, but I think that it was more than anything else for the sake of satisfying my wife that I still approached the Sacraments from time to time; and this was the state of mind that I was in when I first heard of that Capuchin Father,

who was described to me as enduring a living cruci-
fixion, and was working continuous miracles.

'I was filled with curiosity, but at the same time
I hesitated, since this was all happening in the bosom
of the Catholic Church; however, I decided to go
and see with my own eyes.

'I shall not describe my journey, which I made with
much the same feelings that you describe in "From
Doubt to Faith."'

'My first encounter with Padre Pio left me a little
cold. He only made a few rather dry remarks, whereas
I had expected a warmer welcome if only as a reward for my long journey. Shortly afterwards I knelt
down in the confessional, which is God's tribunal.
I leave out all the details and describe only what had
a supernatural quality, a touch of the Divine.

'Padre Pio made me understand at once that in
my preceding confessions I had omitted certain grave
offenses, and he asked me if I had been in good faith.
I answered that I considered Confession a good institution, both socially and educationally, but that I did
not at all believe in the divinity of the Sacrament.
However I was already so much moved by what I
had seen, that I added: "Now, however, Father, I do
believe." Then he said with an expression of deep
pain, "These are all heresies, and all your Commun-
ions have been sacrilegious. . . . You must make a
general confession; make your examination of conscience and try to *remember when you last made a sincere
confession.* Jesus has been more merciful with you than
with Judas." Then casting a severe glance over my
head, he said in a loud voice: "Jesus and Mary be
praised!" and went into the church to hear the

women's confessions. I, in the meantime, remained in the sacristy, much moved and shaken. My head was in a turmoil, and I seemed to be unable to concentrate. I kept hearing these words repeated in my ears. *"Remember when you last made a sincere confession."*

'I hesitatingly made the following decision: I would tell him that I had been a Protestant, that I had been re-baptized conditionally, in view of which, through the virtue of the Sacrament, all the sins of my past life had been wiped out; but that even so, for the sake of my peace of mind I wished to review the whole of my past life, from my childhood.

'When the Father returned to the confessional, he repeated the question: *"Well, when did you make your last good confession?"* I answered: "Father, as I happened to be. . ." But at this point the Father interrupted me saying: "Yes, you made a good confession that time when you were returning from your wedding trip, let us leave out all the rest, and begin from there." I was struck dumb with the overwhelming realization that I had come in contact with the supernatural. But the Father did not give me time to think, concealing his knowledge of my entire past under the form of questions. He enumerated with precision and clarity all of my faults, even mentioning the number of times that I had missed Mass. After the Father had specified all of my mortal sins, he made me understand, with most impressive words, the whole of their gravity, adding in a tone of voice that I can never forget: "You have launched a hymn to Satan, whereas Jesus in His tremendous love has broken His neck for you." He then gave me a penance and absolved me. This absolution gave me a feeling of suffocation at the time, but later caused me such joy and such a sensation of lightness, that returning to the village with the other pilgrims, I behaved like a noisy child.

'I will skip the rest, even my impressions of the Mass, which have been more worthily described by others, and which gave me also the touch of grace, for I understood without other explanation all of the mysterious grandeur and beauty of the divine Sacrifice.

'In order further to emphasize the greatness of Padre Pio in confession, I feel justified in going over certain details, without which it would be easy to minimize the prodigious thing that happened to me. Humanly speaking it was impossible for the Father to know that I had made a wedding journey, and that the confession that I had made on my return was indeed a good one. It actually did happen just as he said. The day after we returned from the trip, my wife expressed the desire that we should both approach the Sacraments, and I complied with her wish. I went for confession to the same priest who had prepared me for my abjuration, and he knowing that I was a novice and little accustomed to such things, helped me with questions, and that is why I had made a good confession.

'I ask myself, however, who but Padre Pio, who had the gift of reading our most intimate thoughts and could scrutinize our consciences, could have had any knowledge of these things. Only as a result of his gifts could he have made me begin my confession at the place that he chose, rather than at the one that I had in mind. As I have already said, I was from the first completely bowled over by hearing things that I had quite forgotten, and I was only able to reconstruct the past by remembering in all their detail the particulars that Padre Pio had described with such precision. Critics and doubters will not be able to say that it is a question of thought-transference, for as I have already said, my intention had been to begin my confession from my childhood.

'In order to make this story of my conversion complete, I will tell you what was also the result of this most fortunate journey. From that day to this, I have been to daily Mass and Communion. I have become a Franciscan Tertiary, and so has my wife, and not only do I believe in the dogmas of the Catholic Church, but in its most minute ceremonies, and I could not lose this Faith without also losing my life.

'I have said all this in order to give glory to God, and thank Him, and to obtain peace and happiness for men of goodwill.

Your affectionate,
Federico Abresch."

On the 2nd of May, 1949, I received a letter from Signora Wanda Bianco, a lady from Piedmont, who for many years had been living in Canada. She wrote:

"...It may interest you to know that several years ago I became acquainted with the humble little friar, Padre Pio, through a Russian aristocrat who later became a Catholic and then a Trinitarian monk, taking the name of Padre Pio. He went to San Giovanni Rotondo and spoke to the Very Reverend Padre Pio, who encouraged him on the road that led to his taking Holy Orders at the age of fifty!

"I beg of you to remember in your prayers this good priest, who was a great friend of mine, and who left this poor earth on the 12th of September, 1947.

Wanda Bianco,
74 Russell Street,
Halifax, Nova Scotia, Canada."

Del Fante wrote:

"This letter interested me deeply, as I had heard much talk about this conversion, but no one had been able to furnish me with accurate and positive information.

"I answered Signora Bianco, begging her to send me more details, and at the same time thanking her for the translation into English of my modest poem on Padre Pio. On the 8th of June, 1949, I received her answer by air mail, in which she replied as follows:

"'...You will find here enclosed the information that you asked for concerning the late Padre Pio, of whom I spoke in my last letter. I am sending you photographs of his tombstone with the inscription in English and in Latin. It would be a great consolation to me if you were to remember him to the Reverend Padre Pio of Pietrelcina when you see him. I am sure that he will be able to remember.

W.B.' "

On a separate sheet she wrote:

"Carl Klugkist was born in Kiev, Russia, in 1871. He received Baptism and Confirmation and made his first Holy Communion in the month of December, 1908. He entered the monastery of San Ferdinando in Livorno in 1921, and here received the habit with the name of Brother Pio of the Holy Trinity. In June, 1924, he was sent to Canada but before leaving Italy he had a special audience with the Holy Father, Pius X, who gave him his blessing as well as his stole, which is now in the Church of St. Joseph in Halifax.

"He pronounced his solemn vows in Montreal, and shortly afterwards he was ordained. He died in Halifax on the 12th of September, 1947.

"Carl Klugkist knew Padre Pio of Pietrelcina. He had contributed to his conversion, for it was he who had encouraged him and told him that he was surely on the right road when he aspired to the priesthood.

"The most Reverend Padre Pio of the Holy Trinity (known in the world as Carl Klugkist) was a painter who had lived most of his life in Rome. For several years he had been tutor to the sons of Princess Del Drago in Rome. Before his conversion he was deeply immersed in the study of spiritualism and theosophy, which he later abjured.

"While he was with Prince Del Drago in Rome, he tried in every way to have himself received in various orders, but was always refused admittance owing to his advanced age. The Very Reverend Padre Pio di Pietrelcina was always a great comfort when he turned to him. He had told him once that the monastic order to which he would later belong would be made known to him through an apparition.

"One day Carl Klugkist, having gone to one of the churches in Rome where he was in the habit of praying, and feeling much depressed, asked for God's help with greater insistence than usual, in order to be shown the right direction to follow. At the moment when the celebrant was lifting the monstrance, and the future Padre Pio was gazing with great faith at the Host, there appeared to him a great light in the center of which was a device that was unknown to him. This was the revelation that Padre Pio of Pietrelcina had told him of. After a prolonged search he discovered that the device which had appeared to him belonged to the Trinitarians. He presented himself to the monastery, and having told his story, he was admitted.

"When the Reverend Padre Pio of the Holy Trinity told me of this, I saw him tremble with emotion, and his face was bathed in tears.

Wanda Bianco,
74 Russell Street,
Halifax, Nova Scotia."

I had heard it said, and Signor Celao Pezzoni of Milan had confirmed it in writing, that Pitigrilli had become converted. I found myself in a Catholic bookstore, and saw a book on the counter called: *Pitigrilli talks about...Pitigrilli.* I bought it together with *The Waters of Siloe* and that very evening began to read the former.

Some years ago I had read other books by Pitigrilli, so that I was familiar with his breezy, brilliant, and powerful style; but the subjects dealt with were different.

It took several hours to read it. To my surprise, or rather my joy, I read this paragraph on page 166:

"My earlier books, published after the first World War, were inspired by a materialism which, at that time, sufficed to answer all my questions, but which is no longer sufficient today. For this reason I have

struck out five of them from my list of works, and
have forbidden that they should be reprinted. My
climb to spiritual heights was slow but constant. Two
contacts contributed to it: those with the actress
Lavalliere, and with Padre Pio of Pietrelcina."

After having told about the famous actress
Lavalliere—the best-known woman in Paris in her
time, who later became a nun in a leprosarium, and
who, before she died, asked to have inscribed upon
her tomb the words of St. Thais, that she had taken
for her own: "I have abandoned everything for God,"
Pitigrilli from page 178, tells of Padre Pio, bearing
out my own observations, except when he refers to
his friend Luigi Antonelli, the comic writer.

Pitigrilli wrote on page 173:

"I stayed at Foggia and its environs for two weeks,
in order to collect testimony and documents. The living document was brought to me by my friend Luigi
Antonelli, a comic writer who had had thirty years
of success. His son Anton, like himself a comic writer,
lives in Rome and Capri, and can testify whether there
is any exaggeration in what I am telling.

"'The doctors,' Luigi Antonelli told me, 'found
here' —and then he moved his hand from his ear to
his shoulder— 'something wrong with me, and wanted
to operate. They said the usual things to me. As far
as cancer is concerned, modern science is where it
was two thousand years ago, when 'opium and lies'
was the treatment. In other words, narcotics and lies
keep the patient from knowing the truth. Today they
lie with more erudite words, and instead of giving
opium to drink, they inject pentapon. I said to my
surgeon, Donati: 'I have now survived the halfway

point of human life, whatever I have left is supplementary, and I am ready to renounce it. But tell me the truth: how much more time have I?' 'With an operation six months; without an operation, three.' 'Operate,' I answered, 'three months must not be thrown away!'"

"I was about to have the operation when someone suggested to me: 'Why don't you go to Padre Pio?' I inquired, and learned from several sources all in agreement, that this monk who performed miracles lived in a Capuchin monastery at San Giovanni Rotondo, 25 miles from Foggia. 'I don't know,' Luigi Antonelli continued, 'whether the word miracle is exact from the theological viewpoint, but you understand me and we will not split hairs upon words. I went to Padre Pio, was present at his Mass, and talked to him in confession. I cannot repeat what he said to me because while he was speaking to me I seemed to be living in a supernatural world. My cancer was checked; I am now writing, as you can see, an article every Sunday in the 'Giornale d'Italia.' I go hunting; for the past month I have been working at a comedy which will be produced in a few months at the Manzoni Theater in Milan. I don't know what the doctors may think about it, I don't know what X-rays and histological examination may reveal—which I moreover, will not have made—but *today I feel that I am miraculously cured!*"

Little by little, as I became absorbed in the book, I found my interest increasing, and—I wish to be frank—also my admiration for Pitigrilli, with whom I had many friends in common, and who are mentioned in his book.

I asked his publisher, Sonzogno in Milan, for his

Upper left: Pio Abresch, Capranica College—Rome—see page 226.
Lower left: P. Pio's niece and her family of six children, July 2, 1952.
Upper right: Pio Abresch, age 12, on the left of P. Pio.
Lower right: Mrs. Emilia Abresch—see pages 223-226.

Upper left: Monastery well.
Upper right: Dr. Sanguinetti, first director of the Hospital (died Sept. 6, 1954).
Lower left: Where P. Pio heard the confessions of women.
Lower right: Panorama of Mt. Gargano, Monastery, Hospital and Hotel.

Upper left: Lining up for P. Pio's Mass at early dawn.
Upper right: Miss Mary McAlpin Pyle—see Preface.
Lower left: Construction of roof addition to the Monastery.
Lower right: Padre Pio's sister.

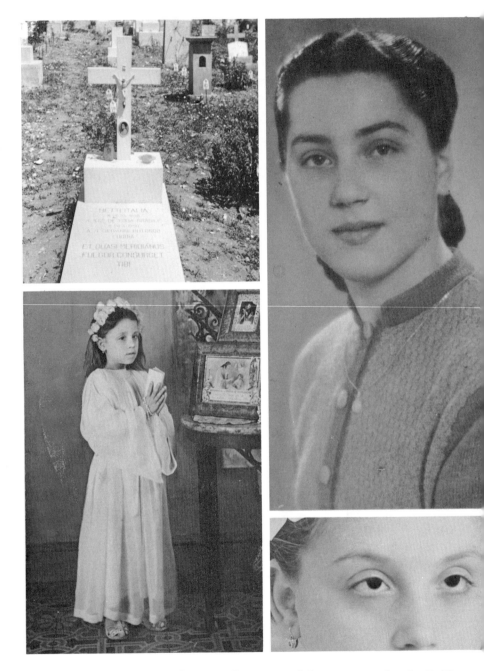

Upper left: Grave of Betti Italia converted from communism by P. Pio.
Upper right: Rosetta Riva cured by P. Pio—see page 78.
Lower left: Gemma Di Giorgi on the day of her Solemn Communion.
Lower right: The pupilless eyes of Gemma Di Giorgi—see page 158.

address, which they kindly gave me. I wrote to Pitigrilli by airmail to Buenos Aires, on February 7, 1950, asking him to tell me of his conversion through the mediation of Padre Pio.

On February 12th, just five days later, Pitigrilli replied:

"I have nothing to add to what I have written in my account. It would merely be a dilution, while I am in favor of condensation. Take from my book anything which may be of use to you. Please say that in my case it is not a question of conversion—that is to say, the renunciation of one faith for another—but of coming back to the Faith from which I had kept myself removed.

"When I wrote in 'Razon': *Pitigrilli speaks of Pitigrilli* in 35 successive issues, and when the chapter on Padre Pio appeared, I was approached by letter and telephone by quantities of sick and tormented people. Why don't you come to Buenos Aires and give lectures about Padre Pio? You would have a great success that could be repeated all over South America.

"I clasp your hand in real friendship, wishing you every success in literature and journalism.

Yours,
Pitigrilli."

"The Mass said by Padre Pio brings tears to the eyes of everyone present," wrote Dino Segre, whose pen name is Pitigrilli.

Pitigrilli followed Pio's Mass hidden away among the faithful, completely unknown to all and to Padre Pio. At the end of the Mass, Padre Pio suddenly turned around and addressed the congregation in these words:

"Pray, brethren, pray fervently for someone who is here among you today who is in great need of prayer. One day he will approach the Eucharistic Table and will bring many with him who have been in error like himself."

Pitigrilli went back to Buenos Aires a changed man and a newly-oriented playwright.

Once the pagan syllogists often tried to attack Christ, without success. Those who deny the supernatural have tried, and are continually trying today to disprove Padre Pio and have never been able to do so.

Christ founded the Christian Church; but in order to be followed, even by His own disciples, the God-Man had need to demonstrate to them and to His followers that He accomplished miracles.

Why? I asked myself. The reasons are various, infinite, and innumerable, wrote del Fante.

Those who deny miracles are usually the atheists, those who believe in nothing at all; the pantheists, who confuse God with Nature, finally the naturalists, who although they do not deny God, neither do they believe in His divine providence. Even if the phenomenon of a miracle is checked and verified by such people, it is not believed, because it might upset all their philosophical concepts which are founded upon castles in the air.

He who denies miracles tends to eliminate God from his conception of the world and of life; he who still denies after the supernatural has been proven, is all the more a slave to the prejudices and conventional lies of society and can no longer think with his own brain.

The great Seneca said: *Veritas in omnem sui partem
eadem est.* (Truth is always the same in all its parts.)
Why, then, deny the truth when it is manifest to our
senses?

Someone might ask me, "Why does not God, who
can do all things, make me believe? I want to believe,
but I cannot, I don't know, I am unable to."

He is in error, as I shall demonstrate at once.

I might answer him: "I also was as you are, I also
never believed in anything. In my prejudice I was unwilling to hear anything about miracles, of the supernatural, of God, of Faith.... All lies, I said, all things
made up for fools, for those who can't think. Now
I believe the opposite. Am I a weathercock? I, who
was unwilling to subordinate my spirit and my
thoughts to such principles, it was I who was mistaken, because instead of checking, verifying, discussing and going to the bottom of the matter, I denied
it *a priori.*

The very first time that I looked at it squarely, but
with a closed mind, unwilling to be convinced and
determined to deny and to prove that I was right,
I had to lower my head and give myself up as defeated.

But I had the courage to avow that I was beaten,
and I felt the need to say to others who thought as
I did: "You are wrong, as I was—I who have seen
things accomplished that my intellect cannot explain,
except by accepting the supernatural."

These things Padre Pio has accomplished; and in
Padre Pio I must have believed, while I was first striving against him. But I was striving without knowing
him, because of illogical conviction.

When I saw him, I repeated to myself what Nicodemus said to Christ: "Master, we acknowledge that Thou art sent by God to teach us, because none other can work the miracles that Thou workest, unless God be with him." I might also have repeated the words of St. Pius X, whom the Father so loved and revered: "I acknowledge and recognize as true manifestations of the Christian religion, the external arguments of revelation, especially miracles and prophecies, and I regard them as highly consistent with the intelligent thinking of all eras, and of all men, including those of our own time."

What is a supernatural act?

It is an act that can be verified, because it is manifest to our senses; but whose nature and character differ from ordinary occurrences; an act which, because of such characteristics, transcends our ordinary conception. I have said that it can be verified; but it cannot be explained, because it is axiomatic. Hence we cannot possibly apply any fixed definition to it.

This definition forms part of the fundamental concept of traditional apologetics, or scholasticism, that seeks to find the formal and substantive cause in every definition.

CHAPTER VI

Miracles

Miracles are a part of our supernatural gifts; they are free gifts which God gives to man as a manifestation of His omnipotence, of the divinity of Jesus Christ and the Holiness of the Roman Catholic Church.

I have said that a supernatural act is manifest to our senses. Well and good; but it must, however, have aspects which stupefy us with wonder, that strike us forcibly, and make us acknowledge Divine intervention.

A miracle accepted by the Church must be instantaneous, such as: to resuscitate a corpse, to cure a sickness on the spot, to restore a missing limb, to restore sight, to multiply loaves and fishes, etc. I believe and maintain that in miracles, as in all things, there are varying kinds and degrees.

Miracles are of the first degree when neither science nor natural law can be agencies, either in the present or in the future.

They are, however, of the second degree, when either science or natural law might, over a prolonged period, have accomplished the act, which in a miracle occurs instantaneously.

There are also so-called intellectual miracles, such as true and sudden prophecy of the future, the knowledge of one or more languages that have never been studied, or the revelation of an unknown doctrine.

Padre Pio predicted events which later occurred. Speaking Italian, he was understood by persons who spoke only some other language; he answered questions regarding any speculation or school of philosophy.

I will say again that the Father brought about unexpected conversions of sinners. He read their thoughts, for if they did not tell him the truth, or if they had forgotten some fact, or some circumstance, he described it exactly, to the amazement of him who came to him.

I do not know what to call the action of keeping a person dry while it is raining in torrents, of warning him by means of his perfume or by his presence if he fails in his devotions; by predicting an approaching event, such as the sex of a child about to be born; by asserting that the finest water one could desire would be found by digging a well five meters from the new monastery of Pietrelcina, although he had never been to the site; of stating that he had aided by touch, the hand of a surgeon who was operating upon a cataract of the eyes to restore the sight of a woman blind for 28 years....Enough, for if I continue to cite examples, I should never end.

On May 5, 1924, several pilgrims from Bologna went to San Giovanni Rotondo to see the Father. As they went up to the monastery, they saw that a stretch of the road along an almond grove was entirely covered by black caterpillars, which were so numerous that they had to trample on them. A man from San Giovanni Rotondo explained to them why so many of these creatures were on the road. The caterpillars had infested an almond tree and the owner, who was beside himself with anxiety, seeing his entire year's crop threatened, went to the Father imploring him to bless the almond tree, in order to rid him of the pest. The Father went to the terrace of the church and blessed the almond trees below. In a few minutes the infested tree was clear, and the street was covered with black caterpillars.

The Father accomplished many similar acts. That is to say, it is always God who accomplishes them; but whoever brings them about is always a certain one of His chosen servants.

But, I might be asked: "Why bother with these things, when one can turn directly to God?" If my reader has done his military service, I reply: "Why, in the army, instead of addressing the Colonel, does one follow the chain of command?" To the one who has not done military service, I answer with a question: "Why does a child who wants something go to his mother instead of to his father? Why, in every institution, in every office, in every place in society, are there directors, vice directors, etc., to whom one turns when seeking a favor from the head man in charge?"

The question is too simple to need an explanation. The heralds of the Lord are our intermediaries; they are the path leading from Him to us.

Is it not perhaps like this?

Whoever accomplishes such acts is always one chosen of the Lord, a soul living in the will of God, according to His laws, and in whom God dwells; wherefore miracles are performed by the Saints alone, either during their lifetime, or after their death; either by themselves or their followers, or by means of others.

Therefore, while a miracle is useful to the beneficiary, it is indispensable to others, for the results that it brings with it.

The miracle helps to bring people closer to God, as Padre Pio indicated every time that he accomplished some extraordinary deed he said: "God has granted you this favor; turn to Him and not to me in your gratitude."

He used the same expressions as the Saints; just as Moses said that what had come to pass was to show the Israelites that there was but one God and that nothing could exist without Him; or Joshua, who said that all the people of the earth must recognize the powerful hand of the Lord, and must fear the Lord their God.

Finally, as Christ Himself was raising Lazarus from the dead, He lifted His eyes to Heaven and said: "Father, I thank Thee for hearing My prayer. For Myself, I know that Thou hearest Me at all times, but for the sake of the multitude which is standing around, that they may learn to believe it is Thou who hast sent Me."

And now I am asking a question:

"Can anyone obtain a miracle?"

Yes, if they comply with the conditions imposed by Jesus Christ; not otherwise.

"Why?" you will ask me.

Because God is not obliged to place His omnipotence at the disposal of His creatures.

In stating this, I do not mean to say that God is ever unjust, no, He is not. God permits a miracle, which is a grace, to occur for those who believe more, or for those who are deserving, or lastly for those who, although not deserving, He wishes to redeem.

Even one whom we consider unworthy can obtain a miracle, because the saving of this soul has come about through the prayers of others—a mother, a wife or children.

God cannot be controlled, and being an absolute law unto Himself, He is not subject to any law, but He upholds and governs them all. His designs, His views and His intentions have so vast a scope, that the eye of man is incapable of grasping it. It often happens in our life, that a certain action is considered reprehensible in one part of the world, and in some other spot will win the stamp of approval. God alone has absolute justice; ours is relative. That which we hold as just and good, is often merely relatively so; we may therefore not pronounce judgment upon Him who judges us.

Now, if certain miracles are conceded to people who, from our point of view, we do not consider to be worthy, it is good to remember that a miracle has for its sole object the protection and furthering of our spiritual and not of our material interests; as for example: a sinner is converted, and through this comes about the conversion of many others. Hence a quantity of people are brought closer to God. They would never have been converted were it not for the conversion of this sinner.

The curing of an illness, for instance, is not so much for the purpose of healing the body, as for directing the soul along the path of righteousness, and hence toward a spiritual recovery.

This was what happened to the man who was cured of cancer of the tongue; he obtained the grace of being cured, also of the ugly vice of taking God's name in vain.

I will close by saying that a miracle escapes all definition.

The accomplishment of miracles is neither an art nor a profession that can be learned or developed and perfected. It is impossible to determine the conditions for obtaining them, nor the manner, nor the place, nor the person.

They happen, and depend upon a free and sovereign will that knows neither restrictions nor laws, and is sufficient unto itself. They can happen to everyone or to nobody. They can come often, or after a very long time.

The reader must note that no pronouncement on these reported cures has been made by the Church. The Church oftentimes passes judgment on reputed miraculous cures only many years after they occur, as in the case of those investigated at Lourdes.

*   *   *

The following facts are attested by the well-known Dr. Ezio Saltamerenda di Lanciotto, Director of the Biotherapeutic Institute of Genoa. From boyhood he had shown evidence of a stubborn and independent spirit. At the age of nine he had lost his faith, which his mother had made such a devoted effort to preserve. He had kept the fact to himself to spare her feelings, hiding his religious indifference until, at fourteen, he openly declared himself.

He did not need God. . . .

It is therefore not surprising that all too soon he knew evil, that he did not try to deny himself any of the pleasures that life showered upon him.

Hungry for reading, he could satisfy his appetite in his father's well-stocked library, choosing at random and in secret, the most varied texts, not excluding those of Sacred Scripture, which he intended to use in laying the foundations of his atheism.

During his classical studies, the young man pursued his taste for physiology and poetry. He even wrote fairly good verse. Of life itself, he had by now formed a purely pagan conception, contrasting strangely with the spiritual struggle which his pride bent toward the desired solution.

War interrupted Saltamerenda's university studies, which he was later able to complete during his military training. The call to arms brought with it severe discipline to his exuberant and rebellious nature. He actually experienced the suffering of a prison sentence in the Regina Coeli jail, as a political suspect, accused of belonging to an anti-fascist movement. He saw the face of death fighting courageously in the front lines of Africa. Having been wounded at Tobruk, he recovered, and was able to return to his regiment. Finally he was deported to Germany, where he endured the horrors of the concentration camps.

As a result of these painful experiences his pride, instead of becoming subdued, came bouncing back, more indomitable than ever. Neither marriage and the birth of two sons, nor his love of art and nature changed his outlook; Dr. Saltamerenda preserved intact that doctrinal self-sufficiency which excluded the intervention of God in the affairs of men. Convinced that man is the sole artifex and judge of his own destiny, he did his best to bring others to his convictions.

"In each experience," he said, "man must go to the very bottom without fear, because life is short and may go smoothly if we dominate it. The body and the mind alone tend to destruction; everything that rebels against the fatal deterioration of matter, becomes knowledge of life. . .God does not exist, but, should He exist, man does not need to fear a divinity made for the weak and the dull-witted."

And thus it went until the first days of March, when a casual meeting took place with Mario Cavaliere, a spiritual son of Padre Pio.

In his study, a large photograph of the monk was enthroned on his desk; Dr. Saltamerenda cast a glance at it, and a strange sudden sensation overcame him, the same that he had experienced a few days before, a sort of tightness in his throat, when he had seen the procession of the Madonna della Guardia.

Mario Cavaliere, who had noticed the glance and a certain expression of diffidence in his visitor, after a few remarks about Padre Pio, gave him a monograph which he accepted rather skeptically, and subsequently passed on to his wife.

That same evening, he left for Rome where, to his great surprise, he expedited in one day some business which he had expected would take him a week to transact. That night he heard suddenly an interior voice, imperious, insistent, which seemed to call him to San Giovanni Rotondo. The bus was not due to leave for three hours, but when he reached the deserted station, there was a taxi waiting, apparently for him! The strange feverish desire to see Padre Pio was too strong to resist; so off he went, covering the distance of forty kilometers across a desert region covered with snow, in the pale light of dawn. His great desire to reach his destination seemed to burn within him. He arrived at the monastery and found a few people waiting for Padre Pio to come down and say his Mass; these were joined by others, until the arrival of Padre Pio became imminent. Three times the young man experienced the same sensation in his throat, and felt at the same time a great inclination to weep. He was shaken by the sound of approaching footsteps. Then everyone rushed to the door, and kneeling before the Capuchin father, tried to reach his hands, covered with half gloves, "the privileged guardians of the sacred stigmata."

Ezio alone remained rigid, standing in a corner, frozen by the struggle with his will, which seemed to deaden all sensation. "Why am I here? What am I supposed to do?" He stood there immovable, as though in a trance, for the whole period of the Mass. He did not know how long it lasted; he regained alertness, seeing Padre Pio going back to the sacristy, and the faithful crowding around him, trying to kiss his hands, bare now, and streaked with red.

Saltamerenda followed him from a distance, when he returned to the monastery for his thanksgiving. Padre Pio was to come back in an hour and a half, to hear confessions. Then he too would approach him, and ask him...what?...nothing, surely, for himself.

When, at length, he found himself kneeling at his feet, he saw the face of the friar darken, and at his request for a blessing for a sick relative he said drily: "He is blessed."

The young man, having nothing more to say, tried to get up, but seemed riveted to the kneeling bench.

Suddenly the voice of the Father boomed out: "Tell me, son, don't you ever think of your own miserable soul?"

"Certainly, Father, or I couldn't go on living!"

"And with what end in view?" Padre Pio retorted with energy. Saltamerenda was bewildered, but managed to answer: "For the propagation of the species."

"Wretch!" snapped back the priest. "Don't you see that your soul is being destroyed?" After a pause, placing one hand on his mouth, he dismissed him: "Go!"

The contact of that hand on his mouth had profoundly disturbed the young man. The Father had dismissed him, but he could not accept it; he must see him again...he must talk to him...otherwise, how could he ever find himself?

In the afternoon, he returned to the sacristy. Padre Pio caught sight of him behind a group of men, and called to him: "Genoese, you have a dirty face! You live near the sea, but you don't know how to wash!" And then after a pause: "A stout ship, without a pilot!"

More bewildered than ever, Ezio Saltamerenda tried to kneel nearby, but Padre Pio sent him away once more. However, all this severity only succeeded in increasing his attraction; the more he humiliated him, the more he loved that friar. "Father," he would have liked to cry out, now that the ice was melted within him, "Father, forgive me!" But he felt that the priest wanted to have nothing to do with him, and he left feeling nothing but despair in his heart. Maybe he would come back some day, when he had understood better. With these thoughts, he wandered out through the fields, like a whipped dog, but always conscious of the perfume of violets still about him.

On his way back he ran into Fra Francesco, who spoke words of comfort, and even persuaded him to stay. He brought him back to the monastery, and took him to Padre Pio's cell, which bears the inscription: "Earth's glory has Sorrow for a companion." While waiting for the door to open, the friar told him of the life of self-denial and sacrifice Padre Pio led, and of what an immense help he was to all about him; of how his effectiveness increased with the use of the scourge.

Fra Francesco knocked at the cell door. Saltamerenda's heart stopped beating. "We will get a scolding!"...The door opened, and the fragrance of violets invaded the corridor.

"What do you want? Don't make me waste my time!" And then: "Go downstairs, and I'll hear your confession."

The next thing he knew, the young man was weeping, with convulsive sobs, his head leaning on the pierced hands of the priest, while Pio, with miraculous clairvoyance, suggested to him, one by one, the faults that had disorganized his life, even the most distant ones, even the forgotten ones. "These were the most beautiful moments of my life!" said our convert.

The Act of Contrition was dictated to him word for word by the Father, full of unusual phrases of his own, pregnant with meaning. In the wave of emotion that overcame him, he exclaimed: "Father, I pray that this suffering of mine, and that my salvation may bring you some measure of comfort!"

"My son," he interrupted, "indeed it has been a great comfort, may God bless you for it!"

That night, Saltamerenda was terrified by the sound of mysterious and loud knockings on the walls of his room, and against the windows and doors. The man who had felt no fear under enemy fire, and who had defied death in the German concentration camps, was now shaking like a leaf, desperately invoking Padre Pio, who soon revealed his presence by invading the room with his own characteristic fragrance. It was only for a moment, but it was sufficient to fill him with a longing to rush to the monastery and don sackcloth. Padre Pio did not encourage this impulse, but merely acknowledged his midnight visit with the words: "My son, we do not know what happens down there!" Then in order to give him courage, he added: "You have now in your hands a marvelous bread, and around you are many starving souls."

"But what must I do?"

"Cut it in slices and distribute it, to feed the hungry; in this way you will serve the Lord. And I shall be with you always."

CHAPTER VII

Writing About Padre Pio

"In order to undertake the journey to San Giovanni Rotondo where Padre Pio di Pietrelcina led a holy life of Franciscan humility, I waited until the cold spell had passed. It was March, and the little village of Monte Gargano was covered with more than a meter of snow.

"Having arrived at Foggia, I went straight to the motion picture theater 'Flabella,' where the bus takes on passengers for San Giovanni Rotondo. The ticket agent said, 'You are going to Padre Pio, you are lucky. There are barely a dozen pilgrims—you see, with this cold weather. . .'

"I took my place in the bus. I had been expecting the traditional warm sunshine of the South, instead of which it rained, a steady rain that had come to stay.

"As soon as we had left the city, we found ourselves on the great highway that goes from Foggia to Manfredonia, straight, interminable, reaching beyond the horizon. After a while we left the high road and took a smaller one to the left, that lovely road that leads to San Giovanni Rotondo.

"The clouds were lead-colored and low; it was snowing. The gray olive trees and the opened blossoms of the almond seemed to shiver with the cold. Only the giant cactus and the century plants greeted the onslaught with a sort of marble indifference. Fat sheep, wandering about, seemed to find food here and there.

"We climbed and climbed, all seized with a great eagerness, the longing to see, as soon as possible, the poor little monastery from which there radiates so much heavenly light.

"After a while, the vegetation became even more sparse, and the ground took on a hard, stony surface. Here man's industry was of no avail; the hostile and intractable soil was more encouraging to grim meditation.

"It seems to me that this road that leads to San Giovanni Rotondo is symbolic. At first you are led through green and smiling country, as though you were being shown the illusions of this world. Gradually, as one climbs higher, the colors fade, the richness disappears, as do the sounds and echoes of the busy world. Our anxious, troubled spirits find relief in a sort of lightness and suspense.

"Finally, the last stretch reveals itself as a lonely road, where the earth only produces stones and rocks, but where one experiences a kind of serene detachment in that clean, enveloping silence. There at the end of the road, all bathed in light, is the Capuchin monastery. In this bare little church, with his hands stripped of the half gloves that for thirty-five years have covered his stigmata, Padre Pio celebrated the Holy Sacrifice of the Mass at five o'clock every morning. Many a distinguished prelate has served this Mass, including bishops and cardinals.

"At San Giovanni Rotondo the alarm clock went off for all alike at four a.m. as it was impossible to stay away from the divine agony of Padre Pio's Mass, for there one saw those hands bathed in blood, the face which seemed to express all the agony of the five wounds, and the dark eyes, in which the pupils were greatly dilated in the light of the heavenly colloquies. The Mass lasted for one and one-half hours, during all of which time, Padre Pio was transfigured.

"When large groups of the faithful came from all directions, in and out of Italy, to go to Confession, they gathered in front of the closed doors of the little church, to register for a number as early as four in the morning.

"At San Giovanni Rotondo there is but one attraction: Padre Pio!

"At San Giovanni Rotondo everything hangs on a mysterious thread: Padre Pio, with his incorruptible wounds, his fragrance, and his gift of bilocation, his reading of minds, his prophecies and cures, and his astounding conversions.

"Whoever went to him for confession, and received Holy Communion from his hands will always be considered his spiritual child, and will feel himself guided, sustained, consoled, and blessed, even from afar. We need him so much, to help us through life, as long as we can, with truth, inscribed on our doors: Earth's glory has ever Sorrow for a companion.

Zaire Fazio."

★   ★   ★

"From the 19th until the 25th of August I stayed at San Giovanni Rotondo for a bit of a rest. The mountain air, six hundred meters above sea level, did me good, but...my soul also benefitted from all that I was able to see, feel, and appreciate in a supernatural sense, in the little church of Our Lady of Grace, which is tended by the Capuchin Fathers of the adjoining monastery.

"The church of 'Le Grazie' is quite far from San Giovanni Rotondo. It was formerly reached by a steep and nearly impassable road; now however one can approach it on a broad highway, a fine avenue, bordered with tidy new houses and villas.

"What a difference between what happens at San Giovanni Rotondo, and up there at 'Le Grazie'! At San Giovanni one leads a natural life, just as in any city or country of the world. At 'Le Grazie,' on the other hand, one leads the life of grace, a supernatural life, because one is near Padre Pio.

"Padre Pio is a Capuchin who leads an exemplary life; he is a man of God. The Father likes to describe himself as a 'humble servant of God.' As other religious do, he says Mass, hears confessions, attends choir, and observes the Holy Rule of his order. He stands out among other religious through his more intense fervor, especially during the celebration of his Mass, which lasts an hour and a half, and from the fact that those who come from afar to go to confession seek him, and none other. Besides, for more than thirty-five years, he has borne on his hands and feet and on his side the wounds of Our Saviour, just as did his seraphic brother, St. Francis of Assisi. Doctors have tried every means of healing these wounds, as though they were from natural causes, but without success. Those wounds are incurable; they are the Sacred Stigmata that were given him by Our Lord, for the glory of His Name, and for the good of our souls.

"Padre Pio bears the gift of the Stigmata with the

greatest humility. He is without affectation. In the evening, he attends recreation for about three quarters of an hour, and is completely natural in conversation, self-possessed and witty, simple and friendly.

"The crowds that come every day to San Giovanni Rotondo and climb to the church of 'Le Grazie' to see Padre Pio are witnesses to the miracle of his life, and the name of this friar with the stigmata is known in every corner of Italy as well as abroad.

"During my short stay, I saw people arrive from Austria, Switzerland and France; and those who come from afar are amazed at our coolness in regard to Padre Pio. To them the Father is a living prodigy that one must know, for whose prayers one must beg. Some may come out of curiosity, but they are soon overcome by the charm of that humble friar; they go to confession, and so become his spiritual children.

"One cannot say that all Padre Pio's visitors are simple people without education. On the contrary, one sees men and women of cultivation, people of means, holding important posts, arriving in handsome motor cars; there are also priests, religious, and sisters. All of these are to be seen waiting before five o'clock in the morning at the door of the church, in order to assist at the Father's Mass; and then join the long queues, the women in the church, the men in the sacristy, in order to have the good fortune to go to confession, to open up their ailing souls, to that soul that is all of God.

"Padre Pio hears hundreds of confessions a day, with the most constant patience. After his Mass and thanksgiving, he stays in the sacristy until about eight to hear the confessions of the men, and then until about ten-thirty in the church to hear the women. After this he distributes Holy Communion for twenty minutes to half an hour. In the afternoon he hears more men.

"There is no preference shown; even religious and priests have to get in line and wait their turn. Confessions are short for all, not over five minutes. However, and here lies the wonder of it, everyone is satisfied, because the Father has used the perfect phrase, and brought peace and tranquillity to their souls. I can attest to this from personal experience, and from having heard it confirmed by others, who after confession seemed to have obtained that peace that they desired.

"The Father does not grant absolution to all. Whoever does not deserve it does not receive it. One evening as I was saying my Rosary before the Blessed Sacrament, a young man came up to me and said: 'Excuse me, Father, tell me what I must do now that Padre Pio has denied me absolution, and I must leave this evening?' I answered: 'You may be sure that if the Father denied you absolution, any other confessor would have done the same; certainly, there is something you can do about it...' The young man answered: 'There is something I can do about it, Padre Pio is right...But now what can I do to receive absolution?' 'A simple thing,' I said to him, 'go, now, and put into practice whatever the Father told you, then go to any confessor, tell him your story and of the remedies you have employed, also tell him of your firm purpose of avoiding what has caused your present humiliation, and you will receive with your absolution, the Grace of God, and peace.'

"Sometimes Padre Pio sent people away before they had a chance to kneel in the confessional. One morning I saw, and actually heard the Father say to someone who had waited in the queue for several hours: 'Go!' 'Why?' I asked someone, who was near me at the time, and I was told: 'The Father sees into the heart, and sends away anyone who is not well-disposed.'

"Holy Mass celebrated by Padre Pio is the first and most important event of the day to anyone who comes from different parts of Italy or from abroad to spend a few days near the Church of 'Le Grazie.' Every day Padre Pio celebrates Mass at five, and every day the church is packed. Padre Pio's Mass lasts for one and a half hours, and sometimes longer; but no one who attends it gets tired or bored, or leaves at the '*Ite Missa est!*' even after it is over; many stay near the altar, for reasons of devotion or to thank God for having sent us such a priest. During Mass, many of those present, from time to time, are bathed in the wonderful scent that comes from the Father. I have never experienced this.

"Why does Padre Pio's Mass last so long? We do not know, because we cannot tell what transpires in his soul, so burning with love for Christ that he wears imprinted on his body the sacred wounds. Nor do we know what happens during the renewal of the Passion of Our Lord on the altar. The wounds that Padre Pio bears tell us how he lives continuously in the Passion of Christ, and that he fulfills in his body that which is lacking in the Passion for the salvation of the men of today. If he has been called to suffer for all, surely his sufferings must increase during the

Holy Sacrifice of the Mass, especially in the moment when Our Lord mystically renews the bloody Sacrifice of Calvary. For this reason, while at the altar, Padre Pio seems to be transfigured with grief, and in certain moments of the Mass, his face shows signs of suffering incredible pain; his eyes seem on the verge of tears, his lips move, as though in intimate colloquy with Our Lord, truly present on the altar from the Consecration to the Communion.

"Whoever, having read these lines, will have, at some time, the good fortune to assist at Padre Pio's Mass, let him rivet his gaze on the Father: during the recitation of the Confiteor,

—when he first kisses the altar,
—at the *'Munda cor meum!'* before the Gospel,
—at the Offertory,
—after the 'Sanctus,'
—from the Consecration to the Communion.

"What goes on in Padre Pio's soul, that is, his intense interior life, we may be able, in part, to understand when he has left this earth for Paradise. Then, perhaps, we shall know why his Mass lasts so long.

"Just as the crowds pressed about Our Lord, to be able to touch Him, receive a smile or a blessing, or hear some word of His, so does it happen at the Church of 'Le Grazie' in the presence of Padre Pio. When, having finished his Mass, the Father returns to the Sacristy, the men surround him, and try to kiss his wounded hands before he resumes his gloves. What a satisfaction and consolation to him who succeeds in kissing the actual wound! To me, this has only happened once. When he goes back to the church at 8:00, to hear the women's confessions until 10:30, it is the women's turn to attempt to kiss his hands, and to say a word to him.

"These are moving scenes, scenes that one will never forget; it is in these moments that he is asked for favors, that children are held up for his blessing, and the sick and suffering of all sorts, that he may heal them, if it is God's will. And Padre Pio, humble and patient, blesses and exhorts all to have faith in the mercy of God, and in the kindness of Our Lady.

"At the instigation of Padre Pio, a magnificent hospital of 350 beds was erected at San Giovanni Rotondo, near the monastery of 'Le Grazie.' A new wing of 900 beds is being built. The engineer and contractor is Mr. Angelo Lupi, once a hater of all priests, and now one of the most beloved of the spiritual sons of the Father. 'For the hospital' is written with all the offerings that come to Padre Pio. Large and small offerings that are hallowed by prayer, and by the blessing of the good Father, so much beloved of God, and of men. They serve to build a house that will be both a house of pain and of comfort.

"The hospital proves that Padre Pio does not live in the clouds, as some say, but on earth and with us; it proves that however much he loves souls, he does not neglect the body. He sympathizes like a brother with those who suffer, and does all he can to alleviate their pain.

"On the morning of August 25, I went to Padre Pio to tell him I was leaving for Barletta, to resume my work in the parish. The Father said, with great humility: 'Pray for me...pray for me!' Embarrassed, and almost stuttering, I said: 'Oremus ad invicem! We will recommend each other to the Heart of Jesus.'

"Padre Pio blessed me, gave me a paternal embrace, and kissed the top of my head. I certainly did not expect or deserve such expressions of fatherly love; I took them as a direct and private message from Our Lord, who called me to greater holiness; and I promised. . . But how feeble I am! I beg of you, who read these lines, to assist me with your prayers, to help me to be truly more virtuous, and never again to wound the Heart of Christ.

The Provost."

IN 1956, BEFORE PADRE PIO'S DEATH, ITALY'S TOP JOUR-
NALIST, ORIO VERGANI WROTE:

FOR THIRTY EIGHT YEARS, THE STIGMATA OF
PADRE PIO HAVE BEEN BLEEDING

Can this be called a scientific mystery? The Church will only pronounce upon this *"Post mortem";* only then will she pass judgment upon these astonishing manifestations, as well as on the humble life of Father Francesco Forgione.

Perhaps someday San Giovanni Rotondo will be as renowned a village as Lourdes, and our grandchildren will come here to learn of the life of Francesco Forgione; just as our grandparents, credulous and otherwise, after reading Huysmans and Emile Zola, went to Lourdes, to that tiny village in the Pyrenees. There they followed the story of the child Bernadette Soubirous, to whom Our Lady appeared in a grotto, and said: "I am the Immaculate Conception!" In Lourdes, in order to recapture those days, a diorama has been constructed, showing the scene of the apparitions with the characters and rustic background of the days of Bernadette. Perhaps something of the sort will be accomplished at San Giovanni Rotondo in fifty or a hundred years, in order to show how it all looked in 1918, and how there lived there, and still lives in saintly and good-natured humility, one Francesco Forgione. If one day the Church will confirm what the people now say, that he is a saint, my grandchildren and great-grandchildren will probably hunt up this ancient copy of the *"Corriere,"* and will read it with the same interest as I would, were I to find today an article by my great-grandfather, dated: "Lourdes, February 11th, 1858," in which was told the story of the first apparition of Our Lady to the little shepherdess.

When it comes to speaking of the 20th of September, 1918, that great and mysterious day, I am sparing of my adjectives, because I know what the Church demands of all Catholic writers when describing such cases as that of Father Forgione. She forbids them to lend any authority to their accounts other than that of human witnesses. I can only say that on that day, in the tiny church of the Capuchin Fathers at San Giovanni Rotondo, Francesco Forgione, known in religion as Padre Pio di Pietrelcina showed to the brothers with whom he had assisted at Mass his hands marked with the blood of the Stigmata.

There have been many changes in the world since 1918, and they tell me that things have changed very much even in this little village, hidden away in the solitary wilderness of the western slopes of Monte Gargano.

There is one thing that did not change up here; the five wounds of Padre Pio never changed. I did not have the good fortune to be present at the events of September, 1918, but what I since witnessed is no figment of my imagination.

I have said that this side of the Monte Gargano is an Italian version of the Thebaid. Mount Carmel, and the hill from which Our Lord delivered His Sermon on the Mount, both had when I saw them the same arid and stony appearance, the same penetrating and desperate loneliness. These are landscapes without comfort that inspire only meditation or flight. Just as in Africa, the spirit becomes "sand-ridden," so I imagine that here, if not illumined by prayer, it turns to stone and dust, and in the end dies slowly of thirst. Whoever has been here has no need to look further, if he is seeking a setting for the ancient hermits.

As a matter of fact, even if the natives tell me that there have been many changes, I soon console myself. In 1956, comparing the countryside to 1918 and probably to a hundred years ago, the gloom and tragic essence of the landscape cannot have changed much, nor its incurable poverty.

There are friars more and less gifted with awareness, in the material sense. It is probable that the best of them have no eyes for their surroundings, but the fact remains that if the view from a monastery window is to be seen as a creation of the Almighty, nature, when seen from the little windows of the monastery of San Giovanni Rotondo wears a very different aspect from what it wears for the friars of Cervaia for instance, or Portofino. This landscape is grim; it is what St. Anthony might have required, in order to put his vocation to the test before starting out for the desert. The road to Paradise is very long, it is a weary, penitential flight of steps. Whoever lives here, will maybe love this arid and bitter earth into which the frost bites deep in winter, and where the summer is burning hot; but if I ask someone from hereabouts the name of a hill or a peak, they never can tell me, as though they had lost their memory from sheer fatigue.

What will Francesco Forgione have thought of his journey's end, arriving here, so many years ago, dressed in the habit of Padre Pio? There were then no good roads or motor cars, and I cannot think that the stagecoach could have survived the attempt to join the mountain to the plain for an occasional peasant. The mule was still the favorite conveyance, but the friars went on foot, or begged a ride on the slowly moving wagons that lumbered up the mountain, grinding out the dust. Up there they would find a tiny church, a monastery with a dozen cells, a small courtyard with a wellhead, a big room where catechism was taught to children; finally, a meal collected from contributions, consisting of a little oil, some nuts, and a handful of flour.

From outside, the monastery looks almost like a small district jail. Since 1918 not a brick has been changed, the buildings have preserved their total poverty. The water that is drunk there still comes from the well.

Francesco Forgione was a peasant's son. Now there is an immense difference between the Lombard and the Tuscan peasant, or one from the region of Benevento, where Padre Pio was born in 1887. It is not necessary to read the regional literature of Southern Italy in order to realize this, nor do you have to seek comparisons between the stories of Ignazio Silone and Lina Pietravalle, or the reminiscences of Carlo Levi about the surroundings of Eboli.

It is very likely that Padre Pio, accustomed from boyhood to praying in a straw shack at the back of his parents' vegetable garden, saw little difference between the hermitage of San Giovanni Rotondo and the setting of his early childhood. He started his Franciscan novitiate at the age of fifteen. It is probable, even certain, that his eyes were not made for seeing his surroundings. One cell or another, one corner of the earth or another must have seemed alike to this simple soul.

It is only in the field of speculation that we worldlings can evaluate the possible effects of the surrounding landscape on one who is certainly isolated by a very different form of vision.

Padre Pio's story is well-known; he was sickly and even threatened with tuberculosis; he was subject to tremendous attacks of fever, which were said sometimes to reach 122 degrees F. Through hard study, he rose from being a humble server to saying Mass and hearing confessions. He was a thin little monk, but in the hours of relaxation he was far from melancholy. Even when he was over sixty-eight, after a life of slow and inexorable martyrdom, he was quick with a good-natured joke or a gay retort; all the more picturesque coming from him, as he used the homely idiom of his native dialect. He was a friar of uncertain health, like many, I am sure, who were serenely looking forward to an early death.

On the 20th of September he was passing through Venafro on a journey and had stopped at the home of his family. After spending an afternoon in prayer in his old straw shack, he came out wringing his hands. His mother seeing his quivering fingers asked him jokingly: "What's the matter, are you playing the guitar?" Padre Pio says that he felt a deep burn in the palms and on the backs of his hands, but there was nothing to see. Only three years later, on the same day, September 20th, while praying in thanksgiving after Mass, he suffered a seizure, for no apparent reason, that forced him to brace himself against the wall behind him, as he knelt in the pew. A lay brother rushed forward to support him and saw that Padre Pio had the Stigmata. The news was kept secret until the arrival of the Father Superior, but the five wounds were there, in his hands, feet and side; the five bleeding wounds of Our Lord.

Forty-five years have gone by since then, the five wounds have never healed; Francesco Forgione is making his painful entry in the group of great ones who wear the Stigmata. Only one, Saint Francis of Assisi, has been recognized by the Church, after a Pope stood witness for him. There have been about sixty others, including the recently beatified Gemma Galgani. I have called it a painful entry, because, even in a simple nature, like that of the peasant friar of Pietrelcina, the pain of the wounds is less tormenting than the spate of arguments and investigations of his case. The Church will not make a pronouncement during his lifetime, but the believers and the unbelievers freely express their conflicting opinions. Medical and psychological investigations come one after the other. The supposed saint is treated as one suffering from a mysterious illness; every effort is made to call it hysteria, auto-suggestion, or some other neurosis, to produce some natural explanation for that gush of blood from the hands, feet and side. Faith stands aside, waiting for miracles, but science converges on San Giovanni Rotondo with chemical analyses and surgical examinations. If this is the road to sanctity, it is a weary and troubled one. On the one hand, science admits that it is confronted by the inexplicable, and on the other it declares that everything can be explained.

In a few years, Padre Pio, who never leaves his monastery, never discusses his troubles, never shows the slightest trace of pride, has become a storm-center of controversy between those who declare that they believe in him now, and those who say that in order to believe, they will have to await his death, and the proof of the miracle.

An immense bibliography, consisting of large volumes, pamphlets, testimonials, bulletins, etc., has grown up around Padre Pio, who is sought out by an ever-increasing crowd of people. They come in droves to the church that is too small to hold them in that remote village, and all they come for is to pray.

Padre Pio is not waiting for his death to prove that his long martyrdom has been a religious phenomenon or a scientific mystery, he is a man who is waiting for the life beyond, which he knows to be the true life, and to one who awaits him, he serenely shows his five wounds. The scientific doubts, as well as the fanatical belief are probably equally distasteful to him, the two extremes are equally hard to bear; he, with his great goodness, finds himself the object of a debate, that has lasted for over forty-five years, and in

Upper left: Monastery garden.
Upper right: Petitions.
Lower left: Watching workmen.
Lower right: Distributing palms.

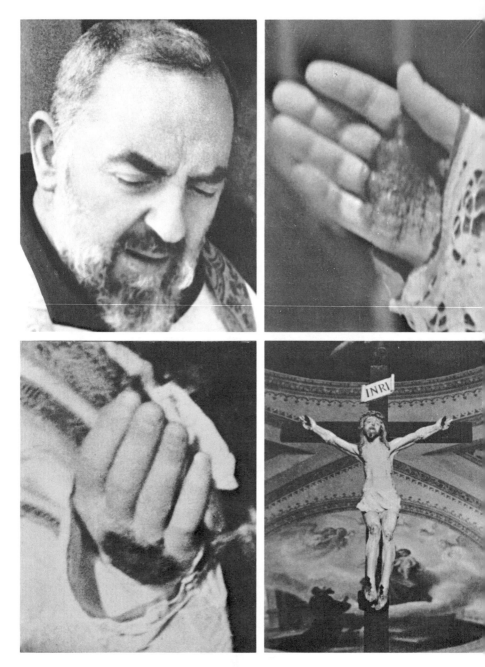

Upper left: In pain.
Upper right: Stigmatized right hand.
Lower left: Back of hand.
Lower right: Visibly stigmatized under this cross.
(Cross of Stigmatization).

**Upper left: Blessing after Mass on Good Friday.
Upper right: Deacon.
Lower left: Preface.
Lower right: Sursum Corda.**

Upper left: Offering of chalice.
Upper right: Memento of living.
Lower left: Canon.
Lower right: Memento of dead.

which the Church reserves her judgment until after his death.

In the meantime, he is still alive, and vigorous in his mission of confessor and priest. Padre Pio hears confessions for ten and even twelve hours almost every day. His penitents come from far and near. Outside of the church, along the road that climbs up from San Giovanni Rotondo, a new city is being born from the human needs common to any pilgrimage site. It thrives on the influx of believers. It is not yet Lourdes, with its 500 hotels and 2,000 shops for religious articles; but there are already Hostels of St. Francis, several inns, and small shops selling photographs, holy pictures, and religious books. It is a little town for the pilgrims, just as in East Africa towns grew around the filling stations for the army trucks.

Padre Pio has lived in seclusion between the altar and the confessional for thirty-seven years, and only looks out to see how the big six story hospital is progressing. He has not interrupted his seclusion for thirty-five years; the little church has not changed, in spite of the fame of her guardian, neither a picture nor a drapery has been moved, and it is still, and will always remain, extremely poor.

The city of Our Lady of Grace is growing on its own account, just as Lourdes grew in a hundred years. The friars watch at the monastery gate to keep off cranks or hoodlums and to protect their dedicated companion from all disturbance. They look like monks of olden times, as one sees them moving through the crowds with quick gestures, like shepherds, herding a flock. They have told me that they are well aware of not being saints, for they often lose patience, and would even raise their fists to defend Padre Pio from the intrusion of fanatical visitors. I liked these friars, with their short, grey beards, their faces tanned by the sun, and their southern invective, their holy fervor and their astuteness. The world begins for them on the steps of their church, which boasts neither bronze nor marble, nor any trace of gilding. Their mission is to defend "The Saint," and whoever reads the Gospel will remember how the Apostles defended Our Lord from the crowds that pressed around Him.

I, too, have mingled with the crowds and have gone into the church, and have seen Padre Pio. What I saw, I will tell you another time.

Orio Vergani.

The following article, also by Orio Vergani, appeared in the *"Corriere della Sera,"* on April 11, 1950. Orio Vergani is one of Italy's ablest journalists.

BEFORE THE CONFESSIONAL OF PADRE PIO

"You came all the way from Milan to see me? An *'Ave Maria'* would have done you more good!"

In the little church of San Giovanni Rotondo, a siege of preoccupied devotees presses its unceasing assault on the most tireless and most patient of rustic friars, all awaiting from him the gift of grace.

The kindly person who accompanied me to Padre Pio's monastery gave me scant encouragement when I asked him if I could see the friar who had worn the Stigmata for 38 years; if I could talk with him, and take pictures, he answered with a hesitating smile, and an equally hesitating skyward glance. He seemed to want to promise anything to the stranger who had come from so far away, but at the same time to give the answer that the Neopolitan recruits would give when asked to take the oath of allegiance: "I don't dare promise you anything. . ."

"Did you want to go to confession?" he asked me.

This question brought me up with a round turn, and gave me the dimensions of the world that I was facing, and of the personality that I was hoping to meet. I might have answered: "I have come to interview Padre Pio." But the word was clumsy, like lead in my mouth. One does not interview a man who for thirty-eight years has worn the marks of the stigmata on his hands, his feet and his side. You cannot stand before a man, pencil in hand, of whom for thirty-seven years people have been saying: "He is a saint." Even had I been a doctor, I could not have said that I wanted to examine Padre Pio's wounds, or in the role of a psychiatrist, that I wished to look into his eyes. The friars of San Giovanni Rotondo do not allow doctors into the monastery anymore unless they are sent by the Father General of the Order. They want no more examinations, diagnoses, or arguments, either for or against. So I asked the host that accompanied me to the door of the monastery: "Is one allowed to take pictures?"

He answered, in the most natural and friendly manner: "It was once attempted by some American photographers, but the monks chased them away. Some moving-picture cameramen came too, but the friars kicked them out because they only spoke English, and the monks could not make them understand that Padre Pio was not a movie actor." After a while he went on: "If you want to go to confession, you may do so in the late afternoon. The morning is reserved for the women, but they have to obtain their tickets days before from the office that is run for that purpose. Padre Pio hears everyone in confession, but the friars have to protect him somehow. The church is already full at five in the morning. The confessional is surrounded by iron bars, and in order to avoid confusion and rows everyone has a number."

"Is it like this in winter and summer?"

"It is always like this." It is impossible to draw the line between the natives and the people who come from elsewhere. There are people here who go every week to confession to Padre Pio, and there are boys who have grown to manhood kneeling every day at his feet in the sacristy. Whoever comes from outside, takes his turn, just like the village folk. People come here from America, especially from Argentina, and every day, motors arrive from the North of Italy; they are mostly people who have had some prayer answered or have been converted through Padre Pio. There are converts, orthodox, and there are Masons who have repented, there are those who have been cured of some illness, who come to give thanks.

"The post office of San Giovanni Rotondo works mostly for Padre Pio. The village has several thousand inhabitants, but the mail is mostly for the monk of Pietrelcina. The oral confessions are continued through correspondence, the many letters tell of worries, illness and sorrow; they beg for the help of him, who through his bleeding wounds, seems to them to be the closest intermediary with Christ. Some books tell us that the Father has the gift of bilocation, and that he has been known to appear in various places at the same time, in order to comfort those who cried to him for help. It has never been said, however, that Padre Pio was able to increase the number of hours in a day. The twenty friars who live in the monastery have been forced to turn one of the rooms into an office in order to handle the mail. The letters are so numerous that Padre Pio can only read a small part of them. Things have been going along in this way for forty-five years, without interruption. Whoever goes to confession to Padre Pio is almost sure to bring with him some letters, holy cards or medals, to place for a moment in his hands, for that which has been near the blood on his hands is holy and blessed. It is easy to see why the friars of San Giovanni Rotondo have often to be prickly in defense of their brother, who besides everything else, is also an invalid whose constitution from his early youth has received some rude shocks.

All this, we must remember, is happening in a little hamlet that seems to be clinging to the rim of the earth, more detached than an island, surrounded by rocky cliffs and desolate hovels; in a world where water is measured in drops, where sheep graze under the walls of the monastery and where whoever speaks seems to be faint from the great silence.

Here is the church, without any real facade, grafted as it is onto the monastery. It is only a little bigger than a chapel, its walls decorated with 19th-century geometric designs, such as the house painters used to copy out of decorators' handbooks. The floor is of tiles, the nave and entrance are whitewashed. The

altar where Padre Pio says his Mass at dawn is just
as it was when he said it on the morning of the 20th
of September, 1918, a few moments before the appearance of the Stigmata, when the friar was seized
by that brief fainting fit as he was kneeling in the
choir. The altar is rustic, dedicated to St. Francis, with
a few unpretentious plaster ornaments.

The whole church, from the entrance to the nave,
from the sacristy to the window frames that face the
garden, is scribbled over with pencil. No *ex votos* are
brought to San Giovanni Rotondo, no little marble
slabs are set into the walls, as at Lourdes in token
of thanksgiving. The name of Padre Pio, for his religious associates, is still that of a brother, even if some
day it will be that of a saint. His name cannot be
inscribed in marble, and silver hearts may not be
placed on altars in his name. The Brothers are always
mindful of the fact that homage of any kind is contrary to the wishes of the Church. But who can stop
people from writing in pencil to Padre Pio? From
dawn to dark, the church is always open and is in-
variably packed with as many of the faithful as it can
hold, who only move away during the brief moments
when Padre Pio goes for a short rest. There is not
a day, nor scarcely an hour, when the little church
in this village of the Puglie does not house three hundred faithful, mostly on their knees. While waiting
to go to confession, fearing that the conversation with
Padre Pio through the grating of the confessional will
be all too brief, many take out a pencil and confide
their late requests in a few words scribbled on a wall.
In this way, the whole church is covered with tiny
messages in pencil; there are an indefinite number

of pleadings, of supplications without end, of open declarations of grief, all of them signed, and many giving their addresses, as though Padre Pio could answer them. The people know that Padre Pio cannot read these notes, but they are sure that he sees just the same, even if his eyes never rest on the actual writing. If they believe in his Stigmata, worn for thirty-five years, why, then, can they not believe that he is able to read these impassioned requests written on the walls of his church. Every few months, the brothers go down into the church at night with a bucket of whitewash and blot everything out, but no one doubts for a moment that the prayers of Padre Pio have interceded for every inscription.

I found myself standing among the men in the organ loft. Two peasants were on one side of me, and on the other was a businessman from Genoa who was here with his wife, who had been cured by a miracle. He told me she had been dying and was now here completely recovered and had just spent her third morning kneeling in the church. Near me were also some young students, with bundles of books under their arms, and an old blind man. Just in front of me was the place reserved for the women, where they kneeled or sat on cane chairs; peasant women, some from distant villages, little girls with flowered kerchiefs over their heads, and old women in black shawls. Many of them had already been to Confession, others would be going when their turn came, tomorrow, or the next day. In the meanwhile, they were all here to see Padre Pio. Suddenly, one of them gave a groan and started to fall fainting on the floor; she was picked up and carried out to the fresh air.

She was a sick woman, and looked half dead. Her grandchildren supported her, praying all the time. The crowd did not look up, they made way and kept their heads bent.

I was not able to go to Confession or Communion, but I stood there for three hours looking at Padre Pio, as he sat beyond his flock on the simple throne of his confessional. I gazed at the friar that I had wanted to interview, and as I did so, I felt as though all my journalism, all my professional life, all the questions that I had planned to ask, melted away before the extreme simplicity of what I saw, with these eyes that have indeed seen so much, and which yet could not get enough of that mysteriously simple picture. What I saw was a peasant friar sitting as he had sat every day for thirty-eight years, in his rustic confessional, giving an incalculable number of interviews, very different from the one I had planned. He leaned over to listen, first on one side, then on the other as the two slow lines of penitents moved up, to listen to all the sins of the world.

I have called him a peasant friar, and indeed he is, being the son of peasants. His face and figure are rugged and remind me of the old herdsmen that I saw, as a boy, in the Roman Campagna, and on the cattle tracks of the *Murgie,* or those ancient shepherds of the high pastures of Calabrian and Lucanian Appenines. His figure is stocky, he has a stiff, stubby beard, and short hair. His asceticism has not left its characteristic traces on his face, which bears, rather, those of a profound and peaceful conviction. Seated on his high wooden chair, he leaned over first on one side, and then on the other to listen, and then would take

into his hands the letters and cards that were given
to him to touch. "Touch them all, Father, there are
only twelve of them!" I heard a little woman say to
him. Every now and then I saw him lift one of his
hands, as though to relieve it from some hidden pain,
and every now and again, he sighed deeply, leaning
over to the right as though to relieve his left side,
weary and aching from the wound. His face never
changed its expression, only he occasionally showed
annoyance when some woman, having finished her
confession, remained kneeling in front of him refusing to leave. He would then dismiss her with a wave
of his big handkerchief. He had been hearing confessions since dawn, and every now and then, he would
make a gesture of appeal to the crowd of women
who were pushing against the railing, begging them
to let him breathe, to stop staring at him, to allow
him to blow his nose in peace! If one may use the
expression "I liked it," when referring to the gestures
of one who was being proclaimed a saint by everyone about him, I will say that I liked his almost rough
straightforwardness, his bringing order, with a wave
of his hand in the two lines of women. I liked his
being pastor as well as shepherd. I looked at his hands,
covered with gloves of brown wool, those hands that
have been bleeding slowly for thirty-eight years, and
I realized how weak would be my faith, if I regretted
too much not being able to see them uncovered.

When he got up to go, it was nearly noon. The
group of women was kneeling in front of him, trying to reach his tunic, his hands and his feet. I could
hear his voice almost impatiently asking them to let
him get by. The two brothers who had come to fetch

him were even more abrupt. Even saints have a limit
to their endurance, and Padre Pio was making way
for himself with vigorous sweeps of his handkerchief.
I followed him into the sacristy with the silent throng
that would not leave him for a moment. I mingled
with the dozens who were trying in one way or
another to give him some object to get him to speak
to them. In the meantime, he was trying to put on
his surplice to distribute Holy Communion. Padre Pio
was trying to vest himself and everyone was trying
to help him, pulling one sleeve and then the other,
making him waste his time, and in fact, putting him
through a mild form of torture. I became ashamed
of having added to the invasion of his privacy. "Do
you want to tear my arms off? Do you really want
to tear them off?" He kept asking, but his eyes were
not cross, even if his voice sounded irritated.

In the midst of the hub-bub of clamoring demands,
he was told who I was, my profession, and that I had
come all the way from Milan to see him. "You made
this great journey just to see me?" he said smiling,
"A fine thing you have come to see! All the way from
Milan too! Haven't you got a prayer book at home?
You could have saved yourself the trip, God bless you.
An 'Ave Maria' is better than any trip, my son!"

The crowd carried him away from me, taking him
back to the church, and forming a group around the
steps of the altar. The women were all kneeling to
receive Communion. Padre Pio standing before them,
had all the simplicity of the early Christians, who
were at the same time shepherds and priests.

Orio Vergani.

CHAPTER VIII

Cures

There was a blind man who lived near the monastery of San Giovanni Rotondo, he was known as Pietruccio to everyone there. When he was fourteen he lost his sight as his father had before him. He went to Padre Pio to ask his help but was told by the good Father that: "Many people sin with their eyes and are lost." In other words he was really better off blind! Pietruccio showed almost heroic virtue and answered the Father's discouraging statement by saying: "I only want my sight if it is good for my soul!" He was a familiar and contented figure around the monastery where he spent his days doing little errands. He took the mail every evening to the post office, and had a cheerful word for everyone he met.

Padre Pio must have felt that Pietruccio's blindness was a sort of guarantee for his salvation, but in other cases he performed some astonishing and authenticated cures. The son of Count Marzotta of Florence, a child of eight, was suffering from a case of advanced myopia bordering on blindness. His parents took him to Padre Pio who urged them to pray very hard for their boy, at the same time promising to pray with them. They stayed for several days at San Giovanni, and by the time they had returned to Florence they noticed a distinct improvement in little Mario's vision. A year later they returned to Pietrelcina and the child was completely cured. He did not even wear glasses.

A very spectacular cure took place in 1947. Gemma Di Giorgi lived in Ribera in Sicily. She was born without pupils to her eyes. The doctors declared that there was absolutely nothing they could do to give her even a limited vision. Her parents accepted this tragic verdict, but her grandmother did not. She undertook the long and exhausting journey to San Giovanni Rotondo with the little girl, full of faith in the powers of Padre Pio. They were both lost in the crowd of the faithful attending his Mass, when at the end while the silence was still intense, everyone heard a voice calling: "Gemma, come here!" The grandmother pushed her way up to the altar with the child and knelt down before the holy man whom they had come so far to see. He smiled at Gemma and told her that she must make her first Communion. He heard her confession and then stroked her eyes with his hand. She received Holy Communion by herself and when afterwards her grandmother asked her if she had begged for any favor from Padre Pio the little girl answered: "No, Little Grandmother, I forgot!" Padre Pio saw them later and said: "May the Madonna bless you, Gemma. Be a good girl!" At this moment the child gave a frantic cry, she could see... The cure was permanent and complete, although her eyes still had no pupils. She was examined by many doctors who testified to the case and were able to offer no scientific explanation.

Padre Pio often told people to undergo an operation when they have been told by doctors that the outcome would be doubtful or even fatal. Grazia Siena had been born totally blind. Medical science had declared her to be incurable and no doctor was willing to operate. She grew up in total darkness but never gave up hope of being somehow cured. She was a frequent visitor to Monte Gargano and well known to Padre Pio. One day he said to her that she must try the inexhaustible resources of science and undergo an operation. The parents protested; they had consulted many doctors in the past and none had been willing to take the risk. Grazia was now 27 years old and her chances seemed even more hopeless than when she was a child. Besides, where could they find enough money to pay for such an operation? Her father's earnings were too meager to allow for such experiments. Fortunately for Grazia a benefactor came forward with not only the money that was needed but the energy and initiative to take her to Bari to consult an eye specialist. The doctor was discouraging; there were grave difficulties involved, and he was about to refuse like all the rest. Grazia's determination to follow Padre Pio's advice made him relent. "I shall try," he said, "but only a miracle can give you your sight." The story has a happy ending, for when the bandages were removed Grazia could see and her cure was permanent.

It is impossible in this case to evaluate the power of Padre Pio's prayer in comparison with the skill of the surgeon. We can only see in all this the manifestation of the will of God and the combined uses to which He can bring His faithful servants.

The healing of Maria Cozzi Giuliano of Ghizzano in the province of Pisa.

Maria Cozzi Giuliano was diagnosed as having an

epithelioma on the tongue at the hospital of S. Maria Novella at Florence, August 18, 1919, and was to be operated on the 21st. She had terrible pain for seven months, and was unable to masticate.

A priest gave her a portrait of Padre Pio before she entered and suggested that she should make a triduum in honor of the Holy Trinity invoking Padre Pio's intercession for a cure. She did so.

The day after her recovery she presented herself to the dentist who was to draw out a number of teeth before the operation could take place. He was astonished to find her tongue completely healed, and immediately called in Dr. Marchetti, who as soon as he had seen her dismissed her from the hospital, declaring her completely cured.

The Cure of Signora Preziosi Paolina of S. Giovanni Rotondo.

At the beginning of the year 1925, Signora Preziosi Paolina developed first bronchitis which then turned into pneumonia. She was the mother of five children. The doctors gave no hope, her coffin was prepared and also her shroud.

Padre Pio's intercession was requested. He predicted her cure would take place during the ringing of the Easter bells. It was then Passion week.

During the night of Good Friday she went into a state of coma. Saturday morning Padre Pio said his Mass and went into ecstasy during the *Gloria*. At the ringing of the bells, Signora Preziosi got up, her fever completely gone.

The Cure of Signora Maria Pennisi. Born in New York, lived in Pietrelcina.

Maria went to school with the Ursulines at Benevento.

In 1922 she became tubercular and was treated at Naples for this malady by Dr. G. Moscato of the University of Naples.

Her case was considered hopeless, she was returned to Pietrelcina with a high temperature accompanied by lung hemorrhages.

Padre Pio did not know the family but went to meet them when they were on their way to visit him. Before being introduced he spoke to Maria and put his hand on her shoulder, saying that she was healed. She was cured, but when taken away from Pietrelcina contrary to the advice of Padre Pio, she fell ill again. She for the second time was cured after being touched with some material stained with the blood of Padre Pio. Bandages, gloves, etc., once belonging to Padre Pio must now be put away and preserved at the monastery.

The Cure of Signora Adelaide Tonelli. Bologna.

She was cured from an illness of the ovarium through the intercession of Padre Pio, after the spiritual return of the whole family to the Faith.

The Cure of Enrico del Fante.

On the 16th October, 1930, after an X-ray examination, Prof. Palmieri confirmed his diagnosis of a high fever being caused by an internal abscess in the kidney. Enrico del Fante was the nephew of Alberto del Fante, then a disbeliever. At the request of his brother-in-law, Tonelli Antonio, who had already received favors from Padre Pio, Padre Pio predicted the cure for a certain day. It took place and caused the conversion of Alberto del Fante who has since written many books about Padre Pio.

The Cure of Silvano Menfredini. Bologna.

Silvano was a twin boy born September 10, 1927. From birth he suffered from bilateral congenital dislocation of the ankles, and of the feet, bilateral hernia and hydrocele.

He was given three months of medical treatment for these illnesses. The child cried continuously.

Through the influence of friends the father put a medal of Padre Pio on the child. After four months the child was X-rayed, and one ankle was found completely cured and the second partly cured without any operation. The father then took the child to Padre Pio to thank him and to ask for a complete cure. Padre Pio promised him this but advised an immediate operation for the bilateral hernia and hydrocele. This was done, and after three months the child was completely cured. Both feet were rectified without any operation.

The Cure of the Dorigo Family of Bologna.

The Dorigo family obtained a solution to financial difficulties and the cure of a child from diphtheria, and another from pneumonia, through the application of a medal blessed by Padre Pio.

The Cure of the Countess Baiocchi of Gavinana. Rome.

The Countess Baiocchi, a native of Rome, Largo di Porta Pia 116, suffered from an illness which no doctor was able to diagnose, so she stopped going to doctors. One day she was walking in the streets of Rome and she heard a voice saying insistently "go to Dr. Festa, go to Dr. Festa." But she could not see anyone. In the evening she asked her husband whether he knew of a Dr. Festa, but did not say where she had got the name. He looked it up in the telephone book, and she made an appointment to see him. Dr. Festa was the surgeon who operated upon Padre Pio for a hernia and a cyst.

She went to see the doctor together with her husband. But he was unable to diagnose the illness any more than the others. She was very disappointed. The doctor then suggested that she should go and see a good friend of his, Padre Pio. He mentioned in speaking about Pio that he had the power of bilocation of the voice. She then told her story for the first time to her husband and to the doctor, as to how she had heard the voice saying, "Go to Dr. Festa."

So she and her husband went to visit Padre Pio. After a brief visit, Padre Pio asked them to come back later, when they had rested from their journey. As soon as the Countess reached her room in the house in which she was staying, she was stricken with sharp pains. The husband became alarmed and rushed off to Padre Pio. Padre Pio told him not to get so agitated and to pray. In desperation he returned to his wife. She was cured.

The Cure of Signorina Annunciata Ventrella. S. Giovanni Rotondo.

Annunciata Ventrella, mother of two sons aged 17 and 19, was dying of a heart disease. The heart was out of place, causing vomiting, and so weakened her that death was imminent. The sons had been called to her deathbed. In the middle of the night—about 11:30 p.m.—the younger son was watching in her bedroom, when suddenly he saw at the foot of the bed Padre Pio, holding out his arms to her, and another Franciscan, St. Anthony, with a baby in his arms. The next day the mother got up, to the astonishment of all. Her heart was quite normal. In a few days she was back again at work.

The Cure of Signor Gattamorta Giovanni. Bologna.
Cured from meningitis at the touch of a reproduction of Padre Pio. 1931.

The Cure of Signorina Giuseppina Marchetti. Bologna.
Giuseppina Marchetti, aged 24, had fractured the bone of the right humerus some four years earlier and had had operations in consequence of it, but the bone would not heal. She and her family visited Padre Pio in June 1930, asking his intercession. On September 17th, the Feast of the Stigmata of St. Francis of Assisi, their home was pervaded by the perfume of Padre Pio. The bone began to heal. The perfume was noticed several times during the year. The following year on 17th of September 1931, the bone was completely healed.

The Cure of Signora Amelia Consolini. Bologna.
Mrs. Consolini suffered for 20 years from vertebral arthritis. She was in a plaster cast when she visited Padre Pio, in January of 1930. She was completely cured, suffering no more pain and a few days afterwards took off the plaster cast, never to use it again.

The Cure of Signor Pierino Muzioli. Bologna.
The young boy Pierino suffered from mental strain due to excessive study. He was in danger of death, running a high temperature, when through the prayers of his mother to Padre Pio, the boy was completely healed.

The Cure of a Baby: Franco Angelini. Bologna.

This baby was suddenly cured from pneumonia after a picture of Padre Pio had been put under the pillow of the baby. The next morning the temperature was completely normal.

The Cure of Signorina Elena Galeati of Imola.

Elena suffered from a malady of the thyroid gland, which was treated for many years by doctors without success. Galeati read the story of Padre Pio in August 1932. In November of the same year when she visited the doctor she was declared completely cured.

The Cure of Alessandro Galeati of Imola.

Alessandro suffered from ulcers in the stomach and was reduced to extreme weakness owing to lack of nourishment. He visited Padre Pio. By the touch of his hand he was cured.

The reader must note that no pronouncement on these reported cures has been made by the Church. The Church oftentimes passes judgment on reputed miraculous cures only many years after they occur, as in the case of those investigated at Lourdes.

Fr. Raffaelle told this story: One man had had a bad accident. His leg was broken, the thigh bone stuck out through the flesh. When he came to see Padre Pio in 1948, his leg was still in bad condition, all swollen, and he had to use crutches. When going to confession to Padre Pio he could not kneel down. As he finished, Padre Pio put his hand on the man's head and told him not to worry. The man walked away and noticed he could walk without the crutches.

When he returned to San Giovanni he told one of the Fathers that when he takes a walk the leg that was cured gets less tired than the other.

Fr. Nunzio also related the following incident: At Montefalcione a hardened sinner was dying. His relatives urged him to receive the Sacraments. They prayed for him, spoke to him about Padre Pio. He said if Padre Pio came he would go to confession. This was like a challenge, because it was evident that Padre Pio could not come—in the ordinary way. He was left alone for a while, and when someone returned to see how he was getting along, the man was all radiant with joy. Padre Pio had been there, heard his confession and brought him peace of heart again. There was also a strong, sweet perfume noticeable in the room.

Fr. Antonio narrates that during the war in Africa an Italian soldier was standing behind a large rock, while a fierce battle was going on. Suddenly a monk stood beside him and pulled him gently by the sleeve, saying he should get out from behind the rock. The soldier did not want to leave what he thought was a safe place. The monk pulled a second time, and was more emphatic. He did not move. Then the monk pulled him out by force. Right after that the entire place where the soldier had been standing blew up. The monk disappeared. Some days after as he was relating this to a fellow soldier, the companion showed him a picture of Padre Pio which he always carried with him. The soldier whose life had been saved exclaimed: "That is the monk who saved my life!" He had never seen Padre Pio or heard of him before.

About ten years ago an Austrian woman came to San Giovanni Rotondo. She was in a state of deep depression as a result of the war and of what it had done to her country, and was suffering besides from a painful swelling in her arm. Shortly after her arrival Padre Pio appeared to her in a dream. He pressed both thumbs on her arm, and when she awoke in the morning she was completely cured. She was able to make her bed and lift furniture, having been unable to do so for many weeks. Several months later she had occasion to ask Padre Pio if it had been he who had appeared to her and had cured her, and he answered that it was.

A few years later she woke very early one morning and was overcome with sadness at the thought of Austria, her native land, that was going through such cruel trials. As she lay there weeping, Padre Pio appeared at the side of her bed holding a large cross which she later recognized as the one in the choir. He blessed her with it and she immediately felt consoled and at peace.

On her name day, the feast of St. Ann which is the 26th of July, she asked Padre Pio in the confessional whether it was he who had appeared to her on the 29th of June and had blessed her. He said "Yes." Then she asked him why he had blessed her. He said: "To dispel the evil spirits." Since she did not understand Italian well, she understood that she had been possessed. She was horrified, but did not know how to ask for an explanation in Italian. But Padre Pio answered her unspoken question: "I did not dispel the devils *out* of you but *away* from you."

The Cure of the Marinelli Boy of Montignana.
A cure was performed on the son of Leonello

Marinelli, of the town of Montignana di Corciano, in the Province of Perugia. This man was superintendent of public works in his town. His son, some years ago at the age of 10, developed a heart ailment. In spite of all the care of the local doctor, the boy got steadily worse. The illness was a functional disorder of the heart, in consequence of which his entire body became swollen. Dr. Schiccollini called in Dr. Calabro of Perugia for consultation. But the doctor could only confirm the verdict of the local doctor, the boy was beyond medical aid. Then one evening after one of the visits of the doctor, the boy turned to his father (who was with the boy whenever he could be) and asked him to go to Padre Pio to beg him to pray for his cure. The father said he would go the next day. But the boy insisted he go immediately. The father left by train for Foggia that evening. At Foggia he went to the home of Dr. Sanvico, told him the story and the purpose of his trip, and asked him to go with him to San Giovanni Rotondo. (Dr. Mario Sanvico was a good friend of Padre Pio and frequently came to the monastery. He was also a member of the building commission for the hospital which was being built.) When they arrived they hardly came into the presence of Padre Pio, when he told the man: "I know why you came. The boy is better and gradually will be cured." The father of the boy had not even a chance to open his mouth. He wanted to leave at once to verify what Padre Pio had said. But Padre Pio persuaded him to stay till morning, assist at High Mass and receive Holy Communion. This he did. The man also went to confession to Padre Pio and was again told the boy would

get well. Before leaving, the man said goodbye to
Padre Pio and was again assured (for the third time)
that the boy would get better and would be completely cured within two months.

When Marinelli came home his boy told him he
had seen Padre Pio as in a dream with his blood-
stained stigmata. From that moment on the boy began
to improve. The doctors who had attended the boy
visited him and attested that all swelling was gone
and that the functional disorder of the heart had disappeared. This happened about the first week of
February. About the first week of March, the father,
Leonello Marinello, and his boy came to thank Padre
Pio. It was at this occasion that Dr. Sanguinetti and
others spoke to both.

The Cure of Lucia Bellodi.

During June, 1952, another miraculous cure was
attributed to Padre Pio.

Lucia Bellodi, a girl of 21, daughter of a farmer
at Mirandola, Prov. of Modena, suffered from a severe case of diabetes for seven years. At the time of
the cure, Corpus Christi, June 12, 1952, she was staying at the home for the aged, since she could not
get into any hospital. The illness first took hold of
her when she was barely 14 years old. For the first
four years she was taken from one hospital to another, without the least improvement. During the fifth
year she became worse. She was accepted in the Home
for the Aged where the sisters did all they could to
give her relief. But there was no cure. Her abdomen
swelled to immense proportions. Her thirst became
insatiable. She drank 100 litres of water (about 105

quarts) daily. A rubber hose was put into her mouth and a jar holding 50 litres placed near her bed. She emptied this twice every 24 hours. It was the only relief she had.

On Corpus Christi, June 12, about 6 p.m., she suddenly stopped drinking water, and called the Mother Superior. She said she felt impelled to go to the chapel to pray. She asked the sister to bring along only one glass of water. The Mother Superior had a presentiment that it was the beginning of the end. Lucia told her with a happy smile: "I will die soon, Mother, Padre Pio came to see me. He was just like the picture on the bureau. He said I could not be cured (i.e. by the doctors). But he also told me to hope, and to have faith in the end in the help of Heaven." Evidently, from the succession of events, she misunderstood Padre Pio. Two sisters assisted her to the chapel. She did not ask for water, and even refused when offered the glass they had taken along. It was now already a quarter of an hour since she had taken anything to drink. After finishing her prayers she was brought back to her little room in a faint. The chaplain was called. The tube was put into her mouth, but she instinctively pushed it away. Suddenly she opened her eyes with a strange smile on her lips. She sat up in her bed and gesticulated joyously, saying Padre Pio had shortly before told her in the name of God: "You are cured. Get up! Come immediately to my monastery. I want to bless you and thank the Almighty with you." Lucia came with two of the sisters on June 17. When they appeared before Padre Pio, he said with a smile: "I was waiting for you," and blessed her.

A Spiritual Benefit, Port Maurizio, September 11, 1940.

"No matter how much I say with regard to the graces received through Padre Pio, I could not say enough, for he procured me a great number, and continued to do so. When I saw Padre Pio for the first time, it seemed to me like a dream, and my heart leapt for joy.

"I assisted at the Mass he celebrated with saintly ardor. I was also fortunate enough to see him at close range, for I was kneeling at the side of the altar; large drops of tears fell from his eyes...in that instant I repented my sins and implored forgiveness for myself and for all mankind. At the Consecration, I was doubly wrapped in prayer, and at the Elevation of the Host I looked up with faith, and to my astonishment It appeared radiant and beautiful. I said nothing about it to anyone that day, but the following day I went to the confessional of the Padre and I said, 'Father, the Host consecrated by you does not look the same as the others.' 'What,' he said, 'is there something special about mine?' 'Yes,' I replied, 'the Host of every other priest looks dull, and there is a crucifix in the center, while yours appears beautiful and radiant.' He did not reply, so I continued, 'Tell me, Father, is this so, or is it an illusion?' Entering into a state of recollection within himself, he replied with gravity, *'What you saw was true.'*

"I could tell some other facts, but I will withhold them for various reasons, partly because they are too personal. I have not told these things to anyone except to a Poor Clare nun, because she is a very holy religious. I would like my name to be withheld with regard to what I have written here. *Deo gratias.*

"Praise be to God, and let us sing His mercy in eternity, and also the glory of the saintly Padre Pio. I enclose a note given to me by a Poor Clare sister which may interest you.

Signature."

The letter from the Poor Clare sister reads as follows:

"J.M.J.

5th September, 1940

"Having heard from Olga...that you are publishing the second edition of the book on Padre Pio, please permit me to submit to you the account which follows:

"My sister Maria M_____ became gravely ill with a disease of the eye for which she had a tendency from childhood. The doctor attending her said that in a few years she would be completely blind. You can imagine how disturbed I was, all the more so because my sister depends on the work of her hands to support herself.

"Once my spiritual director spoke to me about Padre Pio, so I sent him a note asking him to pray for my sister. He replied, saying he would willingly pray for my sister, and assured me she would not completely lose her sight. It is now twenty years since then and my sister continued to work, to the stupefaction of the doctors. I give praise and glory to God, crediting her cure to the merits of Padre Pio."

The Cure of Luisa Carnevali, Widow of Signor Magnanini of Imola. June 21, 1933.
"Knowing how ardently you are following the

miraculous events of the humble Father Pio, and spurred by the duty of gratitude to Our Lord, I am sending you the following:

"On the 15th of February, 1932, a dental surgeon pulled out two roots and teeth for me. The next day I got up with a temperature, and in the evening it went much higher. As the pain persisted, a doctor and the dentist were called and declared it to be a threatening infection. Every medical means was used to stop the dreadful infection, but in vain, for it became worse every day, so that on the 21st of February, in addition to running a high temperature, I began to have tremors and fainting spells. This happened every time I made the slightest movement, such as trying to sit up and swallow.

"The doctor, alarmed by the bad turn of the illness, decided to arrange for my admission to a hospital the next morning. Although in grave condition, I was perfectly conscious of everything, so I decided to have the confessor called to me. On Monday the 22nd, Holy Communion was brought to me, though only a little piece of the Host was given me on a spoon with water. At ten I left the house, surrounded by my weeping family. I was resigned though, and even pleased with the prospect of joining my beloved husband who had died three years before.

"I was carried to the City Hospital of my own town of Imola, directed by the eminent Dr. Francesco d'Agostino. Before entering the operating room I directed my last thoughts, with my crucifix in hand, to the Sacred Heart of Jesus, to Padre Pio, and to my deceased husband; from them all, I drew all the force necessary to endure being operated on without any anesthesia. Our good Lord guided the courageous Dr. d'Agostino[1] who operated marvelously well, but he found my condition very bad, and it remained so until the evening of the 23rd at 8 o'clock. In my room my father was by my bedside, and my eldest son, aged 13, stood at the foot of the bed; all of a sudden I felt someone throw cold water in my face, and I saw our good friend Padre Pio with his hands crossed near my bed. At once I jumped up saying, 'Who has thrown cold water on me?' My father, poor man, thought I was wandering, and told me to keep quiet. 'No,' I said, 'Look!' and putting my hands on my forehead I showed my fingers dripping water. I did not say anything to them about Padre Pio. Only afterwards when my mother came did I mention his visit, but we said nothing to the others.

"Oh great wonder! The miracle was accomplished. Our good Padre Pio obtained it from the Omnipotent Christ, so he saved a poor widow with five children. On the morning of the 24th when changing the dressing, Dr. d'Agostino found that gangrene—that is what he called it—had oozed out onto the bandage. Delighted, he cried out, 'Take courage, you are saved. In a short time you will be well.' And so it was in fact. On the tenth I left the hospital, weak, yes, but with the wound healed and the infection gone. As you see I enclose the diagnosis of Doctor Francesco d'Agostino.

"As a spiritual daughter of the humble Padre Pio I beg you accept this poor account, but it is the pure

---

1. On a postcard headed: Congregazione di Carita Imola—City Hospital, Dr. Francesco d'Agostino had written: Adenophlegmon with gangrene in the lower jaw in serious condition.

truth, and I leave you free to use it when and how you think best.

Yours sincerely,
Luisa Carnavalli, Widow Magnanini, Imola,
Via Cavour 20."

The Cure of Signor Antonio Monari of Bologna.
"Bologna, 16th of September, 1932.

"I am sending for your book the enclosed account so that the world will know more about the greatness of the miracles of Padre Pio of Pietrelcina, and be convinced.

"When I left Bologna to go to San Giovanni Rotondo to see Padre Pio, I was already expecting to see a saint, but I never imagined I would experience what I did, nor that I would be able to return to my home so relieved and contented that I felt like another man.

"I was able to confide to the Father the many troubles that were afflicting me and my family. He listened to me paternally, and with a sweet smile, with so serene a light and expression of goodness in his eyes that I felt that what I was about to say was already known to him. I asked him for a grace for which for many years I had waited in vain through influential people in high positions. He replied with these words, 'Men can do nothing, my son,' then pointing to the skies, 'only He who is above. Persevere in prayer and I will pray with you,' and he gave me his holy blessing. I cannot describe the feeling of profound emotion which invaded me, so much so that when I got up, I lost my balance.

"The Padre on leaving gave me a small slap on

the right side of the head, which I thought was a little affectionate gesture. On the contrary, he meant it as a sign of his grace which he wanted me to keep by me on my way home.

"After the war I came back with my right ear completely deaf. Many people knew about this, including my companions on the journey to San Giovanni Rotondo. Mr. Giuseppe Grazia had to sit always on my left to talk with me more easily, and now on the way back to Bologna, to my great surprise and joy, when Mr. Grazia sat on my right I heard him perfectly well.

"Ever so many times I tested my hearing in the bus, talking to people, and I continued in the train, to say nothing of what happened as soon as I reached home. Imagine the joy of my wife and children, who never wearied of stuffing up my left ear and asking me all sorts of delightful questions in my right ear. My right ear now functions perfectly as in former times, just as my left ear, without any deafness.

"I have written this because if you would like to publish it, it would be a way of rendering thanks and praise to our great and good Padre Pio of Pietrelcina.

> Antonio Monari,
> Via Irenio 39, Bologna."

A few months later another letter was received from Antonio Monari as follows:

> "Bologna, 10 February, 1933

"It is my duty to let you know, for the greater glory of Padre Pio, about his appearance to me in a dream, between the 7th and 8th of the current month.

"It should be noted that my little boy, Sergio, was down with influenza and had remained in bed for some days. Then, after getting up, he again became ill, so much so that on the evening of the 7th he went to bed very early with nausea and shivering.

"In the night I dreamed of Padre Pio. He appeared to me luminous and beautiful in the face, at the foot of my bed, he said to me, 'I have cured your child of a very grave malady.' While I was saying to him, 'Father, I thank you with all my heart and soul for the great good that you have procured for me, because you see, our condition prevents us from spending anything, even the smallest sum for illness,' he tried to write but the fountain pen did not work, and so he folded up the paper and put it in his breast, and said to me, 'Go to Caroli.'

"I got up and ran to my child's room where I saw that he was resting quietly, without fever, so much so that by morning he wanted to go to school.

"I must tell you, too, that just lately I have received another great grace from Padre Pio.

"He has opened the way of Providence, giving me a permanent position which for three years, as well you know, I have sought in vain to obtain. At the end of March I shall start service as assistant gardener to the Princess del Drago at Frosinone.

"These are the many things both spiritual and material with which Padre Pio has enriched me, so that I feel overpowered because I realize I am of so little worth, and that it would not be sufficient if I spent the whole of my life in good works and prayers and in thanksgiving to merit all the good that he has done to us.

> Antonio Monari,
> Via Irenio 39, Bologna."

The Cure of Rosaria Chichine of Mores (Sassari).

On the 8th of May Signor del Fante received a telegram from Professor Calvia of Mores saying: "Kindly inform me of the possibility of direct correspondence with Padre Pio with the hope of a reply. Thanks. Professor Mauro Calvia." Signor del Fante replied by giving the exact address and sending a medal blessed by Padre.

The 10th of May, 1935, Professor Calvia wrote to del Fante: "I thank you very much for your kindness in replying to me and for sending the welcome gift of the miraculous medal which I gave the patient. I was absent from Sardegna for about two weeks, and on my return I found a parcel of books, among which was your great work which one day, after the passing of the saintly Father, will prove to be an abundant source of documentary evidence.

"On my return I found one of my godchildren gravely ill with a complication of pulmonary ectasia. In reading of the powers of Padre Pio, as a good militant Christian I wished to appeal to the prayers of the holy priest of Gargano, to implore the cure of this young girl from Our Lord Jesus Christ, for she lives a good life, full of faith, and was an orphan from birth.

"God will be a Merciful Father in this pitiful case. They are all Christian sons practicing their Faith, and Our Lord will answer their prayers, restoring bodily health to the sick. I telegraphed the Padre as follows: 'I invoke your fervent prayers for a sick person suffering gravely from bronchial pneumonia, relying on the work of Our Lord; May Jesus Christ be praised.'

"This morning the superior of the monastery replied

Upper left: Way of the Cross.
Upper right: Pilgrimage.
Lower left: Waiting for Confession.
Lower right: Listening to opera tenor Gigli.

Upper left: Monastery garden.
Upper right: Casa Sollievo (Hospital).
Lower left: Left window was No. 5 Cell of Padre Pio.
Lower right: Corridor to Pio's cell.

by telegram: 'Prayers for the patient recommended, blessings.'

"I am happy, Signor del Fante, that your guide has been so useful to me in this world, and in preparation for the next...."

Four months afterwards, Professor Calvia wrote again:

"Mores, September 25, 1935

"Dear Brother in Jesus Christ,

"On this day, when the miracle wrought by the fervent prayers of Padre Pio was accomplished, I feel it is my urgent duty to give you a report regarding Rosaria Chichini, child of Paolo of Mores. You will remember my telegram sent on the 8th of May asking you for the address of the venerable Padre Pio, in which I made known the gravity of the child's illness already given up by the doctors consulted. The anxiety of the family was very great. At Mores I came across your good books which I read with the most compelling interest, and a thought flashed before my mind, giving me the idea of what I should do. You know well that tuberculosis is fatal, yet to the glory of this holy priest, the miracle happened, and life was restored to this girl who was most certainly condemned to death.

"The fatherly kindness of Our Lord has prevailed in giving back to her tortured body the health I prayed for.

"On the 15th of August, Feast of the Assumption of the Blessed Virgin, the girl began getting up. The fever diminished progressively, and her life resumed its normal course, for she now sang at her prayers as she used to before her illness. An attack of pleurisy delayed her convalescence. When she was taken to the Medical Hospital of Capoluogo at Provincia some days back for a new X-ray, it was realized what a marvelous change had taken place.

"On interrogating the local doctor, I was told that the fever had disappeared completely, and that her original strength was returning little by little.

"Today, the girl is happy and is beginning to take her first walks out of doors.

"I thank Our Lord fervently for having conceded so much to a family of honest laborers.

"To you, dear friend, I am very grateful for the holy work you are carrying out by the propagation of the Faith.

Prof. Mauro Calvia,
Mores, (Sassari)."

Five years after the preceding letter, Prof. Calvia wrote:

"Would you believe it, the health of my young godchild is excellent, quite normal, the disease has gone and she is living happily. She no longer receives any medical attention. Our Lord, the Supreme Physician, has worked the miracle. Your medal and the prayers of the Padre have brought her health, this is my absolute conviction. Only the Padre can confirm this, as he alone is able to penetrate the mystery. I am glad of the happiness procured...."

Everyone gives praise first of all to God, and then to His herald on this earth, the Saint of Gargano: Padre Pio of Pietrelcina.

A Letter of a Military Chaplain, Don Vittorio Felisati.

"The Sanitorium of Marina Grottaglie (Taranto)

"October 16, 1946

"Dear Professor:

"An introduction is unnecessary—we know each other.

"Since April, 1942, I have been chaplain of Marina, and since January, 1946, I have been in this hospital for the mission, where I continue my apostolate for our dear Padre, to make him known and to bring back souls to the merciful God through him.

"I can affirm by oath anything written here regarding myself.

"I have read and enjoyed your book, which is of the greatest interest for us who know the Padre and his good work. I got to know the Padre about 1934 through the wife of a doctor from Ferrara. Their only son, then eight years of age, was ill, suffering from progressive infantile paralysis affecting his little brain. Given up by all specialists consulted, who estimated he had no more than two months to live, he was taken by his mother to the Padre, who blessed him and said: 'We are at the last stages of the disease.'

"Now he is studying medicine at the university, having become a spiritual son of the Padre, together with his mother. Before the war, I often went with the son, and once with the husband to see the Padre, and I had a cross blessed by the Padre, which I always keep with me; I have put myself and all my dear family under his protection. Members of my family, and especially my brother, a Third Order Franciscan, are devoted to him and speak about him to everybody, having on many occasions experienced his valued assistance in wartime. During the bombardments which were frequent in Ferrara, they remained in the house praying and never had any damage, and the two sons, captains of infantry, returned home safely after having survived many dangers.

"As you will remember, I was sent by the Red Cross to Spain to serve in a hospital, the largest one there, with 1,500 beds. As soon as I arrived I invoked the intercession of the Padre: 'Padre, if you are truly a saint, you must hear me and help. You see how great is the slaughter. Put under your protection all my patients and wounded. You take care of them.' I received the confirmation at once that my prayer had been heard. I was called to the side of a patient so gravely sick that the doctor gave him only another two hours to live. Introducing myself, I asked where he was from. He said, 'from Foggia,' replying with a scarcely audible voice. 'Then you are safe,' I said. He made a sign to the contrary, feeling he was dying. I gave him all the Sacraments. After twenty days, he was in condition to make the journey back to Italy.

"Two men wounded in the head were in a state of coma, and while I begged the Padre's intercession, blessing them with the crucifix they were healed.

"An officer gravely ill with an injured spinal cord and given up by the doctors, invoked the intercession of the Padre. After three months he returned to his post. It was the same with many other cases.

"As I have already declared under oath, in my 24 months of service in this hospital where 37,000 wounded were cared for, only 55 died.

"The wings of the hospital, near the station, were

targets for various bombardments, but were never hit, although several buildings nearby were.

"I gave your book to many to read, and through the intercession of Padre Pio many returned to God.

"In this war Padre Pio never abandoned me. On board the Royal Italian Navy Hospital Ship, 'Citta di Trapani,' I made many journeys to Africa. I put my ship under his care and according to those competent in the matter, it was believed that in the case of a direct hit no one would have had the time to save himself. On the 29th of July, 1940, between Derna and Tobruk at 1:30 a.m. an airplane flew over the ship nearly touching the mast, and then let off five bombs which all fell into the sea about 50 yards away. The bulletin mentions it. After 38 voyages, on the first of December, 1942, at 9:20 a.m. and about ten miles from Biserta, the boat was torpedoed and sunk in nine minutes, but only nine out of 120 people were drowned. I found myself in the range of the blast, having hardly finished celebrating Mass. I was struck all over from head to foot, as these blows caused a concussion and visceral disturbances with vomiting, a symptom of concussion.

"I ought to have fallen down dead. Instead, in this state, with but a ray of intelligence, I liberated myself from the debris, went to the cabin, put on the life belt, took my documents without knowing what I was doing, and still unconscious, without any help, jumped over the railing and descended by a rope ladder till I touched the water, still holding my knapsack. 'Chaplain, throw yourself into the sea, the boat is going down. . .' someone said to me, but I did not understand anything and I stood still, while the ship broke in two and was about to go down. The sea, moreover, was rough and a gunboat was thrown up against the hulk by a wave, and I was taken by a sailor. The ship sank immediately. After three hours I returned to consciousness and found myself on a craft that had come to our help from Biserta.

"A hit on the head is enough to make one fall and lose consciousness, but while I was in that state, I was still able to save myself. Is this not something extraordinary?

"The 31st of January, 1943, I shipped at my own request on board the Royal Naval Hospital Ship, 'Principessa Giovanna.' The morning of April 20, 1943, while they were taking on wounded from the raid on Tunisia, the ship was bombed and shelled, causing little damage and some wounded. I remained unhurt, although close to an explosion.

"The 5th of May, 1943, 800 wounded and sick, and 70 women and children were taken on the ship at Tunisia. On our way to the Cape of Good Hope, twice in one day—at 2:40 p.m., and at 6:30 p.m., the ship was shelled and bombed with about 40 bombs, twenty at a time, which made direct hits and caused a fire lasting 12 hours. One bomb fell a few feet from where I was, but when it burst I found myself on the opposite side. How I got to safety I do not know. I remained completely untouched and unshaken, so much so that with 55 dead and 100 wounded, I was able to run among the flames, smoke, and water to give the Sacraments, conditional absolution and Extreme Unction to burnt corpses and the dying, help the wounded, giving first aid to several among them, giving mass absolution, comforting, etc. For 30 hours the ship was in peril of sinking at any moment—a real end-of-the-world. There was need of my work, and that is why the Padre helped me accomplish my mission, whereas in the ordinary course of human events, I should have found myself among the carbonized bodies. The ship was on the point of being run aground on the sands in the banks of the island of Zembra to avoid sinking, but she recovered herself and made way slowly to Trapani and then on to Naples.

"At the Armistice, my ship had been under repair for three months, and she escaped by a special grace from being captured by the Germans on the way from Spalato to Ancona.

"During the partition of our poor Italy, I found myself still on board ship at Taranto, and I thought of my two nephews, one at Cattaro and the other in Greece, but I had peace of mind with regard to them because Padre Pio was looking after them.

"The one who as first lieutenant in a regiment at Cattaro managed to get on a small boat, and though it was about to sink he was able to get to Brindisi, and after an exhausting search, I found him. My anxiety was rather for the one in Greece, where it was known that officers had been shot by the Germans. A Capuchin chaplain of San Giovanni Rotondo I met by chance at Taranto on his way from Greece confirmed the shooting of Italian officers found there with their troops. I gave this chaplain a letter from Padre Pio, for at the end of December he was about to take his leave. I thanked Padre Pio for his protection and asked him about my nephew. On return from his leave the chaplain told me Padre Pio had said:

'Tell Don Felisati to be at peace regarding his nephew, he is safe and well, and has enough to eat. Let us beg Our Lord to keep him so till the end.' In fact my nephew did escape death, while his companions were not so fortunate. He was taken a prisoner, and after many difficulties he returned home safe.

"A lady gave a letter to the same Capuchin chaplain for Padre Pio asking him about her brother. The Padre replied: 'You must tell her to pray and have confidence,' but the Capuchin chaplain signified that was too little, he must say something more precise. The Padre sighed, 'Do you really want me to be the herald of the bad news?' Shortly afterwards the lady heard that her brother had in fact been lost.

"Many other things could be told, but it would be too long.

"*Memento mei et invicem.*

Yours affectionately,
Vittorio Felisato."

The Cure of Giorgia Roppa from Infantile Paralysis.

The child's mother, Maria Roppa, made the following declaration:

"The 14th day of December, 1940, my baby Giorgia Roppa, four, developed a high temperature, so I called Dr. Vannini and he found the baby had tonsillitis. The day after the visit she had no fever, but was worse than the day before; she had infantile paralysis. I took her immediately to the hospital at Gozzadini where she was examined by Dr. Picherle, Dr. Toni and Dr. Malossi, who confirmed the gravity of the case, and declared her to have polio (poliomyelopathy).

She was kept 35 days in hospital and electrical treatment and massage were given regularly with little results. The right leg totally lacked any reflexes. My husband and I were desperate; but fortunately one day my husband met a friend who had heard about our trouble, and had spoken about Padre Pio, and told him to read his book. My husband did read the book and decided to go immediately to S. Giovanni Rotondo where he asked his help to obtain the grace, and the Padre replied: 'Our Lord helps the bad, and still more the good. If you have come as far as this, certainly you are not bad; pray and I will also pray; put your hope in God.' My husband returned to Bologna contented and full of faith. I also had faith, and from this day forth I did not cry any more and in a few months we obtained the desired grace—my baby was completely cured.

> Maria Roppa,
> Via Timavo 30, Bologna."

Footnote: At the time this book was written, Giorgia was 14 years old. She was tall and strong. She was very well and since that time had had no further illnesses.

The Cure of the Infant Son of Bruno Menicucca at Perugia.

> "Castel del Piano
> 27th Sept. 1946

"We received your kind invitation to report the graces we have obtained through the intercession of Padre Pio, in regard to our son Bruno. We make haste to reply.

"The child, then hardly four years old, was in bed

with an ordinary intestinal fever. His sister, Mirella, only a little older than he, was looking after him for a moment by herself; all of a sudden she realized that the baby was dying, and thoroughly frightened called her mother. She ran at once and saw with terror that Bruno was quite still, with eyes staring, lips tightened and violet, covered with an icy sweat, and showing no sign of life. She ran for the doctor, fearing the worst, then returned to the little one, and in her immense anguish she had a divine inspiration. She recommended her baby to Padre Pio, placing a picture of the Padre on the child's head; at once Bruno began to move and breathe and soon returned to normal.

"His mother had promised on the spur of the moment to go with all the family to thank the Padre personally. They kept their promise in 1942, and Bruno thanked the Padre for his intercession in his innocent way, and got the reply: 'I prayed so much, I prayed so intensely for you!' The remembrance of the Padre remained vividly in the family, so that after the war, when the time arrived for little Bruno to make his First Communion, the whole family went again to Padre Pio, followed by a number of pilgrims. The 13th of September 1946, Bruno received Jesus in the Holy Eucharist for the first time from the hands of Padre Pio, who said he had made a beautiful confession, adding that the final one would be still more beautiful.

"Full of gratitude towards the all-powerful God for having sent so holy a minister among men, and invoking again His everlasting protection, the family devotedly publish these events.

> The family of Guiseppe Menicucci, Perugia."

The Miraculous Cure of the Baby of Gianfranco Cuccoli.
The child's mother, Clementina Cuccoli of Bologna wrote as follows:

"My little Gianfranco, aged 4 years and 4 months, had been in bed for 15 days with acute peritonitis. I had written to good Fra. Gerardo of San Giovanni Rotondo asking him to recommend my little one to Padre Pio.

"On December 23rd I received a reassuring reply from Fra. Gerardo, saying that the Padre had said the child would be cured and the doctor in attendance, Renato Paltretti, a pediatrician, held the same opinion. But the night of 23rd to the 24th of December, my Gianfranco woke up at 1:30 a.m. and complained of a bad pain in his left side. I thought it was a chill. I took his temperature which was 99°. I gave him half a grain of morphine and applied a hot water bottle. The child fell asleep, but at five in the morning he awoke complaining of acute pains. I took his temperature again and it showed 103.1. At seven the doctor came and after a more careful examination, in which he found the temperature now at 106.5, he said unwillingly, that the child had bronchial pneumonia with resultant meningitis and atrophy of the limbs. To reassure me, he said the next day he would use penicillin and if it were necessary the child would be taken to the hospital. For the moment he would use sulphurmethane. A half hour afterwards the fever started to go down; at 8 p.m. it was down to 101.3, and at 11 p.m. to 96.8. With the lessening of the fever, the little one began to lose consciousness. While he could still speak he said often, 'Padre Pio, make me well!' A crib had been placed near him. Kneeling by his side, repeatedly I called him without getting a reply. I wrote again to Padre Pio, begging him to look after my little one and I prayed ardently.

"A friend of the family, Ada Soligo, who had been to see Padre Pio during the month of September, suggested I should put the photograph of the Padre under the pillow together with a reproduction of Our Lady of Grace. I touched the lips of the child first with one and then the other, and he kissed them without speaking and then turned his head the other way, made some strange sounds, and began to move his hands in the air. All of a sudden, he turned his eyes towards the chest of drawers and looked fixedly on the crib and joined his hands together. I thought I would die of sorrow for he did not say a word to me nor look my way. I went out so as not to cry and I entrusted him to my family who were around his bed. I was told later that after remaining in the position of prayer for a few minutes he moved his head to the other side and seemed less agitated.

"My friend Ada Soliga again advised me to have faith in Padre Pio and to invoke him ardently at midnight when he would be saying Mass in San Giovanni Rotondo, assuring me that Padre Pio would hear me and would come to my assistance. I repeated the prayer before a photo of Padre Pio which I had brought from San Giovanni Rotondo, and asked him again for the cure, my only joy in this world. I again sent a letter by express to the Padre and a letter to Fra. Gerardo, which I posted on Christmas morning.

"About two o'clock the child sat himself up in bed, and without any coughing, a quantity of mucus came out of his mouth. I lay down near his bed because on several occasions he tried to get out and escape. I remained till 5 o'clock in the morning. At that hour he was sitting on the side of his bed as though he had had nothing the matter with him, and he asked for a drink. It seemed to me as though I was dreaming, I was so happy to see my Gianfranco as he was when well, for he was happy and gay. Once more without coughing he emitted mucus. Then he asked me where I had put his Infant Jesus of Sister Elizabeth, and with his hands joined he turned to the crib and repeated, 'Infant Jesus, make me well.' I offered him a glass of milk which he took very willingly and then went to sleep quietly. At eight o'clock on Christmas morning Dr. Paltretti came, and he was stupefied when he saw that the fever had nearly gone. All day my little one remained in bed playing and reciting a sermon to all who came and asked how he was, fearing to find him in a very different condition.

"On the day of St. Stephen in the morning I received a letter by post from Fra. Gerardo. The letter runs: 'I thank the good God with all my heart that you have received the cure of beloved Gianfranco. The Padre told me he would be cured and, in fact, he is cured; whereas in the case of my nephew, he said nothing, but looked sad. And this meant there was nothing to be done, it was already an established event; in fact a month afterwards my nephew did die. So be happy that you have been found worthy of this great grace....'

"I was mad with joy. When the doctor who had looked after my child with such devotion came in the afternoon, after a careful examination he said to me, 'Your son has no longer anything the matter with him.'

"I cannot describe what I experienced by this new proof of Divine power.

"His grandmother then asked Gianfranco what he had seen when he held his hands joined that holy night, feeling convinced that he could not have remembered, but the child replied immediately and sincerely, saying, 'I saw the Infant Jesus on the chest of drawers, dressed in white and with a flower at His feet. I said, "Baby Jesus make me well and make Grandma get well." And He replied: "I will make you well," and then the angel carried Him to the crib.'

"Now Gianfranco is well, lively and happy, grateful to the Padre, who has done so much for him.

Clementina Cuccoli,
Via Gombruti 10, Bologna."

To insure veracity and to give greater weight to the letter of Clementina Cuccoli, the doctor's certificate was requested. Dr. Renato Paltretti wrote on his letterhead:

"I certify that Gianfranco Cuccoli, 4 years of age, infected with congestion of the lungs with resultant meningitis, obtained a clinical cure in 48 hours.

Yours faithfully,
Dr. Renato Paltretti."

The Cure of Francesco Fazzetta.

Adelaide Fazzetta sent the following report from Naples:

"22nd of June 1948

"To the greater glory of God and to express my gratitude for the graces received through the intercession of Padre Pio of Pietrelcina, who obtained from God the cure of my husband Francesco Fazzetta of Casoria, in the province of Naples, I send the following account together with the medical certificates.

"On June 13th, 1946, my husband went to bed with a high fever. The local doctor was called, and after a careful examination he declared it to be a case of consumption, but in order to be certain he considered it desirable to get the advice of two other doctors, well known in Naples, who diagnosed it as a lung abscess.

"All instructions and prescriptions were scrupulously observed, but the fever continued during September of 1946. The doctor advised an X-ray. I report the certificate given by the Institute:

Instituto Foto-Radio-Terapico
Radolfo Stanziale
President: Prof. Candido Maderna
Pliclinico
                                   Naples 25 September 1946
No. of Registration: 40320

Fazzetta Francesco
The examination by X-ray gives the following evidence:
On the left: Apex and area of the lung is clear. Adenopathy of the hilus with nodes and sclerotic channels.
On the right: Infiltration in the upper and middle lobe of exudates of diffused type with diminishing lung expansion.
                              The Chief Radiologist,
                              Prof. Carlo Guarini.

"The physician, Dr. Corrado de Rose, who came especially from Naples, after reading the certificate given by the Institute, did not let my husband know the seriousness of his case, and in order not to depress him advised him to undergo the treatment of collapse-therapy, and he advised me to use different crockery than my husband, prescribing isolation. And afterwards he said to me: 'Tuberculosis, madam, is a terrible malady, only Heaven can help you. Be careful with the child, because the young are prone to contagion.' These words troubled me greatly, but what was I to do? I asked Our Lord for help, and I put myself in His hands.

"The next day, I said to my little Antonio, my only son, nine years old: 'Daddy is ill, the fever won't go down and he coughs all the time, so you must not kiss him.' My son, however, replied with determination: 'He is my father and I shall always kiss him.' I embraced my son and turned my thoughts to God and said: 'Lord, Thy will, not mine be done!'

"My husband would under no circumstances undergo the lung treatment, and would listen to the advice of nobody. He got weaker every day, the cough did not allow him a minute of rest, either by day or by night, and when I noticed blood in the sputum, I feared the end was near.

"In December 1946, my husband's brother and sister-in-law came to visit him, and we all tried to persuade him to undergo the lung treatment, but my husband would not hear of it, nor listen to any of our advice.

"My sister-in-law, seeing it was all useless, said: 'Tomorrow I will send you a photograph of Padre

Pio of Pietrelcina, a Capuchin Father who is at San Giovanni Rotondo in the province of Foggia. Put the photograph under the pillow of the sick man and pray with faith, asking for the grace,' and she added: 'A son of a friend of mine was healed in this way.'

"The next day I received the photograph of Padre Pio, which I gave to my husband, who after kissing it with deep Christian faith, put it under his pillow as suggested. I must add that even to this day every evening before putting it under his pillow, he kisses it and in the morning he puts it in his pocketbook, declaring that he cannot be without his Padre Pio.

"Besides turning our thoughts constantly to God, we thought of writing the Padre to ask if the patient should undergo pneumotherapy, asking also for his prayers. The letter was written by Rev. Don Domenico d'Auria of Casavatore the 28th of December, 1946, and I also wrote on the 31st of December. We waited with anxiety for the answer. I never tired of praying, and I made a promise to give the money we would have spent on the cure to some welfare work.

"The evening of January 3, 1947, as usual, my husband took his temperature. The thermometer showed 97.9. We tried and tried again, as it seemed impossible to be that, but we had to convince ourselves that it was the case as the thermometer always remained at 97.9. 'That is what it is,' I said to my husband. The next morning we took his temperature and again it showed 97.9.

"The 5th of January 1947, the reply came addressed to Dom Domenico d'Auria, who sent the letter on to us. Fearfully I read it, while my husband cried with joy. Padre Pio affirmed the cure and sent his benediction.

"Re-reading the letter, I noticed that the date—3rd of January 1947, was the day on which the fever ceased.

"All those present were deeply moved. I gave thanks to Jesus with a hymn of love saying: 'Lord, I am not worthy of so much joy; how great is Your bounty!'

"My husband was cured on the 3rd of January 1947, for from that day on he began to get back his strength, the cough disappeared, and not long after he took up his usual work again. In our nothingness we shall always be grateful to Our Lord, who through His faithful servants concedes such graces.

Adelaide Fazzetta Sandomenico,
Casoria 22 June 1948."

The following is the medical certificate:
"Dr. Corrado de Rose
Internal Medicine
Infectious and Respiratory Diseases

"Naples 12th June 1948
Corso Umberto 365

"Signor Francesco Fazzetta was treated in October 1946 for: 'Extensive infiltration of the right lung following pleuro-pneumonia, acute exordium.'

"At present, the patient is clinically cured.

Dr. Corrado de Rose."

Father Domenico d'Auria wrote the following letter regarding the above-mentioned cure:
"Everyone knows that I often see Padre Pio and that is why I was asked to write to him on behalf of the patient. To be more certain that the note would

reach the Padre (knowing what is apt to happen with him), and wishing a quick reply to reassure the family, I wrote to my great and good friend, Signor Tonelli. Within a few days I got a letter from him assuring me that the Padre had prayed and sent his benediction.

"I went to see the patient's family in order to tell them the news. What was my joy on hearing that the patient was already healed, and precisely on the day on which Signor Tonelli had sent the letter assuring the patient of the prayers and benediction of the Padre.

"This is the truth.

Rev. Domenico d'Auria,
Casavatore, 11 November 1948."

The Cure of Signorina Mariuccia Ghislieri.

Cascina Alata di Sale
Allessandria.

In March of 1947 Mariuccia Ghislieri went to San Giovanni Rotondo to visit Padre Pio. She was in the company of two cousins, Maddelena and Maria Curone of Castelnuovo Scrivia. At that time she had developed tuberculosis due to a neglected case of pleurisy. Dr. Sanguinetti Gugliemo of Borgo San Lorenzo, at S. Giovanni Rotondo, examined her and was forced to the conclusion that she had not had proper care and should have been sent to a sanatorium, where she could have tried the pneumono-therapy. The X-ray photos verified the infection of tuberculosis. But the belated treatment of the Institute was of no avail, and she left the sanatorium in a worse condition than when she went in.

Mariuccia, seeing that the physicians of this world could do nothing, turned to the Divine Physician, God, and chose the humble Capuchin of Pietrelcina, Padre Pio, as her intercessor. She had dreamt about him several times, and had been going to him for spiritual guidance. The cousins went to the Padre several times on her behalf, and whereas the doctors held out no hope, he always said: "She will be cured, she will be cured."

On returning home to her family she felt no further pain. In September 1948, Mariuccia Ghislieri went to see del Fante, full of joy and happiness, in order to tell him of her good fortune and her family's gratitude and to ask him to publish the story of her case for the glory of God, for it was only by the prayers of Padre Pio that she had obtained her cure.

The Cure of Anna Grillo.

"Castion di Zoppola,
Province of Udine.

"Having been asked to put into writing the cure received by me through the means of Padre Pio of Pietrelcina, I will try to narrate it in a few lines.

"I come from a poor family. My mother put me to learn dressmaking when I was very young, by my own choice, and I am still engaged in this work. But at the beginning it was a great struggle owing to ill will, especially on the part of my father. There was so much unpleasantness that in the end it affected my health, and I began to have very bad headaches which left me no peace. My detractors rejoiced at this and added the worst of calumnies. I visited a doctor, who found me extremely weak. I took the prescribed medicine but without effects. I had my teeth extracted, thinking they were the cause of the trouble, but the pain instead of diminishing became worse. I visited a specialist for a second time and I was sent to Dr. Gabrielli of San Vito at Tagliamento, who found my blood in a bad condition.

"Now I did not know where to turn for help, and neither did the doctors know what to prescribe. There was nothing more to be done. One day I found out that in the province of Foggia there lived a friar who worked great graces. A friend of mine gave me a book to read on the life of Padre Pio. I was so moved reading the pages, that there was born in me the hope, and moreover the feeling of trust, that I also would be granted my wish. I wrote at once to Padre Pio giving him the story of my life. On the 4th of August 1943, I received a reply with the promise that Padre Pio would pray for me. A few days afterwards the ill feeling at home ceased, to my joy, and the headache though not altogether cured became bearable.

"At the end of the war, I wrote again to the Padre asking him to celebrate Mass for me. The reply reached me on the 18th of January 1945. From that day my headache completely disappeared, and the fever little by little went also. I threw away all my medicines, because I felt absolutely all right, as I do now and have for three years. May God be thanked, and his faithful servant Padre Pio!

"This is what you asked for and which I am most happy to send.

Anna Grillo."

The superior of the Convent Sanatorium, Madonna di Rosa of San Vito at Tagliamento confirmed the story of Anna Grillo as true.

The Cure of Angela Lunardon of Chatillon (Aosta).

"Chatillon, 18th June 1948

"I read your books with great interest and spirit of veneration for Padre Pio.

"I also have had the good fortune to have experienced the power of intercession of that beloved Padre. About eight months ago, I was in the hospital of Aosta to undergo an operation. I had an abscess on the kidney. I had already received treatment for several months in another hospital, but without any efficacious result, as the abscess quickly reappeared. The surgeon of the hospital of Aosta, Dr. Bertone, decided unwillingly to operate because he feared that I had both kidneys affected, and because it was the kind of abscess which generally recurs. Nevertheless he attempted the operation. But as soon as he had made the first incision, the surgeon was obliged to limit the operation to the insertion of a small tube to help drain a large amount of purulent matter— several pints—intending to operate on the kidney later.

"Meanwhile, some people who were concerned about me had written to Padre Pio asking him to intercede in my favor, before God. After this first incision, as just related, my health rapidly improved contrary to the expectations of the doctors of the hospital, and in a short time I found myself completely cured without any further surgery needed. For several months I have been working again and my health remains good, and I have had no recurrences of the malady. The grace of physical recovery was accompanied by a spiritual one. Being a widow with three small children to look after, I felt demoralized because of my illness which prevented me from attending to my work. But after turning to Padre Pio with faith I felt myself inundated with a holy joy, which helped make my stay at the hospital a happy one, and I passed on my joy to those in bed around me.

"Another point worth mentioning is that the condition which I was in should normally have caused a high temperature, whereas even during the first few days after the preparatory operation, I was almost completely without fever, which astonished the doctors and the sisters of the hospital.

"I am intensely grateful to dear Padre Pio, and also to you who are his meritorious biographer.

Angela Lunardon."

The Cure of Ida Cuccana in Puglia (Modena).

"5 February 1949

"The wife of the sacristan of the cathedral, Ida Cuccana in Puglia, via Stretta Duomo No. 1, Carpi, 55 years of age, about forty days ago had a very high fever which would not leave her. It was a case of congestion of the lungs, and the little effort of just coughing could have had disastrous effects.

"Several doctors visited her without results. The last, Dr. Lugli, considered it necessary to take her to the hospital for an X-ray, which took place on December 15, 1948, with the family at home weeping.

"Having heard of this desperate case, I invoked Padre Pio and remembered poor Ida Cuccana in my prayers, and I sent her a little piece of chocolate blessed by the Padre during my visit to S. Giovanni Rotondo. The poor sick woman in desperation invoked the Padre at once and ate the chocolate. By the will of God and by the intercession of the prayers of Padre Pio, who heard the invocation of the poor woman from afar, the fever went down immediately after she ate the chocolate. The next morning she was examined by two doctors and by Dr. Balderi of the hospital, who found the patient without fever. They looked at each other, surprised and astonished, and made some statements in favor of the fact that such a reduction of the fever was outside the scope of science.

"Ida Cuccana in Puglia has given me the full right to speak of this grace received for the glory of God and to make the merits of Padre Pio better known.

> Nara Pedrielli,
> Via Brennero 5, Carpi."

Ida Cuccana confirmed the foregoing letter as follows:

"I confirm the account given by Nara Pedrielli; it is the absolute truth. I owe thanks and all gratitude to Padre Pio of Pietrelcina.

"For greater clarification, I add that the fever, which was extremely high, completely stopped after forty days, and on the same day I entered the hospital, before I started any treatments. It was only by the invocation of Padre Pio and the chocolate he blessed that I received this great and unmerited gift. What an unforgettable joy! I thank God that by means of his faithful servant I am healed. My cure astonishes the doctors and the professors.

> Ida Cuccana in Puglia,
> Via Stretta Duomo 1, Carpi."

The Cure of the Baby of Pettinello Littorio.

Dr. Angelo Breccia of the city hospital of S. Antonio of Bagnorgio (Vitterbo) gave the following certificate:

"The baby, Pettinelli Littorio, was in hospital from January 3rd, 1949 till January 12th, 1949. He was diagnosed as a case of encephalitic meningitis characterized by Kernig's Paralysis, extension of the upper left and bottom left limbs, motor aphasia. After a medication of 3,000,000 units of penicillin in all, the condition of the patient remained the same. Prognosis reserved, the family took the baby home on January 12th, 1949.

"The parents turned their prayers to God and asked the humble Capuchin of Pietrelcina to intercede for them and they obtained the grace of a complete cure of their baby."

The Cure of the Baby of Pietro Antonietta.

The baby at six months was diagnosed, too late for treatment, as suffering from toxemia. Due to the insistence of the mother injections were given, but to no effect, as was foreseen by the doctors.

The mother prayed with fervor, invoking Padre Pio. On the 29th of October she noticed a strong perfume. On November 2nd the doctor said the toxemia was arrested but the child was still weak. However, after a few more days all anxiety passed and the child recovered. The doctor confirmed the cure.

The following is the doctor's certificate:

"Dr. Francesco Tagliaferri
Medical Specialist for Infant Diseases
Director of the Ass. Prov. le of O.N.M.I.
Ragusa
Via Dt. Pluchino 12

"13th of June 1949

"I declare that during October 1948 I had the baby Pietro Antonietta, 7 months old, under treatment. She was affected by acute lactant toxemia and was in such a grave condition that death was to be feared at any minute.

F. to: Dott. Tagliaferri."

The Cure of Adelle Faccini of a Mastitis Cyst.

"23rd of January 1949

"Dr. Rino Faccini, Medical Surgeon
Orthodontist
Noceto, (Parma)

"For the greater glory of God and in honor of the Capuchin stigmatist of San Giovanni Rotondo, I beg you to publish in your book the miraculous cure of my sister Adelle, married in Ghiaroni, resident of Reggio Emilia.

"In October of 1947, she noticed the growth of a neoformation in the region of the right breast, with the characteristics of a fibromastitis cyst of the 'Reclus.' Dr. Razzaboni, director of the surgical hospital of the University of Parma, confirmed the diagnosis, and in the beginning of November, he cut out the growth which by histological examination was verified to be as diagnosed. After a few weeks the same kind of growth started in the other breast, but as there was no great urgency for an immediate operation, the date was fixed for the end of the following January. For several other ills, my sister had resorted to other well-known doctors in Parma, who on seeing the new neoplasm, were all agreed on the diagnosis of the mastitis cyst.

"Meanwhile my mother had completed a novena to Padre Pio asking him to intercede to Our Lord requesting the cure. When my sister came to us from Reggio to enter the hospital, our joy and excitement was great when it was observed that the tumor had disappeared. The astonishment of Prof. Razzaboni was no less than ours, when after examination he said: *'There is no longer anything there, you can go home.'*

"We give thanks to the almighty and merciful God for this immense benefit received; after a few days we joyfully made a pilgrimage to San Giovanni Rotondo to fulfill the vow.

"*Laudate Dominum omnes.* Praised be Jesus Christ.

Dr. Rino Faccini,
Noceto."

The Cure of Amelia Magnani of Levata, Cremona. (After her grave had been prepared).

"26th of October, 1949

"For a long time now I have been meaning to let you know about the benefit I received through the intercession of Padre Pio. In June of last year, I went along to Padre Pio, but owing to the great number of the faithful, it was impossible for me to confess to him. I nevertheless returned home contented, feeling sure that Padre Pio had seen my tears, repentance and love, and that he had blessed me.

"One day, owing to a very great vexation, I was suddenly taken ill and brought home more dead than alive. The doctor was called and held I was suffering from paralysis, as the left side of my body was immobile. For ten days I was between life and death. The Sacraments were brought to me, and my grave was prepared in the cemetery. My mother and brother who looked after me considered taking me to the hospital, but realizing my condition, feared I might die on the way. However, I ardently invoked Padre Pio and put all my trust in him. My brother, a parish priest of Levata, Don Ettore Magnani, telegraphed to Padre Pio asking him to pray for me. The superior of the Capuchins replied: 'Padre Pio is praying, good wishes, imploring divine protection and fraternal benedictions.' On reading the telegram, I immediately began getting better, now I can say I am completely cured, as I can walk, and I have taken up my employment again. The Blessed Virgin has granted it to me through the prayers of Padre Pio. This year I have also been with my brother and other people to see the Padre at San Giovanni Rotondo.

"I give you every liberty to use the account of these miraculous events.

Amelia Magnani."

In reply for request of witnesses of this event, Amelia Magnani sent the following note:

"The medical physician of my town is Dr. B. Agazzi. The doctor who attended me at the hospital, and who more than anyone considers my cure to be miraculous, is Prof. Aristeo Bertola.

"My brother is a parish priest, Don Ettore Magnani, and the sacristan, Sign. Nino Ardigo.

"After taking Communion at the Mass of Padre Pio, Gina Angelini was cured of a semi-ankylosis of the knee due to a fracture in 1944, certified by the doctor, director of the city hospital of S. Lorenzo, Borgo Valsgana, January 8, 1949."

The Cure of the Little Boy Giovanni Fernander, Hamrum, Malta.

The boy aged 4, was diagnosed as having undulant fever, known as Mediterranean fever, with swelling of the left knee, which was put in plaster cast. His mother had read your book about Padre Pio, and sent a telegram asking his prayers for the child. The following answer was received: "The Father is praying and sends blessings." Signed by the superior. The cure was obtained. The specialist noted the case was better and took off the plaster cast, considered no longer necessary, and after a few days the cure was completed.

On request the doctor sent a letter by airmail certifying the cure in English. This was translated into Italian. Here re-translated into English from the Italian:

"Anthony Debono, M.D.
D.M.O.
33 Father Magri Square
Marsa, Malta

"16 February 1950

"This is to certify that John Fernander, 3 years old, living in Hamrum, 738 High Street, was put under my care suffering from 'Brucellosis Synovitis' of the left knee, beginning the first week in December. Towards the middle of January 1950 the joint was cured without surgical intervention."

The Cure of Maria Restanti, Mantova, Via le Piave 20. (A maternity case).

Maria Resanti sent the following letter dated Mantua, 25th of October 1949:

"I was in the sixth month of pregnancy when on three consecutive days, though without pain, I suffered hemorrhage in the morning, which worried me. An obstetrician was called in from the Hospital of Mantova. He told my husband that it was a very serious case of placenta praevia, dangerous both for me and for the child. I was very unhappy at the thought of losing my child.

"It was then that I thought about Padre Pio and turned to him for aid, with all fervor and faith. In agreement with my husband, I made the promise that if the baby were born we would go as soon as possible to thank Padre Pio. My sister brought me a small relic of the Padre which had been sent to her. I put this on my breast full of faith and I began a novena to Padre Pio, always with the faith that he could obtain the grace. To the stupefaction of all, I completed my nine months, and gave birth in the most natural manner, without any assistance, to a very healthy baby to whom we have given the names of Guido Mario Pio Bruno.

"We are sure that the grace was obtained through Padre Pio.

Maria Restanti."

The Cure of Gaspare di Prazzo. Cianciana, Agrigento.
(From Mediterranean fever).

The following report is given by a priest:

"Gaspare di Prazzo of Leonardo, Cianciana, in the Province of Agrigento, on December 8, 1943, fell ill of Mediterranean fever, which then developed into pernicious malaria. The doctors were unable to do anything. At the end of the month of December he went to a cousin's house in Agrigento for a change of air, in care of Dr. Giannone, where he remained till the end of February 1944, continuously delirious and with a very high fever. Signora Vaccaro, a widow and the mother of the present Vice-Secretary Vaccaro of the municipality of Agrigento, knew there was no remedy for this case despaired of by the doctors, but she came one evening to Dr. Giannone's house and said to Signora di Prazzo, the patient's wife: 'There is a certain Padre Pio of Pietrelcina, a Capuchin, who has the stigmata and is still living; he is truly a saintly person, who by prayer obtains graces and miracles from Our Lord. Here is his photograph; recommend yourselves to his prayers. I will lend you this photograph for some days, and then please return it because it is the only one I have.'

"The patient kissed the photograph of Padre Pio, and begged him to cure him. A few days passed when at 6 p.m. one evening the patient said to his wife: 'Put someone at the door and don't let anyone in, because Padre Pio is coming, and I do not want to be seen by anyone.' The wife nodded assent and assured him that their servant's nephew was already at the door.

"Late at night, at eleven o'clock, when all were in

bed and only his wife was sitting up by the patient's bedside, and the patient had a fever of 107.6 degrees, he said to his wife: 'Put out the light because Padre Pio is about to come, and I don't want to be seen by anyone, not even by you.' His wife obeyed and put out the light.

"All of a sudden the patient started to speak, very joyfully: 'Oh! Padre Pio, you are here to heal me. I thank you. Pass your hand from my head to my feet. I cannot go on anymore, and I do not want to die so young, I do not want to leave my wife a widow. . .' The patient saw and felt Padre Pio near his bed. He passed his stigmatized hand over all his body. His wife saw nobody, but understood that Padre Pio was beside the bed of her beloved spouse, and trembling in a corner of the room on her knees, she also prayed to Padre Pio, weeping: 'As you have come, Padre Pio, ask Our Lord for the grace of my husband's cure.'

"After a few minutes, the wife asked her husband if she could put on the light, and the patient replied: 'No, because the Padre has not gone out yet, he is still by my bedside.'

"Another ten minutes passed, then the husband told his wife to put on the light, because Padre Pio was gone. After putting on the light, his sister and Dr. Giannone came around the bed of the patient, whose eyes were shining, and who was emitting deep sighs. He said he felt better, and then told the following:

"'A little while ago I found myself in a beautiful church, where Padre Pio was celebrating Mass, and I was on my knees. I saw the Holy Ghost in the beautiful form of a dove above the altar. After Mass, I drew closer to him, and he said to me: 'Have faith in God. But you must go to confession and you must not swear any more.' Being thirsty, I asked Padre Pio for water, and he accompanied me to a cistern. I filled a bottle with lovely fresh water; groaning with pain I drank it in one draught, burning with fever. As soon as I had drunk the water I smelt a perfume, which resembled vanilla. Then the Padre went away.'

"After this account the patient repeated that he felt better. The cousin, the medical physician, examined him and noted a big change: the fever had already diminished; the next morning he was without any, and the fever never returned. Early in the morning Signora Vaccaro went to visit him—she lent him the photograph of Padre Pio—and joyfully she said:

"The grace has been given! I dreamt of Padre Pio last night and he said to me: 'The grace has been given.'"

"And truly the grace had been obtained, for a few days afterwards, the patient got up cured and went to the church to thank Our Lord. Later he had a solemn day of the Blessed Eucharist celebrated in the Church of the Liguorini, where he confessed and received Holy Communion, after having been away from the Sacraments for ten years. From then on Signor Piazzi has never sworn again and he is very grateful to Padre Pio, whose photograph he always carries about with him.

> Padre L. M. da C.,
> Monastery of S. Francesco, S."

The Cure of a Boy Considered Incurable by the Doctors.
In February 1950, several newspapers published a story of a boy cured through the intercession of Padre Pio.

The paper *"Gazettino Sera"* of Venice, in the latest edition of Saturday 11th to Sunday 12th, February 1950, N. 36, published on the front page an article entitled: "Miraculous cure of a boy pronounced incurable," and with the subtitle: "The cure predicted by a Friar comes true to the astonishment of the physicians." This article is not reproduced here, but rather one published in the *"Nazione"* of Florence— newspaper of Perugia—in the issue of the 9th of February 1950, N. 34, because it gives a more detailed account of the same cure:

"A miraculous event, the details of which will no doubt arouse many different opinions, has been verified in the little center of Matignano of Corciano, where the Marinelli family lives, whose head, Leonello, carries on the profession of Superintendent of Public Buildings.

"For some time past the family had been weighed down with the sorrow of seeing their little boy of ten lingering with a terrible illness for which they could find no cure, despite repeated treatment from specialists. Lately, moreover, in spite of the devoted attention of the local physician, Dr. Tommaso Schioccolini, who had attended the child since the beginning of his illness, his state became worse and all hope of saving his little sick body had been abandoned. It was a case of a serious heart disease which had produced extensive swellings all over the body. The doctor called in Dr. Calabro from Florence for consultation. But he also had to give the same opinion: 'Prognosis unpropitious.'

"One evening, after a useless medical examination the boy turned to his father, who had never left him for an instant, and in a weak and almost inaudible voice asked him to go at once to Padre Pio of Pietrelcina, at Foggia, to beg him to obtain his cure. The father promised to go to the priest the next day, but the boy repeated his request to go at once without waiting. His poor father took the train the same evening. After arriving at Foggia he went to the house of Dr. Mario Sanvico, originally of Corciano. He told him his story and the reason for his journey, and asked to be taken immediately to Padre Pio. They reached the Monastery of San Giovanni Rotondo, and as soon as Marinelli was in the presence of the priest, before he had said a word, the priest assured him his son was better and would slowly be cured. Much moved, the poor man could not wait to get back home to let them know what the Padre had said. But the Padre advised him to stay till the next day, to hear his Mass and receive Communion. In the confessional, the Padre repeated what he had already said to Marinelli, and reassured him a third time that his son's condition would improve. Padre Pio added that in about two months the boy would be completely cured.

"On returning home Marinelli heard from his own son that on the same night of his meeting with Padre Pio, the boy had had a dream in which the priest appeared to him with bleeding stigmata in his hands. After this vision the boy grew slowly better, the swellings went down and the cardiac condition almost disappeared. When the doctors examined him, they were all of the same opinion with regard to the progress observed in the boy's body. The two months are now coming to an end, and the boy has entered convalescence, at the end of which he will be completely cured.

"The thing that surprised Marinelli and the doctors most was the manner in which Padre Pio was able to communicate with the sick child, for as soon as he saw Marinelli, he was able to give the good news of his son's gradual cure."

The Cure of Rodetta Redaelli Zappa. Romano Brianza, (Como).

The parish priest of Romano Brianza wrote the following:

"Please permit to send you the enclosed account, so that if you think it suitable you can publish it. These are the facts, do not fear the slightest untruth of any kind, not even in the smallest detail.

"His Eminence Cardinal Schuster, to whom I told the story on the 5th of April 1949, when he was on his pastoral visit here, said to me, 'It is certain that Padre Pio is a man of great virtue and in union with God.' At that time all of these events had not taken place.

"Today, now that every fact is so clearly in evidence, it seems to me that to be silent would be ungrateful to the Divine Redeemer, who by means of the stigmata of Padre Pio of Pietrelcina, wishes to manifest His divine and merciful love to this world again, to this strange world, inviting all humanity to contemplate the mystery of the Cross.

"With my kindest regards, yours devotedly in Jesus Christ.

Sac. Carlo Frigerio, Pastor."

This is the account:

"On the 8th of May, 1949, a little girl named Pia

Zappa was baptized in the parish church of Romano Brianza, born of Emilio and Rosetta Redaelli Zappa, who were married April 15, 1939. Our Lord had blessed the family with five children. The first, however, at about the age of two, died of gastroenteritis, and so there remained four: Ermanno, six; Giuseppe, five; Alessandra Maria, three; and Maria Pia, nine months.

"It should be observed that Rosetta, when young, owing to a lack of proper care of pleurisy, spent a period in a sanatorium for lung treatment. When she married Signor Zappa she confidently accepted maternity, taking the precaution of an appropriate strengthening diet at the first signs of pregnancy and again in the sixth month, always with excellent results.

"Now, it happened that this last time she was pregnant she thought the treatment unnecessary since she felt quite well and had confidence in herself. It was a real disaster: she suffered from nausea, being unable to take the minimum amount of food, weakness, followed by a fever of 104 degrees, hemoptysis, and a whole complexity of ills, so that the worst was expected. It was suggested that she should undergo an illicit operation which, however, the good Rosetta refused to do, even though she did consider this sad suggestion as a last resort. The doctor saw the uselessness of the remedies he was giving her and decided to send her to a hospital for tuberculosis for examination before going to a sanatorium.

"I met her husband just at the moment when he was going out to get a car to take the sick woman to the tuberculosis hospital for examination, and he hastened to invite me to visit his wife in order to give her a blessing. I accepted at once as I was already aware of her condition.

"What a sorrowful scene presented itself to me when I opened the door of the room where the sick woman was suffering! She was lying up on three cushions, very pale, with a high fever, evidently very weak. Two children, Ermanno and Giuseppe, then respectively four and five years of age (little Giovanna had been taken to relatives) played on her bed, ignorant of the situation, and the sick woman did not have the force or the will to look after them.

"The mournful sight made me stand still for a moment. My thoughts flew to Padre Pio and I thought: if he were here, certainly he would supplicate Our Lord. Then with an inexplicable force within me I said: 'Rosetta, there is nothing the matter with you. If you do what has been suggested to you, you will die. I know the name of the child that you will give birth to.' I gave the blessing and went away.

"Rosetta no longer wished to go to the hospital for examination and in the evening of the same day a woman came to my house and told me that the doctor on hearing what I had done said, 'What is the Pastor thinking of, taking the responsibility of this sick woman whose lungs are all eaten away?'

"I attached no importance to the words, but the day after when celebrating Mass, at the moment of the Remembrance of the Living, I recommended the sick woman, and...My God, what a turmoil of thoughts came to my mind— 'You are proud, you want to force Padre Pio to do miracles! Who do you think you are? Padre Pio is prudent, and always says first, "Do what the doctor says." Then he prays—but what do you mean by doing the contrary?'

"'O, Lord!' I said, 'help me! If Padre Pio had found himself before the scene of misery that I beheld yesterday, he would not have hesitated to call on You.' Besides, Padre Pio said to a lady who had asked his advice regarding an operation which would have prevented her from ever being a mother again, 'Very well, my daughter, do not do it, you would be ruined forever.' He obtained the cure for her.

"This last thought quieted me, and I continued the celebration of the Mass in peace. In the afternoon of the same day I went to take a rest and darkened the room. I had hardly laid myself down on the bed when I heard in the passage the characteristic sound of a monk's sandalled feet with the click of the rosary. I am a careful listener and I know I am not mistaken. As at that time a Passionist Father came to the parish on every first Thursday of the month to help with the confessions and to prepare people for Holy Communion of the First Friday, I thought that the Father had arrived. But then I remembered that the next day was not Friday, and still less the first Friday of the month and meanwhile I felt, without my door being opened, that the feet came up to my bed and the air passed over my face as when a person comes by. Immediately I sat up in bed, put on the light and I called, 'Who is there?' I did not see anyone. Suddenly a thought passed through my mind, 'Padre Pio has been here to assure me that Rosetta has obtained the grace,' and a great sense of joy invaded me.

"Meanwhile, Rosetta got worse and four days afterwards was taken to the tuberculosis hospital for examination. I was tranquil and sure of the outcome.

After a careful examination the doctor declared that
Rosetta had nothing the matter with her and that
she was at the end of the period of suffering that
had accompanied her pregnancy.

"After a few days Rosetta began to get better, and
after three weeks of inconvenience caused by two ab-
scesses due to injections, she very soon became entirely well. Now she holds the child Maria Pia with
joy to her heart, a child doubly dear because given
to her by God, and blessed by God through the good
services of Padre Pio.

(signed) Sac. Carlo Frigerio,
          Pastor of Romano Brianza.
          Rosetta Redaelli in Zappa,
          Emilio Zappa."

*The Cure of the Baby Anna Clara Lacitignola of Bari
from Infantile Paralysis.*
The following letter was received.

"January 8, 1950

"It is my duty to inform you of the enclosed
account so that you can join my name to the large
number that have been benefitted by Our Lord
through the intercession of Padre Pio of Pietrelcina.

"On the 8th of January 1947 my three-year-old
granddaughter, Anna Clara Lacitignola, daughter of
Mario and Adele Violante (my daughter), living in
Via Imbrianai 73, was suddenly afflicted by infantile
paralysis, as the doctors and professors who were called
to attend her can verify. All the treatments they tried
had no effect, so they consulted other specialists whose
names I can give to you, if necessary.

"After three months of treatments the child showed

no signs of improvement though she had received a blood transfusion, injections of different kinds, X-ray examination, electrical treatment, etc. The little body of the child remained paralyzed in the limbs, retaining only some strength in her neck, for she could still hold up her head.

"The family saw what a sad condition their little one was in and reached the point of wishing the child would die rather than remain paralyzed all her life.

"Although every remedy was tried, and a real patrimony spent at great sacrifice by her father, by Easter, 1947, the child was still in the same condition.

"I, her grandmother, had a special love for the child, and without telling the family, I decided to go to San Giovanni Rotondo, but without meeting the Padre— though I had heard he was a living saint, full of goodness and charity for the suffering for whom he begged graces from God. I left Bari with great faith, hoping I would obtain the grace from God, which I had so much to heart.

"I arrived late in the evening at the town, but at five o'clock in the morning I went to the monastery. I assisted at the Mass, and then went into the sacristy to wait my turn at confession. As soon as I knelt before the Padre I was unable to open my mouth, but what was my surprise when Padre Pio said before I had mentioned a word; 'What. . .you have come for the baby?' A shudder of emotion invaded me and I sobbed, kneeling in the confessional without the courage to ask him what I desired. He sent me away saying: 'Go home, go home, you will find your baby better: take courage, pray to Our Lord for the cure.' All confused, I kissed the stigmatized hand of the

Padre, and I went away deeply moved and very happy.

"As soon as I was outside the monastery, I could not rest, for I had to be away from Bari for several days for a business reason, while the Padre had said without doubt that I should go home that evening. When I reached home, I knew that it was at the hour when I knelt before the Padre that the child for the first time after three months sat up spontaneously in bed, and showed improvement in her condition. The miracle was proclaimed, and it was admitted that it was my decision to go to Padre Pio that produced the good results.

"From that day onwards little Anna Clara continued to get better, until she was completely cured. Now she is five and a half years old; she is robust, healthy, very bright and very pious, she never forgets Padre Pio, to the extent of arousing the admiration of the Sisters of the Institute of St. Rose of Bari, where she now attends the first elementary class. Last year I took her to Padre Pio, who blessed her.

"If you wish for any further information, please ask, I will always be at your service.

Sincerely,
Violante Gaetano,
Via De Giosa 107, Bari."

Padre Pio Cures a Child of Bronchitis, Pneumonia, Meningitis.
Mr. F. Flaman, 6009 8th Avenue, Brooklyn, N.Y. (U.S.A.) on the 12th of April 1950 sent a letter to del Fante from Signor Pietro Mazzone of S. Felice a Cancello (Naples) in which he gives the news of the cure of his daughter Nicoletta, which happened many years ago, but which he now wishes to release

for publication in order to give greater glory to God and honor to Padre Pio.

"27th of March 1950

"Cesare and Nicoletta have written to me from Milan, saying that they wish me to give you an account of the cure of my daughter Nicoletta. Here it is:

"In April 1919 or 1920 (I do not remember precisely) my daughter Nicoletta developed bronchitis, pneumonia, meningitis and delirium, causing brain damage and tongue paralysis. She received medical attention from Tardio Antonio Francescatonia and Lauricella. From the beginning of the treatment, my Nicoletta lost the use of her tongue, and could not recognize anyone of us. This state lasted six months.

"Seeing their treatment was useless, the doctors told us that they were unable to do any more for the poor sick child, and considered it of no avail to continue to visit her as only God could operate the miracle of the cure. They also told us that even if she got better, she would remain dumb, blind and deaf. This sad prediction persuaded us to no longer ask Our Blessed Lady for the cure of our daughter, and to pray instead that she should be taken from us, fearing that she would remain as the doctors told us.

"Later, owing to the insistence of my family, who had heard of the miracles worked by Padre Pio of Pietrelcina, I went to San Giovanni Rotondo to see the Padre, despite my skepticism. When I recommended my daughter to him, the Padre smiled and replied: 'Go home and be happy, the Madonna of Grace will make her well.'

"Thinking that the Padre could not understand the

gravity of my daughter's illness, I told him what the doctors had said, that only God could save her, and that if she got well she still would remain mute, blind and deaf, and continue to suffer from 'delirium tremens.' I added that I had left her at home almost in the last agony, and that I despaired to find her still alive.

"The Padre was a little annoyed: 'Man of little faith! I repeat, go home, and be glad because the Madonna of Grace has healed her.' I returned home. My wife— that is your sister—and my mother came to meet me with joy and said that the dying child had spoken without difficulty, syllable by syllable, saying she was hungry. From that day onwards, day by day she improved until she was completely well, and no defect remained.

"When I met the doctors who attended her on the road, they stopped to see her and were astonished, saying she had returned from the grave.

(Signed) Pietro Mazone,
Via Roma 633,
San Felice a Cancello. (Caserta)"

The Cure of Casperini Clementa from a Chronic Disease.
The following letter was received from a priest.

"Canovaccio di Urbino
Parish of St. Stephen
of Gaifa
"April 4, 1950

"I am sending the medical account regarding the cure obtained miraculously from God through the intercession of Padre Pio. I have been to San Giovanni

Rotondo six times and I have found Padre Pio always more saintly and closer to the Divinity.

"Please have the kindness to publish the following cure of Clementa Gasperini of the Parish of S. Mario a Pomonte (Canovaccio di Urbino) who was affected by so many illnesses that inevitably she would have died. It was sufficient for her only to look at Padre Pio and she was healed.

"Wishing you a happy Easter,

Don Gino Palazzi, Pastor."

The following is the doctor's certificate:

"Dott. Scoccianti Emilio
Medical Surgeon
Urbino, (Pesaro)

"4th of March 1950

"Clementa Comollini in Gasperini of Celesio, aged 38, resident in Urbino (Canovaccio) has been repeatedly under my care during the years 1947-48, for hepatic disturbances, colic, anorexia, tracheobronchitis, causing pleurisy in the right lung which had been affected before, arthritis and ischialgia on the right side.

"All these foregoing illnesses, of which each required a period of constant and intense treatment, have rapidly and greatly diminished contrary to expectation since 1948, so that no further treatment is required.

Dr. Emilio Scoccianti."

The Cure of Mrs. Amelia Abresch.

Mrs. Amelia Abresch was married January 10, 1925, and in April of 1926 she was disturbed by a hemorrhage which Dr. Casanova diagnosed as its cause a small tumor in the uterus. Other medical advice confirmed the diagnosis and the need of an operation. She debated over the advice of the doctors and lived in hopes of avoiding surgery or of submitting to X-ray treatments. An operation would render her sterile.

In July of the same year she had an abortion caused by the tumor, as the obstetrician Dr. Orsini certifies. The doctor informed her husband on a succeeding visit that if she had carried the fetus through the usually required months a Caesarean operation would have been necessary for delivery, because the tumor was in such a position that it would obstruct the natural parturition. It is necessary to note that the tumor was at that time very small.

She had other hemorrhages, but never could make up her mind to submit to an operation. In May of 1928 she was advised to consult Dr. Nigrisoli who immediately said to her, "You have a tumor. You know it, don't you? For tumors there are no cures outside of surgery." He then spoke to her husband, who longed to have a son, and he explained that maternity must be avoided because of the danger to the child as well as the mother, and added that almost always in the first months of pregnancy abortion takes place when a tumor is present.

Having said this the doctor registered her name in his day book (which he still preserves) and made even a diagram of the tumor, indicating to her husband where it was in the uterus, adding also that it was as hard as a knee cap. Although all doctors were of the same opinion, she went and consulted the obstetrician Dr. Tassinari who gave her the same advice.

One more year passed. She returned to Dr. Tassinari, who found the tumor so enlarged that he warned that the operation could not be postponed much longer. He wrote a letter, which she still preserves, to the surgeon concerning the operation.

Miss Carolina Giovanni of Bologna gave her illuminating counsel and in particular acquainted her with the life of Padre Pio, whom she and her husband were now anxious to see.

Mrs. Amelia Abresch tells of her visit to Padre Pio in these words, "I confessed my sins to him, then I wished to say something about what was so dear to my heart, but the grace that I wanted to ask of God, through His intercessor, was so great that I did not know how to find courage, nor the words, and in order to say something, I began:

"'Padre, the doctors tell me that I should submit to an operation.'

"'Follow the advice of the doctors,' he answered to me.

"Stunned, grieved, bewildered, I supplicated:

"'Padre, then I can never have any children.'

"After this phrase he raised his eyes for an instant to the heavens, then with an unforgettable sweetness said to me: 'Well, then, my daughter, no instruments; you would be ruined for the rest of your life.'

"And with such words that filled me with a new joy, I returned happy to Bologna, definitely decided to see no more doctors.

"In fact, the hemorrhages ceased and I remained in perfect health.

"About two years after, to my husband who went to visit him, he prophesied my maternity, and my husband sent me a telegram saying, 'Happier than ever; prepare a baby trousseau.'

"As the gestation progressed and the baby grew, Mrs. Abresch began to have doubts and feared the tumor was coming back. One morning just before rising, Padre Pio stood at the foot of her bed holding a pillow on his hands on which was a baby boy. He said: "Do you believe it now?" Before she could call her husband, Padre Pio had disappeared. Mrs. Abresch died a holy death, Aug. 7, 1949, at 2 a.m. It was the boy's birthday. Shortly before she died she gave Pio, her son, a crucifix as a gift for his birthday."

June 25, 1952, I personally visited and photographed this boy, Pio Abresch, whose birth was a miracle. He is now a priest of the diocese of Bologna.

Mrs. Amelia Abresch and her convert husband moved from Bologna to live within the shadow of the monastery. Mr. Abresch has granted me permission to use his photographs of Padre Pio which are in this book. Literature in Italian on Padre Pio is sent out all over the world from his religious goods store at Via Cappuccini, San Giovanni Rotondo, Foggia.

The Cure of Signora Emma Bonardi.

Signora Emma Bonardi of Genoa was suffering from progressive paralysis. She was practically dying, her limbs were contracted by tetanus, and she was unable to open her mouth; it was necessary to force a little broth through her tightly clenched teeth. She had been in this state for a fortnight, and the doctors had as good as given her up. I wrote to Padre Pio, recommending her to his prayers. The Rev. Father Warden sent me a little medal and a prayer from Padre

Pio. I gave them to the woman's husband, and after a few hours she was able to get up, to walk and to eat.

Six years have gone by, and although Signora Bonardi happens to be ill at this moment, she usually goes out unaccompanied, goes to church and is in relatively good health.

The Cure of Maria Palma Carboni.

Maria Palma Carboni, a fifteen-year-old girl from Lagaro, a small hamlet outside of Bologna, was the daughter of very poor parents. For 17 days she was the victim of diabolical possession. Her possession was widely known in and out of Italy as a result of the front page press accounts which aroused great excitement among her neighbors, who were frightened by the sufferings the unfortunate girl had to endure. Neither the particular prayers and blessings of the pastors of Lagaro and Sparvo, nor those of Monsignor Brini of Bologna, were able to free the girl from Satan and from the delirium which tormented her many times during the day.

Maria arrived at San Giovanni, June 19, 1952, accompanied by her brother Antonio, an intimate friend, Silvia Manizze, and by the two pastors of Lagaro and Sparvo, Don Francesco and Don Antonio, two young priests who sought the aid of Padre Pio in liberating the girl.

Since they arrived at 9 p.m. they could not obtain an interview with Padre Pio, and they were directed by Miss Mary Pyle of New York and San Giovanni to the Lombardi Hotel for overnight accommodations. In this hotel Maria Palma Carboni, very solicitously assisted by the two priests, by her brother and intimate friend, passed another violent night under the influence and power of the devil, who incited her to rail frequently against the two young priests.

The young girl, in one attack that was more violent than the preceding ones, hurled herself on the bed alternately laughing satanically, reciting or singing verses without surcease. In moments of quiet she called on Padre Pio for help. According to the manager of the hotel, Luigi Francavilla, and his family, who were eyewitnesses of the strange and terrifying spectacle, the girl was imitating the barking of a pack of dogs, or the mooing of cows, and was scratching the glass on the windows. It was only the reassuring presence of the two priests which prevented the family of the manager from fleeing in fright.

The next morning Maria Palma Carboni appeared quite pale and exhausted. In a moment of quiet she declared that at 10:30 a.m., after meeting with Padre Pio, she would be freed of the evil spirit. In fact early in the morning the two priests went to the monastery to obtain for their victim a special interview, which was immediately granted by Padre Pio, who through the grace of his usual clairvoyance was already aware of every detail pertaining to the girl.

In the corridor between the church and the cloister, about 10 a.m., the young girl finally was able to kneel in the presence of Padre Pio, who immediately rested his merciful and stigmatized hands upon the head of the unfortunate girl and blessed her in the name of the Lord. At this contact the girl fell into a swoon and was taken immediately into the church, where she revived at 10:30 a.m., freed of diabolical possession.

With tears of joy coursing down her cheeks and
in a state of great emotion, she asked for Padre Pio
in order to express her gratitude to him. Besides those
who travelled with her to San Giovanni Rotondo,
many of the faithful, Mr. Francavilla and his family
were the eyewitnesses of the spiritual favor for which
all intoned a *Te Deum* of thanksgiving to the Lord.

The Cure of Giovanni Savino.

Giovanni Savino was a young laborer engaged with
his companion, Genarro, in blasting rocks in the
monastery gardens at San Giovanni Rotondo. Every
day before going to work in the garden Giovanni had
asked Padre Pio for his blessing and kissed his hand,
after Pio's Mass in the sacristy. Three days before he
was injured in the monastery gardens Padre Pio embraced him and said, "Courage. Don't worry." The
morning of the accident, February 14, 1949, Padre
Pio did the same. Giovanni asked what he meant.
Padre Pio did not answer. Giovanni in a few moments
knew what he meant, for that morning when he and
Genarro started to blast the rocks with dynamite one
charge suddenly exploded into Giovanni's face. Father
Raffaelle of the monastery gave him first aid until
the doctor came. The right eye was completely blown
out and there was nothing left in the eye socket. The
doctors at the hospital at Foggia, which is 25 miles
away, did not give much hope for Giovanni to see
out of the left eye after several weeks of treatment
because the left eye was still full of pellets of rock.

Giovanni relates the following: One night, weeks
after the accident, while he was sleeping in the hospital, Padre Pio slapped him slightly on the right side

of the head, and after a few days he could see out
of that eye (which certainly must have been a new
eye, for the doctors testify that there was no eye left
in the right eye socket). Giovanni left the hospital
to pay the visit requested by Padre Pio. He met Padre
Pio in the sacristy on Holy Saturday of 1949 and
wished Padre Pio a *Buona Pasqua* (Happy Easter), and
thanked him for the salutary and all-healing slap. Padre
Pio laughed and said, "Here, Giovanni, is another one."
Padre Pio slapped him slightly on the left cheek. Then
Padre Pio added seriously, "Let us thank God that
you didn't get killed." Giovanni had become able to
see quite well out of both eyes and he did not use
glasses. His picture in this book shows no evidence
of scars.

CHAPTER IX

Spiritual Maxims of Padre Pio

"Through the study of books one seeks God; by meditation one finds Him."

★

"The life of a Christian is nothing but a perpetual struggle against self; there is no flowering of the soul to the beauty of its perfection except at the price of pain."

★

To someone afraid of doing wrong, Father Pio said: "As long as you have fear you will not sin." This person added: "Perhaps so, Father, but I suffer so much." "Certainly one suffers, but one must distinguish between the fear of God, and the fear of Judas. Too much fear makes us act without love; too much confidence prevents us from reckoning with and fearing with intelligent caution the danger we must overcome. The one must help the other, ever going along together like two sisters. We should make this our practice always, because if we are aware of being overly frightened, we must then run to confidence; if we sense we are too confident, we must seek to have fear, for love tends toward the object loved. In process of going forward spiritually one's vision is darkened, but holy fear gives light."

231

Speaking of temptations he said:

"If you succeed in overcoming temptation, this has the effect of washing on dirty clothes."

★

"Whoever does not meditate," he once said, "is like someone who never looks in the mirror before going out, doesn't bother to see if he's tidy, and may go out dirty without knowing it.

"The person who meditates and turns his mind to God, who is the mirror of his soul, seeks to know his faults, tries to correct them, moderates his impulses, and puts his conscience in order."

★

Someone asked the Father one day: "How can one distinguish temptation from sin? And how can one be sure of not having fallen into sin?" The Father smiled and replied: "How do you distinguish an ass from a reasonable being?" "The ass lets himself be guided, the reasonable being instead does the guiding." "Quite right," replied the Father. "But how is it that when the temptation is past there is a sensation of suffering?" To this the Father replied: "Listen, I will give you an example: have you ever felt the tremor of an earthquake? While everything trembled, you trembled too, but you didn't get caught under the wreckage."

★

"If we are calm and persevering, we shall find not only ourselves, but our souls, and with that, God Himself."

A man came one day to ask Padre Pio to cure his mother. He showed a photo of her to the Father and said: "If I deserve it, bless her." Padre Pio answered: "Eh, what deserve! (*Ma che merito!*) In this world not one of us deserves anything. It is the Lord who is kind to us and it is His infinite goodness which grants us anything, because He forgives all."

Padre Pio does not like the maxim: "Everyone for himself: God for all." That is too selfish, too worldly for him. To this he opposes one of his own: "God for everyone: but no one for himself alone."

★

One day, to someone who asked his advice on penance and mortification, the Father expressed himself in these words: "Our body is like an ass which we must beat, but not too much, because otherwise it will fall down and it won't carry us any more."

★

"The demon has only one door by which to enter into our soul: the will; there are no secret doors. No sin is a sin if not committed with the will. When there is no action of the will, there is no sin, but only human weakness."

★

Someone complained to the Father of being excessively distressed by the sins he had committed. The Father replied to him: "That which you feel is pride; it is the demon which inspires you with this sentiment, it is not true sorrow." The penitent replied: "Father, how can you then distinguish what comes from the heart and is inspired by Our Lord, and that which instead is inspired by the devil?" "You will distinguish it," replied the Father, "always by this: The spirit of God is a spirit of peace, and also in the case of grave sin, it makes us feel a tranquil sorrow, humble, confident, and this is due precisely to His mercy. The spirit of the demon, on the contrary, excites, exasperates, and makes us in our sorrow feel something like anger against ourselves, whereas our first charity must be to ourselves, and so if certain thoughts agitate you, this agitation never comes from God, who gives you tranquility, being the Spirit of Peace. Such agitation comes from the devil."

*

To someone in a position of responsibility towards souls, and who asked what to do in the case of a person who would not listen to truth and goodness, and was made nervous by every effort to attract him, the Father replied: "Try with love, lots of love, spending all you have, and if that is useless....rebuke him. Christ who is our model has taught us so, since He created Paradise and also Hell."

A good scolding or slap given dutifully is sometimes more in order than a kindly reminder. On several occasions the Father said to his spiritual children at San Giovanni Rotondo: "Beatings and bread make beautiful boys."

*

One day a boy told him he was afraid he loved him more than God. The Father replied: "You must love God with an infinite love, through me. You love me because I direct you to good, and to God the Supreme Good, and I am just the means that carries you to God. If I directed you not to God but to evil, you would not love me any more."

★

Signorina Maria Pennisi one day complained that she could not stay away from Padre Pio because being with him made her so happy. Father replied: "For the children of God there is no distance." But she was not convinced, so Father Pio took out his watch and said: "Tell me what is in the middle there?" "The pivot, Father." "Exactly," he replied, "the pivot is like God who is immovable, and the hands circle round, attached to the center, and indicate the time. The distance between the center and the numbers telling the hours really is no distance, as the hands bridge the center to the hour. God is the center, the hours the souls, but there is also Padre Pio, one of the hands, who makes a bridge from the center to the hours."

★

Signorina M.B. who was leaving San Giovanni Rotondo for a village in the Trentino, expressed her doubts to the Father: "It seems to me," she said, "that God cannot grant my request, because I seem to have become cold in my faith, although my love of God has not diminished." "Remember," replied the Father, "always have prudence and love, for these two must stay together."

Prudence has the eyes, love the legs.

Love that has the legs, would wish to run to God, but the impulse of rushing towards Him is blind, and sometimes can cause one to stumble if not led by prudence, who has the eyes. Now about prudence. When prudence sees that love should be restrained, she lends her eyes. In this way love is held and guided by prudence, and acts as she should and not as she would like it.

★

A young and lovely woman, wife of a member of parliament who died very young, overcome by sorrow, wished to retire from this world and to found a new religious order. She already had a special audience with the Holy Father. But lacking the means for actuating her proposition, she went to see Father Pio to ask his opinion. The Father listened and then said: "Madam, before you sanctify others, think about sanctifying yourself." Note: This lady is today in a Carmelite convent.

★

To a converted Mason Father Pio one day said: "All human ideas, no matter from where they come, have their good and bad points; one must assimilate all the good in them and offer them to God, and eliminate the bad."

★

One day, a lady speaking with Father Pio admitted to him that she was a little vain, the Father replied in this way: "Have you ever seen a field of corn fully ripe? You can see that some ears of corn are standing straight up, and others are bent down to earth. Try and take the ones standing up, the more vain ones, and you will see that these are empty, but those bending down, the more humble, are laden with grain. From this you can conclude that vanity is empty."

★

A lady asked the Father what prayers were most acceptable to God. The Father replied: "All prayers are good, when these are accompanied by the right intention and good will."

★

One day some people referred some sentences to him which were being reported as his own. The Father listened and then said: "They often change what I say." In meeting these people they asked him to pray for them. He said: "I will pray for you. You pray for me. Pray, and continue to pray so you won't get rusty, and I won't become cold towards you....I will repay you with the same money."

★

A spiritual daughter, one day, expressed herself in the following manner: "Father, I fear lest I love you more than Jesus." Father Pio did not reply, and after she had finished her confession he absolved her. After a few days, this penitent came to him in the sacristy to kiss his hand in the same way as all the others. The Father in a tone of command told her to go into the village and say an impossible thing to a certain person. "Father, I would never do such a thing." Father Pio insisted: "I command you, do it under obedience." The poor penitent was astonished at what he requested and did not comply. When the Father saw that she was firmly convinced that what was requested was wrong, he said: "You see now, you do love Jesus more than me. Don't you see that when I order a thing obviously contrary to the will of God that you do not obey? Are you convinced now?"

★

The Father said one day to a builder: "You have built badly, tear it down, and build it again as it should be."

Prayer should be insistent when insistence denotes faith.

"Man," said Father Pio, "is so full of pride that when he has everything he needs and good health, he believes himself a god, and superior to God Himself, but when something happens and he can do nothing, and others can't do anything about it either, only then he will remember that there is a Supreme Being."

★

"God enriches the soul which empties itself of everything."

★

"In the spiritual life one must always go on pushing ahead and never go backwards; if not, the same thing happens as to a boat which when it loses headway gets blown backwards with the wind."

★

"It is not a loss of patience if one asks Jesus to take away pain, when this becomes insupportable to us and beyond our strength, nor does one lose the merit of the suffering which is offered, by asking this of God."

★

"Beneficence, from wherever it may come, is always the child of the same mother, that is Providence."

★

"The lie is the child of the demon."

★

"The habit of asking 'Why' has ruined the world."

★

"Humility is truth, truth is humility."

★

To a penitent, speaking of human frailty, the Father said: "Remember always that God sees everything."

★

"Prayer is the best armor we have, it is the key which opens the heart of God."

★

"Remember that the axis of perfection is charity; who lives centered in charity, lives in God, because God is charity, as the Apostles said."

★

In March, 1923, a lady asked the Father what she should do to sanctify herself. "Separate yourself from

the world," he replied. A friend knowing what a retired life this lady lived, made a gesture of surprise.
The Father turning said to her in a rather severe tone:
"Listen to me: one person can drown on the high
seas, another can choke to death on a glass of water.
What is the difference between these two persons;
aren't they both equally dead?"

★

"Remember, said the Father to one of his penitents, "A mother in the beginning teaches a child to
walk holding onto it, but afterwards the child has
to walk alone. You must learn to use your own reasoning powers."

★

To one person complaining because she was unable to do anything for him, the Father replied: "Only
a general knows when and how to use a soldier. Wait
till your turn comes."

★

Someone once asked him if he thought he, the penitent, could hope to remain always devout and respect-
ful to the laws of God, and whether Padre Pio thought
him worthy of being a spiritual son. The Father replied: "But does it seem possible to you that I should
leave a work unfinished?"

★

"Sin against charity is like piercing God in the pupil
of the eye"—and he added—"What is more delicate
than the pupil of the eye? To sin against charity is

like a sin against nature."

★

"A good heart is always strong, it suffers, but with tears it is consoled by sacrificing itself for its neighbor and for God."

★

"Love and fear must go united together, fear without love becomes cowardice. Love without fear becomes presumption. When there is love without fear, love runs without prudence and without restraint, without taking care where it is going."

★

"Where there is no obedience there is no virtue, where there is no virtue there is no good, where there is no good there is no love, where there is no love, there is no God, and where there is no God there is no Paradise."

★

On a holy card on which there was reproduced the image of the Cross, the Father wrote one day these words: "The Cross will not crush you; if its weight makes you stagger, its power will also sustain you."

★

For Mr. Andrea Lo Guercio, who had come from America, he wrote on a holy card with a reproduction of the Sacred Heart on it: "Humility and purity are the wings which carry us to God and make us almost divine. Remember: that a bad man who is ashamed of the wrong things he is doing, is nearer to God than a good man who blushes at doing the right thing."

★

To a man who had come to Father Pio for spiritual direction and who asked him if he considered him his "spiritual son," Father Pio replied: "I have bought you with the price of my blood."

★

An intelligent Sicilian teacher, who for several years had been teaching in a lovely neighborhood near Bologna, had heard about Padre Pio, but being a rationalist by principle and a realist through his studies, he did not feel any attraction for Father Pio, and it seemed to him that all the talk about him was carried on by people mentally ill with mystical ideas. He did not like him, but to be honest, he did not oppose him. "It may be as you say," he said, "but in my personal opinion, and that of other recognized teachers, I cannot believe in this being you say has supernatural gifts."

One day, however, he was staying in a house in the vicinity of Father Pio's village when someone gave him the book *Dal Dubbio alla Fede,—From Doubt to Faith*—the first book written by Alberto del Fante on Padre Pio. The evening of the 27th of August, 1940, after having finished the book, he went to sleep thinking about Father Pio. About three in the morning he felt that someone was in the room. Waking up, he saw in front of him a Capuchin monk like Padre Pio as pictured in the book.

Upper left: Confessing.
Upper right: Villas near monastery.
Lower left: San Giovanni viewed from Monastery.
Lower right: Monastery viewed from front of Hospital.

Upper left: Padre Pio at cloister door.
Upper right: Padre Pio as a young monk.
Lower left: Photo of stigmata taken under obedience.
Lower right: Trunk marks place where he was invisibly stigmatized o
Sept. 20, 1915.

Upper left: Sanctus.
Upper right: Pouring wine.
Lower left and right: Offering chalice.

Upper left: Offering chalice.
Upper right, lower left and right: Pater Noster.
Showing ungloved stigmatized hands.

Rubbing his eyes he thought he was dreaming; he felt quite frightened but was not too shaken to turn to the Father and ask him who he was and whether he was by any chance Father Pio. "Yes," replied the monk, "I am Father Pio. Do not be astonished at my visit, my mission is precisely to console the afflicted, especially those in spirit. I know that you are frantically seeking happiness and truth, that is God. The first thing you are seeking is not possible for you or anyone on this earth, which is a valley of tears where everybody must carry his cross. Happiness, in fact, is not of this world.

"The second thing, God, you can find, if you want to, but you are on a wrong road, for knowledge is useless except to reveal *HIM WHO IS*. Science, my son, great as it may be, is but a poor thing, and less than nothing when compared with the formidable mystery of the Divinity. You must take another path. Purify your heart of every human passion, humble yourself to the earth and pray. In this way you will certainly find God, who will give you serenity and peace in this world and eternal beatitude in the next.

"I HAVE SPOKEN.

"I must go, because other unhappy people are waiting for me to give them consolation. Before going I bless this house where goodness and virtue are blossoming; whose perfume rises to Eternity and consoles and cheers those who live nearby. *MAY JESUS CHRIST BE PRAISED."*

The teacher, as soon as the Father disappeared, got up from his bed, where the Father had been sitting, and wrote down at once what he had said, fearing to forget some of the words, but while writing it seemed to him that his hand was being guided when he was not sure of the exact word.

In the morning he looked up in the Bible and found that the Patriarchs and Prophets use precisely the words *HE WHO IS* to signify God, a phrase hitherto unknown to him.

Returning to his home and on showing the phrases he had written to del Fante—the writer of the book on Father Pio—he confirmed the habitual use of the words *HO DETTO (I HAVE SPOKEN)* by Father Pio when the penitents tried to find a wrong reason for something, and the Father used it as a form of imperative.

The last words, *"MAY JESUS CHRIST BE PRAISED,"* are used habitually by every Franciscan at the end of a sermon.

The teacher permitted del Fante to publish this account, but asked him to leave out his name.

★

To Signor Natal Selvatici, of Bologna, Arcoveggio 1084, one day the Father said: "Remember that man has a mind, that he has a brain which serves him for reasoning, then he has a heart for feeling, he has a soul. The heart can be commanded by the head, but not the soul, so there must be a Supreme Being who commands the soul.

"Remember, it is impossible to exclude a Supreme Being and I will explain why. Supposing that this Supreme Being is inferior to us. If that were the case there would be no reason for seeking such a being because we would be superior, and would have nothing to gain. Suppose that we are equal. Then we would be capable of doing what He does; but He has created us and we are not capable of creating Him. Given that we cannot do what He can do, then we must be inferior. As we are therefore inferior, it follows that we must be subject to Him, who is our Superior."

★

One day he said to one of his spiritual daughters: "In the spiritual life, the more you run the less you get tired; moreover, peace, the prelude to eternal joy, will come upon us, and we shall be happy and strong according to the extent that we live in this study of making Jesus live in us, and of mortifying ourselves."

★

One day, the Father asked one of his spiritual sons, in confession, if he ever told lies. "Yes, Father," replied the penitent, "and you are the cause." The Father looked at him searchingly and asked him the reason. The penitent replied: "Father, some people come to me asking me to speak to you about them, but I can't always do so. If I reply 'Yes,' and then do not do anything about it, I tell a lie. How can I comply with so many requests, without committing this fault?" The Father lifted his eyes to Heaven transfigured, and murmured a sentence as though speaking with the Invisible always present, and then replied: "Call me, and I will answer you." The penitent was very troubled and did not know what to say, but then said frankly: "But, Father, I am not worthy, I can't do that alone, that is without your help, I can't assume such a thing. I live in the world, among temptations, and I should have to live in complete purity to assume such a

burden; your help is absolutely and constantly necessary." The Father smiled and said: "And have I ever
abandoned you?"

*

To a penitent who had previously lived in vice and
who asked whether if he changed his life completely
he would obtain pardon from God, and if he would
die in His law, the Father replied: "The doors of
Paradise are open to every human creature, remember Mary Magdalene!"

*

To Signorina Carmencita Borgognos, a secretary
of Catholic Action in the parish of Cartegna, Spain,
who had written to Father Pio asking him to pray
for her, he sent her word not to stop knocking at
the Heart of Jesus asking Him to turn His eyes on
her to help her accomplish the good work of the
apostolate she was doing and added, "Charity is the
measure by which Our Lord judges all things."

*

"Time spent in honor of God and for the salvation
of souls is never badly spent."

*

"Keep well dug into your minds the words of Our
Lord: In patience you will possess your soul."

*

"Pray that God will console you when you feel
the burden of the Cross, for in doing so you are in

no way acting against the will of God, but you are placing yourself beside the Son of God who asked His Father during the Agony in the Garden to send Him some relief. But if He is not willing to give it be ready to pronounce the same *'Fiat,'* 'So be it,' that Jesus did."

★

"What does it matter to you whether Jesus wishes to guide you to Heaven by way of the desert or by the fields, so long as you get there by one way or the other? Put away any excessive worrying which results from the trials by which the good God has desired to test you; and if this is not possible, resign yourself to the Divine will."

★

"It is just as well to make yourself at home with the sufferings that Jesus is pleased to send you, as you must always live with them. In this way, when least you are expecting to be liberated from them, Jesus, who cannot bear to keep you long in affliction, will come and relieve you and comfort you, giving you new courage."

★

"Those strong and generous in heart do not complain except for a strong reason, and even then it does not affect them intimately."

★

"The impetus to be in eternal peace is good and holy; but it must be moderated by complete resignation to the Divine will: It is better to accomplish the Divine will on earth than to rejoice in Paradise. 'To suffer and not die,' was the motto of St. Teresa. Purgatory is sweet when one suffers for the love of God."

★

"The demon is like a dog on a chain; beyond the range of the chain it cannot bite anyone. And you, therefore, keep your distance. If you get too near, it will get you. Remember the demon has only one doorway by which to enter your soul: your will. There are no secret or hidden doors."

★

"Temptations, discomforts, worries are merchandise offered for sale by the enemy. Remember this: if the demon makes a lot of noise, is is a sign that he is still outside, and not inside. What should frighten us is when he is at peace and in harmony with our human soul."

★

"Your temptations come from the devil and Hell, but your sufferings come from God and Paradise: the mothers come from Babylon, the daughters from Jerusalem. Despite temptations and embrace tribulations. No, no, my child, let the wind blow and don't mistake the noise of the leaves for the sound of battle."

★

"Let us climb Calvary without getting tired, carrying our Cross and be certain that the climb will lead us to the beatific vision of our dear Saviour."

"If Jesus manifests Himself to you, thank Him; if He hides Himself from you, thank Him likewise: it is all a game of love. The Blessed Virgin continued to obtain from the ineffable goodness of Our Lord, the force to sustain as many proofs of love that were given to her, to the very end. I hope you will persevere to death with Christ on the Cross, and that at the end you will softly exclaim with Him: *Consummatum est!* (It is finished.)"

★

"Divine Goodness does not only not reject penitent souls, but goes out in search of obstinate souls."

★

"The sacred gift of prayer is in the right hand of Our Saviour, and according to the measure that you empty yourself of yourself, that is of love of your senses and of your own will, and make progress in rooting yourself in holy humility, to that extent the Lord will speak to your heart."

★

"Have patience in the perseverance of the holy exercise of meditation, and be content to begin by making little steps until you have legs to run with, or rather wings to fly with. Content yourself with just making an act of obedience, which is never a thing of little importance for a soul who has chosen God for her portion, and resign yourself for the time being to be a little baby bee in the hive, which soon will become a full-grown bee, able to make honey."

"The heart of our Divine Master knows only the loving law of sweetness, humility and charity....Put your trust often in the Divine Providence of God, and be certain that rather will Heaven and earth pass away than that Our Lord should fail to protect you."

★

"Walk with simplicity in the way of the Lord and do not torment your spirit. You must hate your sins, but with a tranquil hate, not worryingly or restlessly."

★

"Rest like the Virgin on the Cross of Jesus and you will not be deprived of comfort. Mary stood petrified before her Son crucified, but it cannot be said that she was abandoned. On the contrary, He loved her so much more for her suffering, she could not even cry."

CHAPTER X

Letters To His Spiritual Children

J.M.J.
D.J.C.   12/10/1914

May peace, mercy and grace be with you forever
and with all those who sincerely love Our Lord Jesus
Christ. So be it.

I wrote you a letter now a long while ago, but
up to now I have not received any from you. How
are you? Since I know you to be a correspondent
of great faithfulness and exquisite courtesy, I am all
the more disturbed by your silence.

I am hoping that the infinite Divine Mercy will
concede me the grace of knowing that it is only your
work that has stopped you from sending me your
news and has made you forget him who continuously
offers prayers for you and gives thanks to the
Heavenly Father. I am waiting with impatience for
your letter so as to have exact news of all your family, more especially regarding Giovina, to whose
prayers, as also to yours, and those of Rosina, I recommend my spiritual well being.

I have been assured that your health is better, and
I am very pleased about this, but not having heard
from you, I am assailed with disturbing thoughts and
the doubts that perhaps this time I have been de-
ceived. Moreover, some days ago, the Lord permitted

251

me to visit Giovina, and through me the Good Jesus is bestowing on her many graces, and it seemed to me then, that she was in better health than she was before. I am not worried. Reassure me with a letter and I pray you, at the same time not to mention anything about my visit to Giovina. (It is a good thing to keep the secret of the King.)

I fear greatly that your long silence is a subterfuge of the enemy, for whose guile be always on the lookout, and never listen to him. Do not consider it out of place if I show concern and preoccupation for your salvation; you must remember that I have espoused you to Jesus and I am jealous lest others ensnare you. Please remember that I took upon myself a strict obligation always to keep watch over you, an obligation which forces me to shield you from every pestilent breath, so as to present you a chaste virgin to the Divine Spouse, when He comes to call for you. Woe betide me if I fail in this task. I entreat you by the gentleness of Jesus Christ and by the bowels of compassion of the Heavenly Father never to grow cold in doing good, and never to depart from my suggestions; for goodness sake do not render unfruitful the graces of the Lord, which have been so plentifully given to you by the Sacraments. Be vigilant always and never let yourself slip. Be careful ever to advance in charity: enlarge your heart with confidence in the divine inspirations which the Holy Ghost is so intent in shedding on you. Now is the time of the sowing; if we want to gather a lot, it is not so necessary to sow a great deal of seed as to sow the seed in good ground. We have already sown a lot, but it is still very little, if we wish to rejoice at the

time of the harvest. Let us spread, let us spread the
seed again and then we shall not be saddened when
the seed grows by the heat and becomes a plant, and
we then must take great care that the weeds do not
suffocate the young plants.

D.J.D. 12/12/1914

May the Father of Our Lord Jesus Christ enrich
you always with His divine grace and render you
always more worthy of His Divine Son. So be it.

Our letters have crossed on the way. I am astonished
at the lateness of the arrival of your much desired
letter. In this there is the hoof of Satan, who would
have liked to have mislaid your letter, but thanks to
the Immaculate Virgin Mary, this was not permitted.
This has been another failure for that beastly rude
person. I cannot tell you how my heart rejoices in
the midst of my miseries in again having your confirmation regarding the state of your health as also
that of Giovina. The Lord continues to have mercy
and to console us in the events of our life. I do not
know really how to tell you of my thankfulness
towards so good a Father for so many benefits which
He continuously grants us, in spite of our unworthi-
ness, more specifically my own, which have reached
the zenith. May He be always praised and blessed by
every creature. I am not embarrassed to thank you
again as is only just for the prayers and the novena
which you are making to the Madonna of Pompeii
for me, knowing how poorly I could do it myself.
I wish you every recompense from Jesus.

Whilst admiring and praising your sincerity in letting me know that you do not feel it desirable to

supplicate the Spouse of souls to break the chains
which hold me in this body, yet I cannot hide from
you that this again is a sword that pierces my heart,
making the agony greater. Come now, why deny me
this charity? I do not dare to call you cruel any more
because you are sincere, but by the bowels of the
compassion of God Incarnate, force yourself to do
so in the future, otherwise you will make yourself
an assassin. I shall be alone in praying for such an
end. It will never be answered, as I have a heart
clogged with faults and a tongue surrendering itself
to the worst sacrileges.

D.J.D.   12/29/1914

This is to follow up the preceding letter, in which
I advised you to be at rest as regards your love towards God. I do not cease to make the same exhor-
tation. I assure you of this, and I repeat with insistence
that your love of God is becoming ever firmer. Your
fears are without ground, and you are mistaken on
this point from the beginning in thinking that you
are deprived of this love as you do not feel it in your
will, nor in your heart, nor any sweetness in your
love of God. It is painful, and I understand this state
of your soul very well, but it is said to be necessary
for a soul called by God to a high form of perfection. (God calls to Himself a soul to entice it.) I said
that this constitutes for a soul a painful state, and
for a good reason, for the poor creature is forcing
itself to serve and please God in everything, and this
from its own point of view, and there is no blame
in the way it is working for God because in every
devotion it experiences a parching in the will and the

heart without any feeling for supernatural things, and
what is worse, very often the soul feels in itself a
horrible division. With the superior part of the spirit
it feels pushed towards God, in the inferior part, that
is in its lower appetites, it finds itself afflicted with
troubles, with dryness and other painful effects. But
do not let us be frightened when confronted with
this state in which the soul finds itself. Lucky soul!
even in the midst of this dense darkness, it can still
receive a little light so as not to fall into despair. Let
us reflect a little on the virtue of the love of God.

What is the love of God? Before answering this
question, we need to distinguish between the substantial love of God and the accidental love, and this
last is divided again into accidental sense love, and
accidental spiritual love. Given this point of distinction, we can begin to answer the question.

The substantial love of God is the simple and sincere preference with which the will places God before every other thing, by reason of His infinite
Goodness. He who loves God in such a manner, loves
Him with substantial charity. If the substantial love
of God is accompanied with suavity, and this suavity
is altogether in the will, we have still the accidental
spiritual love; if then the suavity enters the heart and
makes itself felt with ardor and sweetness, we have
accidental sense love. Only God, when He wants to,
by His infinite Goodness, lifts up a soul to high perfection and carries it to Him as a mother with her
babe. Observe the wisdom of a mother's care.

She is completely given to her little one. As soon
as the babe is born, she does not immediately bring
it to her bosom to nurse: and there are two reasons

for this. The mother is anxious not to injure the baby's health with milk not yet altogether purified from the heat of her maternity. And this is not the only motive that makes the prudent mother act in this way; the milk before she has recovered, would not be agreeable to the baby's palate, and so she is properly concerned that the baby, nauseated by the distasteful early milk not yet purified, might not afterwards be put off from normal nursing. She therefore begins by feeding it with sweet foods, such as sugar. Having begun in this matter, when her milk is purified she then takes the baby to her bosom to nurse. When the baby is old enough to be weaned, little by little, other foods are given. The weaning certainly causes discomfort to the little one in the beginning so much so that generally the baby pines away for a while, but then afterwards it blossoms again with health, grows stronger in its limbs, and becomes one day a well-formed man, which it could never have done if the mother had never weaned it.

Similarly, and in a still better way God deals with our souls. He seeks to win us by making us experience abundant sweetness and consolations in every one of our devotions, both in the will and in the heart. But who does not see what perils surround such a love of God? It is easy for the poor soul to become attached to the accidental part of devotion and love, neglecting the substantial devotion and love; the very qualities that render us dear and acceptable to God. To counteract this peril Our Lord hurries to our assistance. When He sees that the soul has become stronger in His love, affectionately united to Him and already withdrawn from earthly things and from the occasion of sin, and has acquired sufficient virtue to remain in His service without all these attractions and sensible sweetness, and wishes to advance the soul to greater sanctity of life, then He takes away the sweetness of the affections, which up to now have been experienced in all devotions and meditations, and what is more painful for the soul, He takes away the faculty of praying and of meditating and leaves the soul in the dark in a complete and painful aridity. In the face of such a change, the soul at first is terrified, thinking that it is due to some grave sin into which it has fallen, and afraid of being in disgrace before God. And so without losing time, the soul begins to make an examination of conscience, and passes every action before His judgment, but not finding any reason that could account for such a misfortune, concludes: I have been abandoned by God, in punishment for past sins, or as a penalty for my daily faults. But what a mistake! What the soul thinks to be abandonment is none other than an exceptional grace of the Heavenly Father. This is the transition to the capacity for contemplation, dry at the start, but afterwards, if it perseveres, the soul shall be lifted from meditation to contemplation, and all becomes sweet and pleasant. The aim is to acquire contemplative prayer which cannot be achieved without first being purified from that so-called accidental sense love. The preoccupation of the soul with this type of sense love is the reason for the state of pain. But, alas! the poor soul cannot get peace, there is no comfort, because the soul thinks that no one has realized its real condition. And if the soul does not take some comfort in the assurance given it, the comfort is slight, and almost at once the soul gives way again and thinks: I am deprived of the love of God. Oh, if the soul could understand that this pain is not caused by its own fault! If the soul could realize that the impossibility of resting the imagination on a point of meditation is due to God's having subtracted from the fantasy that great quantity of light which helps the imagination work on supernatural things. The light now removed formerly enlivened the meditation and made it efficacious. Oh, if the soul only could, I say, know that the withdrawal of this light by God is done only to infuse at the same time a better light in the intellect, a much more spiritual light, and a purer one, enabling the soul to fix the mind on God and on divine things without any discursive reasoning, contemplating with a simple vision, ever so sweet, delicate and divine. One could object that if this light is so much better, the soul should, by its spiritual powers of intellect and will apprehend and recognize this new light of contemplation. But go slowly! We are not that far along yet.

Here, as a rule, it happens as with those not accustomed to anything but coarse and heavy foods. If you give them more delicate foods, at first they do not appreciate them at all, on the contrary they would willingly pass the better food by for the other. The same thing happens usually to the soul, which not having been accustomed to spiritual food is greedy for the coarser food and the more material sense consolations. For this reason it will not feel, nor be able to discern this more delicate light of contemplation, except after progressing through aridity as a purification until is is able to remain detached from every sense. That is how it is, my dear Raff, your soul is not deprived of love of God. In spite of the aridity and darkness you are involved in, you have not withdrawn from the service of God. On the contrary you can observe in yourself that you are more careful in the service of the Lord, and you are most attentive in seeing to it that you do not go backwards. You feel in yourself a certain vigor and a kind of holy arduousness in your steady perseverance in virtue.

Now I ask you: where do you think your soul gets all that strength to act so virtuously at this time of aridity and darkness? It certainly does not come through your senses, for they are in a condition of desolation; therefore you have every right to conclude that this force comes from your spirit. My God! Even though the spirit is in darkness, one has to admit that in all this obscurity there is still a simple light, pure, soft, delicate and divine, as I have just mentioned. This light is indiscernible to you, but it is this light which gives you force and vigor in the service of the Lord. This light is for you the beginning of contemplation, and this contemplation cannot reach your soul until the soul has humbly permitted itself to be purged of attachment to the senses. My good friend, contemplation is an entirely spiritual thing, and as long as the soul has not become completely spiritual it cannot possess contemplation completely or know it entirely. But we are still at the time of the weaning: I beg you remember the great care of the mother with her babe. To make this child become an adult man, strong and well formed, the mother must begin to give him more substantial foods. For in order for the soul to pass through adolescence, it must submit itself to new tests, much harder than we have so far discussed. Jesus in His compassion calls you to this. Let us see what is that other test. You still find yourself in the period of the purging of the senses, that is, you are passing through the stage which we have already considered. After this, as I have mentioned, the Heavenly Father has provided to submit you to another test called the purge of the spirit. Be faithful, and do not be frightened and forsake your purpose. All this new testing is so you may liberate yourself from the so-called accidental spiritual love and devotion. The principal means of attaining this is by going through spiritual aridity, which means you will be deprived absolutely of every comfort of the spirit. Your present state is very painful, but since your task here is to purge your love and devotion to God of everything that can be felt as sweet or pleasing to the sense appetite, in the ordinary way, in these devotions and various movements of love toward God, you will not feel even in the point of the spirit any of that refreshment and comfort which we call an accidental spiritual devotion and love. And precisely it is in the privation of this refreshment and comfort that the last purge consists.

Then it will please the Lord to put you into a state wherein your soul will suffer a pain so acute that it surpasses any other concept of pain that we have ever formed. Remember, however, that the love of God is continuously growing in the soul. The sign by which to distinguish it is this: you will always feel more ready for anything that is in the service and honor of God even though it will be without the minimum attraction, utterly devoid of feeling in your spirit. On the contrary you will feel yourself surrounded by thick darkness and all acts of the spirit will be done with great difficulty and repugnance. You then will be loving God with a purer love, without knowing it, and you will do good without being aware of it. And this lack of consciousness on your part will be due to God having withdrawn the reflected light, by which we get to know and love God and begin to act virtuously. When all this happens, comfort yourself, for then that love and devotion is already yours.

After all this I do not know whether the purge will finish here. It seems to me that there is still another grade of contemplation to which Our Lord invites us. And if it is true, as I hope and my inner convictions affirm, that the Divine Doctor will lift you still higher, then I will not add another word except to exhort you to be faithful and humble, keeping the example of the Great Mother of God before the eyes of your mind, who the more she was exalted, the more she humbled herself. Sure in my mind, that God wishes to lift you up to mystical union and perfect love, I warn you that for the purging of the spirit at this point aridity alone is not sufficient, nor is the privation of reflected light. There is need of another interior cause of affliction, which penetrates the whole of the soul, piercing it intimately and renewing it completely. This other cause is no other than a very high light which transfixes the soul in its sins, and so upsets the poor soul as to put it into a state of extreme affliction with interior pains of death. And yet this light which at first surrounds the soul in such a desolating and painful manner, is that which eventually lifts up the soul into mystical union and transforms it. But how that happens, I do not understand, only I say without fear of making a mistake, or of telling you a lie, that it will happen in this way and not in any other way. To say it in my weak way, it seems to me, that it must be so. This very high light will join the soul to the Divine Spouse in a perfect union of love, but when at first it finds the soul indisposed for such a high union, it invests it in a painful and exceedingly desolating manner, and instead of remaining in a state of illumination, the poor soul becomes obscured, and instead of being consoled it is pierced, filled with extreme afflictions in the sensate appetite and interior pains of death in its spiritual powers. The atrocious pains which the soul then feels are so penetrating, that they somewhat resemble the suffering of souls in Purgatory if not actually the damned in Hell.

When the light which is the cause of this atrocious suffering shall have rendered the soul pure and capable of receiving the kiss of the perfect union of love, this same light will clothe it in an illuminative manner.

D.J.C.
J.M.J.   2/12/1915

In your last letter you asked me to give you an explanation of what the Apostle says in his letter to the Philippians, Chapter 1, verses 23 and 24. Here I will satisfy your wishes, excepting always that there may be a better interpretation, and I write subject to the judgment of the Church, in whom I profess my wish always to live and die. To understand the Apostle properly, it is necessary to consider in what circumstances he found himself when writing the epistle. He was in Rome imprisoned for preaching the Gospel, during the reign of the Emperor Nero. So he found himself suspended between death and life, for there was a possibility he would be given his liberty, as in fact came to pass. (But the second probability seemed to him likelier at the time.) His mind being now in this state of suspense, before anything else he declares to the faithful his readiness to accept all things for the love of Christ; he has strong faith that all, even the chains shall be useful to him for salvation and that anything to come shall be advantageous to eternal life. (And this was said also for your comfort, for all things will turn to good for those who love God.)

He rejoices at the thought that nothing shall be lost and that Jesus, as always, will be exalted in his body, quickened in the midst of chains. If he lives it will be his life for the glory of Jesus Christ; and a chance to go on preaching even in prison; if he is martyred he will glorify Jesus by giving his head. Then he declares openly that life for him is Christ, the soul and the center of all his life, the mover of all his works, the object of all his hopes. Then he says death is a gain for him, because his martyrdom would be a solemn testimony to Jesus of his love, his communion with Jesus would be rendered indissoluble, and it would augment the glory which awaits him. And as the Philippians might suppose that he preferred death, he added at once that if living in the mortal body for some time longer were more gainful for the increase of the glory of God and for the salvation of souls, in this case, he would not know which to choose.

He was so uncertain at the time of writing that he did not know which to choose, to live or to die. And to make them better understand this perfect love, he says he is torn between the two: he desires to be dissolved and to be with Christ, which is far better, but remaining in his body is necessary for their sakes. Being dissolved in order to unite himself to God in perfect union of glory was the best for him, but remember, his preference to die rather than live proceeded from his love of God.

To me, it seems, my dear Raffaelina, that the saintly Apostle received a revelation from Our Lord.

One desire proceeded from the perfect love that he had for his neighbor. The other he saw was more useful for him, and he desired as ardently as any soul can, to unite himself to God; the desire to remain in this life with its worries and weariness in order to procure the salvation of souls is less attractive. Filled as he is with the Spirit of God, St. Paul sees it as more necessary for them, or put it this way: having received the revelation, as seems indicated by what follows immediately afterwards, he resigns himself and suffers it for the love of the faithful. Unfortunately the faithful are ever eager to leave this exile and unite themselves to God, and as this wish, for inscrutable reasons, is not always accomplished by God in the way they want, they carry on with the burden of the present life with the sole aim of pleasing God, if it is to be in this fashion. But they suffer atrocious pain in thinking of themselves on this earth of exile. We cannot form even the slightest idea of what these souls suffer, even in satisfying the most normal needs of life, such as eating, drinking, and sleeping. And if the merciful God did not come to their help with a kind of miracle, by taking away this reflection by such in the fulfillment of these acts necessary to survival, they would go through such torment in performing only one act of this kind, that I find nothing to compare it with, except possibly that which the martyrs must have experienced when burnt alive or otherwise brutally put to death for testifying their faith in Jesus Christ.

Perhaps some people will consider this comparison altogether exaggerated, but I know, my dear Raffaelina, what I am saying. For such incredulous people, I would like to ask the bountiful God to give them first-hand experience of such facts.

And after all this, you will still remain indifferent to supplicating the good Heavenly Father for my dissolution?

For goodness sake, if you refuse this for egotistical reasons of your own, I entreat you at least to cease praying for my remaining in this life. Will you at least give me this assurance? Answer me on this. If I knew I were of some value by remaining in this life, I would resign myself to go on supporting the burden that it brings me. But I fear, and my fear is well grounded, I may not fulfill my sacerdotal ministry and therefore render useless the graces given to me by the Bishop's laying on of hands in priestly ordination.

To undertake such a burden as this is to be like a son who tenderly loves his father and shows his affection by subjecting himself to all humiliations, even to the point of performing certain base forms of employment which the father has commanded him to do, not only just to avoid crossing his father's will in the slightest way, but also to please him. But this good son, who thus willingly subjects himself for the love he bears his father, does not cease to feel the burden of the sacrifices. But why lose ourselves in comparisons of natural and imperfect love of this base world? Is not what the holy Apostle felt the same as what all just souls desire?

PADRE PIO

I.M.J.F.
D.C.   9/28/1915

With repeated blows of the salutary hammer and with diligent repolishing the Divine Artist prepares the stones that must enter into the composition of the eternal Edifice.

This is what our loving Mother the Holy Church sings in the hymn of the Divine Office for the Dedication of the Church, and so it really is.

Every soul destined to eternal glory, can rightly say of itself that it is a stone destined to build up the eternal Edifice. A builder, in order to put up a house, needs to make preparations and to clean up, so the Heavenly Father does the same with the elect soul, who from all eternity has been destined for the composition of the eternal Edifice. Before this soul can become part of the building of the eternal Edifice it has to be polished with the blows of hammer and chisel. But what are these hammer and chisel blows used by the Heavenly Father for the preparation of the stones? My dear sister, these hits of the chisel are the shadows, the fears, the temptations, the afflictions of the spirit, the spiritual tremors with some aroma of desolation, and also physical illness. Let us therefore, thank the infinite mercy of the Heavenly Father for the things He is doing to our soul. Why not glory, my dear sister, in these affectionate traits of the best of all Fathers? Open your heart to total abandonment into the arms of this most holy Father, for He is treating you as one elected to follow Jesus closely by the way of Calvary, and I observe with joy and interior emotion the action of grace within you. Be sure that all that is happening to your soul is ordained by Our Lord and do not ever fear it as an occasion of offending Our Lord: It is sufficient for you to know that in all this you are not offending Our Lord, but on the contrary giving Him glory. If He hides Himself from your view, it is not because He wishes to punish you for some act of unfaithfulness, but rather to test your faithfulness and to purify you once again of certain affections that the carnal eye does not perceive. I intend to speak of those faults, which even the saints are not free of, for it is written in the Scriptures that the just fall seven times. Believe me, if I did not see you so dejected I would be less pleased because I would see you had been given fewer jewels by Our Lord. Therefore, take courage, and dispel all doubts to the contrary, in the name of Jesus; believe that in all these struggles of the spirit you are not offending God, you are not sinning. Dispel again all those doubts which cloud your soul, causing you to think that you are deaf to the Divine call and that you resist grace. All this, I tell you is not true, it is a plot contrived by Satan. Pray continually to the Heavenly Father asking Him to make you hear His loving voice always more clearly and respond gratefully. Ask the Spouse of the Canticles with confidence that He draw you to Himself and make you sense the fragrance of His ointments, so that you may follow Him always, wherever He goes.

Hold firm to what I have explained, for this is the map that will conduct you to the place of salvation, and this the divine armor that will put victory in your song. It is the complete and blind submission to Him who is to guide us through the shadows, the perplexities and the struggles of this life. The Holy Scriptures infallibly confirm this: *"Vir obediens loquetur victoriam*—The obedient man shall sing victory."* If Jesus manifests Himself to you, thank Him; and if He hides Himself, thank Him just the same. It is all a joke of love. I hope that you attain to dying with Jesus on the Cross, and that you can softly exclaim with Him: *Consummatum est.* The desire that you have to see God in all things, the annoyance that you feel drawn to when confronted with creatures is an unusual grace of the Divine piety which is not vouchsafed to all poor travelers. Know how to profit by this, therefore, and give thanks to Our Lord. Do not listen to what your imagination tells you, that is, that the life you are living is inadequate in doing good. For in this you do not reason rightly; the grace of Jesus is watchful and will hold you to good. Be certain that the more a soul loves God, the less he feels it.

The thing seems strange and impossible in terms of the fallen love of creatures, but in the realm of the love of God, it is quite different. I do not know how to express this truth, but be sure that it is like that. God is incomprehensible, inaccessible, so that the more a soul enters into the love of this Supreme

Good, so much the more this sentiment of love towards Him seems to diminish, to the point of seeming that one does not love Him at all. And truly in some cases it really appears so, but the facts afterwards prove quite the contrary. Those continuous fears of losing God, the saintly prudence which makes you careful to put your foot where it will not slip, that courage with which you fight the enemy, the resignation in all adversities of life to the Divine will, that ardent desire to see the Kingdom of God established in yourself and in others, are the most enlightening proofs that your love towards the Supreme Good is in fact alive and reciprocated.

Jesus says in the Gospels that only those who do the will of His Father are His brothers. And wouldn't you want to conform yourself to the Divine wishes in every act? Would you not give your life rather than determine to go against the Divine will? Of this you are quite sure; well then, this is the yardstick by which to know whether your life is really lacking in good. Oh! how far away you are from that which your feeling would lead you to think. Say rather that you love, and that you wish to love with a perfect and consummate love. This good cannot be obtained in its completion except in the next life! Oh, the miserable state of our life! May the Spouse of Souls rend the curtain which separates us from Him and finally concede to us the consummate love we sigh after with so much mourning and weeping!

You have besides interpreted too rigorously what I said about your sister. I do not doubt for a moment that her soul is not acceptable to Our Lord, I only said that I saw with displeasure the way in which she regards the Eucharistic Communion. In these sad times of dead faith and triumphant impiety and because we are continuously surrounded by people with hate in their hearts and blasphemy on their lips, the best way of keeping ourselves immune from their pestilent contagion all around us is to fortify ourselves with the food of the Eucharist. This immunity is not easy to obtain by those who live months and months away without replenishing themselves with the immaculate Flesh of the Divine Lamb. How much the physical condition of your sister distresses me, I cannot tell you, and only the Lord knows how much I pray for her spiritual rather than physical health. Blessed is the person rendered worthy of following Him who has willed to give us His Blood for our reconciliation with His Father. May my weak but nevertheless continual prayer be acceptable to Him who governs all things for our good and to His glory.

I do not cease to pray for all those souls which you have kindly presented to me. And you complain that I do not comply with your requests and gently reprove me. I have no alternative but to ask your pardon, and do not condemn me before listening to my defense. You know that for some time past I have been suffering from forgetfulness in spite of all my good intentions to satisfy you. I realize that this is a great grace by which Our Lord makes me remember only those things which He Himself wishes. He indeed, on several occasions puts before me persons that I have never seen nor even heard spoken about for the sole reason that I should pray in their favor, and does not bother if He does not listen to my supplications. On the other hand when the Lord does not wish to grant me my request, He makes me forget even to pray for that person although I had the best and firmest intention of doing so. My forgetfulness at times reached even those things that are most essential such as eating and drinking and such things. But I thank Divine Providence that I have never forgotten those things pertaining to my priestly state.

Now judge if I am guilty or worthy of your compassion. However, if on any occasion you see I have not replied to some point, please ask it again a second and third time without human respect. And if also in this case you still receive no reply, then adore the Divine Judgment and rest assured that Our Lord will not leave every one of your good thoughts without a reward. For some days past my soul feels as though it were encased in a circle of iron, please ask the Heavenly Father to give me the force to support with resignation this burdensome wish of His. I should be most grateful if you would add to your prayers the three novenas to the Virgin of the Holy Rosary of Pompeii, for a grace which I see will be to the glory of Her Divine Majesty. But if you cannot do this without grave inconvenience please dispense yourself.

PADRE PIO

J.M.J.
D.J.C.

I am forcing myself with a trembling hand to scribble these few lines. Yesterday I returned from Morcone where within a few days I was reduced to a state of extremity. Now more than ever I am suffering the results brought on by this new trial demanded by Jesus. I have become absolutely dry; weak to the extreme, I can hardly carry on for fear that Our Lord will reward me only in this life. Pray to Jesus, who has willed to try His servant with the test of fire!... You also, my sister, thank the infinite mercy of Our Lord for not permitting the enemy to touch my spirit in this extreme trial, and this without any merit on my part. How sweet it is to live always in the shadow of the Lord in His holy cloister! Perhaps I am not worthy to rest in this holy enclosure and this is the reason why Our Lord is nearly forced to turn me out.

May His will be done who wishes to put the loyalty of His servant to this extreme test. The Lord, to my disadvantage wills to listen to the prayers of all those devout people who, as it seems, absolutely insist on keeping me among them. This is not just a simple conjecture, no, they have demonstrated it on various occasions. For instance when I last returned, on entering the village the people came out and added *"eviva"* to their thanks to Our Lord for my return. I was moved to tears. I am trembling, however, for fear lest Our Lord will reward me in this life only. Pray to Jesus and ask Him to preserve my reward for the next life. You say that you fear your own malice and ask me what you are to do to liberate yourself. Humble yourself before the Lord and do not fear anything. Besides, your malice is not the sort that would disgust the Divine Lover. Entreat the gentle Jesus to take away your excessive fear of yourself. Keep present before the eyes of your mind the goodness of the Heavenly Spouse who sees, knows and weighs all our actions. And you need not fear because all your actions are directed to a good end.

I try to believe that you have offended Our Lord, but I see you walking too well before Him to believe it, and this tempest that is raging around you in the end only adds to the glory of God and to your own merit, and the good of many souls as well. I, however unworthily, pray constantly to the Lord for all the intentions requested by you. Be of good cheer, the Heavenly Father never permits the enemy, in these bitter trials, to touch your spirit or that of your sister. Take courage, I say again, my sister, be sure that God is with you, and what shall you fear?

Let yourself be led by the Divine grace and be calm for He will glorify Himself in you. I am unwillingly forced to stop for the present. I feel completely exhausted. Forgive me if I am not able to satisfy all your holy and just desires, and be assured that it does not arise from wrong intentions.

Meanwhile do not deprive me of your correspondence.

Pray for him who so desires your sanctification.

P.S. In thanking you for the prayers offered for me, I would like to know if you have finished the novena in honor of the Virgin of the Rosary. It does not seem so to me.

PADRE PIO

J.M.J.
D.J.C.

May Jesus console you, guide you and bless you always and make you understand ever better what He says in the Holy Gospel: "My yoke is sweet and my burden light." Please understand how much your

letter has delighted me—may God be thanked and
blessed for it. I thank you very much for the nice
things you have said in my favor in your letter, but
in respect for truth, you should know that I do not
merit either praise or thanks, as nothing good is in
me which is not the work of God and nothing is
bad within me which is not my doing! I am only
capable of sinning, my dear madam, and then...noth-
ing else but more sins. Comfort yourself, dear madam,
comfort yourself because the hand of the Lord has
not ceased to guide you. Oh! if He is the Father of
all, He is so in a very special manner for the unhappy, and in a still more special manner for you
who are a widow and a widowed mother as well.

Banish the dark clouds that gather round your spirit
which the malignant spirit seeks to spread to make
you if possible fall into despair. The Heavenly Father
wishes to make you like His Divine Son in the agony
and in the ascent to Calvary. Let this be a true comfort to you in the midst of all the humiliations for
which you have been rendered worthy, without any
merit of your own. And let this spur you on, never
to pause on the road of Our Lord. Humble yourself
under the powerful hand of God. Accept with humility and patience the tribulations which He sends,
so that He will lift you up at the time of His coming
giving you His grace and His glory in the established
time. Cast all your worries to Him, He has the greatest
care of you and of the three little angels of sons with
which Providence has adorned you. These sons will
be a comfort to you by their conduct in the course
of your life. Be always careful regarding their education, their scientific as well as their moral education.

Upper left: One room birthplace of P. Pio.
Upper right: Back wall of the one room birthplace of P. Pio.
Lower left: Shady nook where P. Pio prayed and studied.
Lower right: The vaults where P. Pio's father and mother are buried.

Upper left: Niece of Archpriest Pandullo.
Upper right: New Monastery and Church fulfilling prophecy of P. Pio.
Lower left: Church where P. Pio was baptized.
Lower right: Libera Cardone, who cared for P. Pio in his infancy when his mother was ill.

Upper left: Altar of St. Francis where P. Pio said Mass.
Upper right: Monastery chapel where P. Pio made his thanksgiving.
Lower left: Where P. Pio vested for Mass.
Lower right: Choir where P. Pio was visibly stigmatized Sept. 20, 1918.

Upper left: Lucia Bellodi cured of diabetes—Corpus Christi, 1952—see page 169.
Upper right: Blind Pietruccio—see page 157.
Lower left: P. Pio's brother, Michael.
Lower right: Giovanni Savino with his new eyes—see page 229.

Be vigilant in all things and hold them as the apple
of your eye. Together with the education of the mind
by good studies be sure there is also the education
of the heart and instruction in our holy Religion, without which, my good lady, the human heart suffers
mortal harm. You ask my advice regarding a visit
to Florence about the business which you describe
in your letter. What counsel can I give you about
this except not to delay in putting your scheme into
execution? Do not think about the humiliations which
you will have to face in the presence of the Mar-
chese. Our Lord, who is leading you to this, will give
you all the strength and the courage necessary to ask
help for your little sons.

I do not know what will be the outcome of this
visit but my heart tells me that it will go well according to the heart of God. But if it is unfruitful,
according to your way of seeing, console yourself that
you have done the will of Our Lord in this thing.
Meanwhile let us pray to Jesus for happy results so
all will work out for the glory of God and the salvation of souls.

Do not grieve because Our Lord who is so good,
will not fail to open the way for you. I conclude,
my dear madam, I cannot continue, I didn't go to
bed so I could give you a prompt reply to your kind
note.

Pray for my poor soul, so that it will not become
unfaithful to Our Lord.

Meanwhile be sure that I, however unworthily, have
never ceased to remember you with tears and thanksgiving before the Lord.

PADRE PIO

J.M.J.
D.J.C.   S. Giovanni, 8/23/1919

My Dear Daughter,

May Jesus reign in your heart to fill it and make it abound in His saintly love! I am sorry I have not the strength to reply adequately to all the points made by you in your last letter. I have been ill for the last three days, and I have got out of bed for a brief respite in order to answer yours, but you will forgive me if I am brief. In general I wish to assure you that you can be at rest regarding your state of soul, which is pleasing to God. I cannot believe what you conclude, and therefore neither can I dispense you of your period of meditation just because you think you are not profitting by it. The sacred gift of prayer, my good daughter, is in the right hand of the Saviour, and according to the amount that you empty yourself, that is, of corporal love and of your own will, and root yourself well in humility, the Lord will communicate with you in your heart. Have patience in the perseverance in this holy exercise of meditation, and be contented to begin by little steps until you have strength to run, or better to fly: be contented to make the act of obedience, which is never a little thing for a soul that has chosen God for its lot, and resign yourself for the present in being a little bee in the hive which soon will become a big bee able to make honey. Humble yourself always and lovingly before God and men, because God speaks to those who really keep their hearts humbly before Him to be enriched by His gifts.

But the real reason that you do not experience or

rather do not succeed to do your meditation well, is due if I am not mistaken, to the following: You approach meditation with a kind of arrogance, with a great anxiety to find some subject that will please and console your spirit and this is enough to have you never find what you are seeking. Your mind is not in the truth you are meditating on, and your heart is empty of affection. My daughter, you know when someone is looking for a thing with haste and avidity, he will touch the thing with his hands and look at it a hundred times without noticing it. By this vain and useless anxiety you will only become spiritually very tired, and your mind will not be able to rest on the subject you are considering, and from this arises as from its own cause, a certain coldness and stupidity of the soul, more specifically in what concerns positive effects.

I do not know of any remedy other than as follows: Get rid of this anxiety because it is one of the worst traitors to real virtue devotion can have: it pretends to get us warm for good works, but it does not do it; it chills us rather, and only makes us run in order to make us stumble, and for this reason you must, as I have often told you when speaking to you, be careful on every occasion and particularly in prayer. To succeed better it is as well to remember that grace and the taste for prayer do not draw from the earth but from Heaven, so not even if we use all our strength can we make it fall at our bidding, though we must make every effort to dispose ourselves with the greatest care. Yes, but always in humility and tranquility; it is necessary to hold the heart open to the heavens and wait for the heavenly dew to descend.

Do not forget to take this thought with you, my daughter, when in prayer, because with it you will be able to draw near to God, and you will put yourself in His presence for two principal reasons.

The first is in order to give honor to God and the homage which we owe Him. This can be done without Him speaking to us or we to Him, for this obligation is fulfilled by the recognition that He is our God, and we His miserable creatures, prostrate before Him awaiting His commands. How many courtiers who come and go in the presence of the King, not to speak to Him or hear Him but simply to be seen by Him, and thus manifest ourselves as His true servants? This way of being in the presence of God just by declaring with our will to be His servants, is a holy and excellent one, pure and of great perfection.

You may laugh, but I am speaking seriously.

The second reason why we put ourselves in the presence of God in prayer, is to speak to Him and to hear His voice by means of internal inspirations and illuminations, and generally this is done with much pleasure, because it is a significant grace for us to speak to so great a Lord, who when He replies causes to descend on us a thousand perfumes and precious ointments which produce great joy in the soul. Now, my dear daughter, one of these two goods cannot be missing in prayer. If you can speak to Our Lord, praise Him, hear Him; if you cannot speak for uncouthness, do not be unhappy, but in the manner of the Spirit, shut yourself in the room, and like a courtier pay Him homage. He who sees you will be glad of your patience, He will favor your silence and another time you will be consoled, when He takes

Upper left: Our Lady of Grace.
Lower left: Padre Pio's hospital.
Upper right: House of Relief of Suffering.
Lower right: Dedication May 5, 1956.

Upper Left: Day of dedication.
Upper right: Cardinal Lercaro cutting the ribbon.
Lower left: Cardial Lercaro blessing the corridors of the hospital.
Lower right: Padre Pio, celebrant.

Padre Pio, celebrant of the Mass officially opening
the Hospital May 5, 1956.

Padre Pio, celebrant of the Dedication Mass May 5, 1956.

you by the hand, speaks to you, walks a hundred times with you in your company in the paths of His Garden of Prayer, and even if that never happened, which is really impossible, because the kindly Father could not bear to see His creatures in perpetual fluctuation, be contented all the same because our obligation is to follow Him, and consider it too great an honor and grace that He should take us in to His presence. In this way do not trouble about speaking to Him, because the other way of just standing by His side is not less useful, perhaps even better, though maybe less to our taste. So when you find yourself with God in prayer, consider the truth, speak to Him if you can, and if not remain there, make yourself seen and don't make yourself a nuisance.

Regarding anticipating your return, it is always better to subject yourself to the will of others, that is of that of your family, and so avoid further trouble.

My prayers, for which you ask with insistence, will never be lacking for you because I cannot forget what has cost me so many sacrifices and that I have given birth to you to God in extreme pain of the heart; I have confidence in your charity, that in your prayers you will not forget Him who carries the Cross for all.

I bless you with all the tenderness of my soul and I recommend myself to you.

P. Pio, Cappuccino.

To Father Angelo da Camerino
Republic of S. Marino
Very Reverend Father,
May Jesus be always the Supreme King of our hearts, and comfort you in your trials to which He

may be pleased to subject you, and render you worthy of the glory of the blessed.

I am extremely grateful for the Divine grace which procured me the advantage of knowing your surroundings and your precious letters, and I should be still happier to know you personally.

I shall not forget to pray for the intentions which you have asked. May it please God to accept my requests which I have put before Him. Do you not forget either to keep me present in the treasures of your prayers. How can I show you my gratefulness for having counted me among the number of the devout of your celebrated sanctuary? My gratitude forces me in my poor way to declare it before Jesus.

May the Divine Grace accompany you and sustain you everywhere.

I remain yours respectfully, and I embrace you with all my heart.

Affectionately yours in the Lord,
Padre Pio of Pietrelcina, Cappuccino.

S. Giovanni Rotondo. 5/7/1919

CHAPTER XI

Medical Reports

Padre Pio's hands, which the faithful could see while he celebrated Mass, were covered with blood, and the wounds seemed bigger than they were in reality. Washing them with water, the stigmata appeared as circular wounds, about two centimeters in diameter, in the center of the palm. Equal wounds were found on the back of the hands in such a position that they gave the impression that the wounds met each other and the hands were pierced through and through or transfixed, so that a bright light should be seen through the stigmata.

It is properly on account of the depth of the wounds, transfixed from back to front, that Padre Pio could not completely close his hands. Theresa Neumann wrote with great difficulty, as did Padre Pio. Visually, one could not see the depth of Pio's wounds on account of the soft skin which covered the surface. The skin every so often fell off to give place for the formation of new skin.

As St. Gemma Galgani sought to hide her stigmata, so also Padre Pio immediately sought to hide his stigmata. The regulation for wearing gloves was made by the Superiors General, after they were satisfied with the various examinations and reports. Padre Pio was required to wear gloves except at Mass. He was forbidden by his superiors to show his hands to anyone. Even saying Mass he tried to cover his hands with the long sleeve of the alb. He even, in the first months, believed it useful to put iodine on the wounds twice a week in the hope that such an application might diminish the too copious flow of blood. After the visit of Dr. Bignami, he gave this up. The wounds on his feet presented the same characteristics as the hands. A wound on top of the foot corresponded with a wound on the bottom of his foot. The stockings were always stained with blood on the top and the bottom. Different from the other Capuchins who wear sandals, Padre Pio wore shoes, but special shoes that were flexible, soft and partially made of cloth. They were sent to him as a gift from Switzerland. In descending the altar steps to give Communion to the faithful he appeared to me to step down backwards because of the intense pain in his feet. His gait was always uncertain, slow, and hesitating.

The stigma on his side was the strangest of all, because it emitted a greater quantity of blood even though the wound seemed more superficial. He lost about a cup of blood each day from the wound in his left side.

Once Dr. Festa applied a clean white handkerchief to the left side of Padre Pio at nine in the evening. After ten hours, at seven the next morning, Dr. Festa found completely saturated with blood and serum not only that handkerchief but also another cloth of equal size which Padre Pio had applied above the handkerchief during the night.

The Capuchins of the monastery never threw away the clothes bathed in blood, but jealously stored them away. The Holy Office forbade them to give out his gloves or anything worn by Padre Pio. One glove applied to the body of the dying Mother Teresa Salvadores, Superiora dell'Escuela Taller Medala Milagrosa of Montevideo, brought about her immediate miraculous cure from cancer. She was dying from a double disease, cancer of the stomach and lesion of the aorta. She could no longer retain food. Monsignor Damiani, the brother of the famous opera tenor, Damiani, when at San Giovanni Rotondo had obtained a glove of Padre Pio. When he returned to Montevideo he applied the glove to her stomach and to her throat. Immediately the dying nun fell asleep and when she awoke she was cured. She narrated that while asleep Padre Pio touched her side, then breathed on her while saying heavenly words. (November, 1921).

All of Padre Pio's organs, the lungs, the heart, the kidneys, and the spleen were perfectly healthy. His lungs, once diseased with tuberculosis, were sound and normal. After a surgical operation in 1925 for hernia, and in 1927 for a cyst on the neck, the healing of the surgical wounds was quick and without any sort of complication.

The duration of the stigmata of Padre Pio is the longest which is recorded in the long list of stigmatics. At the time this book was written, it was the 45th year since the visible stigmata appeared on his body, September 20, 1918. This long duration is more remarkable because his stigmata did not appear only on Thursdays or Fridays, as in many other stigmatics, but for 45 years without interruption he carried them night and day on all the days of the week.

DR. FESTA'S REPORT ON THE STIGMATA

In the palm of the left hand, corresponding to half of the third metacarpus (bone from the carpus to the fingers) there was an anatomic lesion of the tissues in circular form with clear margins, about four-fifths of an inch in diameter.

Dr. Festa found no change in July, 1920, from the time of his first examination in October, 1919. This lesion was covered with a reddish-brown scab. Padre Pio affirmed that from time to time this scab detached itself first at the edges then little by little toward the center until it fell off completely. Then the lesion appeared in all its detail with dark red color and always bleeding. Because of the presence of this scab it was not easy to judge the profundity of the wound. The Provincial Superior, who visited him shortly after the stigmatization had the clear impression that the wounds observed on the palms of each hand went right through to meet or join the wound on the back of the hand.

In a conversation with me on this point, he declared textually: "If I were interrogated by superior authorities on this particular question, I would have to answer and confirm under oath, so much is the certitude of the impression received, that, if one fixed one's glance on the wounds in the palms of his hands, it would be easy to recognize in its detail written matter or an object previously placed in the side opposite or back of the hands."

The edges of the palm wounds had a limit of demarcation that was so clear, that the skin immediately surrounding, even observed with a magnifying glass, presented neither swelling, redness, infiltration, nor even a single trace of inflammatory reaction.

In the back of the left hand a little nearer to the joint of the third finger, and therefore not in exact correspondence to the palm, there was another lesion, analogous to the first in form and character, but the edges were more confined and with an apparently more superficial scab. With equal characteristics one could describe the lesions existing on the back and in the palms of the right hand.

While Dr. Festa examined them, small and continual drops of blood bled from their edges. Invited to close his fist, he did not succeed in closing it completely. This author noticed while Pio was vesting for Mass, that he held rather loosely and tied very slowly the cincture. He could not close his hand firmly around the cincture or cord used to tie up the long, white alb worn by priests during Mass.

Dr. Festa said: "During my examination, in order to be able to study also the lesions of his feet, I myself helped him remove his stockings, which I immediately observed were abundantly stained with bloody serum. On top of both feet, and precisely corresponding with the second metatarsus (part of the foot between the tarsus and the toes), I found here also a circular lesion, of reddish-brown color covered with a soft scab, which duplicated exactly the origin and characteristics of those described in the hands; perhaps these were a little smaller and more superficial. There was perfect completeness of the metatarsus bone lying under with full length; there was no trace of infiltration, no swelling, no inflammatory reaction in the skin which surrounded it; also here there was light but continuous drops of bloody serum.

"On the bottom of the feet and at a point corresponding to the top of the feet, there appeared at my observation two other lesions; one in each sole of the foot, well outlined in their edges, perfectly identical to the top wounds, and bleeding.

"Direct pressing of any of the wounds caused very intense pain and the mere touching of the tissues that surrounded the wounds gave pain, but less pain. He had pain in both feet and this caused him to walk slowly with an uncertain gait. This author noticed that when Pio descended the altar steps to give Holy Communion, he had to turn around and step down backwards. There was less pain in the feet by stepping down backwards."

HEART WOUND

In the anterior region of the left side, about two fingers under the nipple there was another lesion in the form of an inverted cross.

The length of this measured about seven centimeters or two and three-fourths inches. The width of the short arm of the cross was four centimeters or one and one-half inches. They intersected at right angles.

This figure of a cross was very superficial. The width of the wound in both the short and the long arms of the cross was about one-third of an inch. The color was the same as the hands and feet. A soft and small scab covered the central part, and not even here did the surrounding tissues offer traces of reddishness, infiltration or swelling. The painful sensitiveness caused by touching it was far greater and more extended than in the normal tissues of the other wounds.

Although so superficial, it bled much more freely than the other wounds. Padre Pio said he lost one cup of blood each day.

Dr. Festa held that there is absolutely nothing in science that can give reason for this phenomenon. They came visibly upon his body *all at once* while he was genuflected in prayer of thanksgiving after Mass and not one by one as in the case of Theresa Neumann. After 45 years, the longest record for any stigmatist, the wounds were the very same in character as when they appeared on his body, September 20, 1918. Down through the years a soft scab formed, detached itself from the edges, then the center, until it fell off completely to give way for the formation of a new scab. In 45 years they did not show the least sign of healing or ceasing to shed blood. Theresa Neumann's hands shed blood only on the Fridays of Lent and not on the other Fridays of the year when she shed tears of blood and bled profusely from the wounds of the scourging. The reddish-brown color of his five wounds was the same color as when they first appeared on his body. The extreme sensitiveness he had in them in the beginning did not diminish. The issue of blood and serum was of the same amount every day for 45 years. Dr. Festa testified that the wounds could not be the product of a traumatism of an external origin or due to chemical substances that are powerfully irritant. The lesions did not have the characteristics of wounds made from blows for there was absent the redness, the swelling, and the infiltration common to all wounds. Padre Pio, who in his profound modesty considered his condition as a true humiliation, endeavored as much as he could to hide the wounds which he had, and the pains he received from them. He had hoped to stop the flow of blood entirely by applying iodine which availed him nothing. After the visit of Dr. Bignami in July 1919, he no longer applied the iodine, yet they conserved always the same identical characteristics as when they first appeared.

REPORT ON SURGERY FOR A HERNIA

"The evening I arrived at the monastery was Monday, September 28, 1925," says Dr. Festa, "and the episode, apparently insignificant, which I now recount happened on the succeeding Tuesday.

"Having passed a great part of Wednesday in cheerful conversation with Padre Pio, on the following Thursday, the first day of October, while I was with him in his cell, talking about indifferent things and alternating our chat with jokes and pleasantries, the good *fraticello* suddenly interrupted, and almost changing the expression of his face murmured:

"'I wanted to ask you a question, but at this moment it slipped my memory. Patience, if it comes back to me I shall tell you.'

"We exchanged some more thoughts and then, stopping again:

"'Look,' he said, 'this is what I wanted to ask you. Do me a favor of examining me a little; it is already a long time that I have been suffering and I am truly not well.'

"Surprised at that unexpected digression from a merry conversation and at a manifestation of physical pain as severe as that which appeared again at that moment on his face, and surprised by the facility with which, in conversing, he forgot himself, I began to question him on the causes and the nature of his suffering.

"'It is already several years,' he answered briefly, 'that at intervals I am stricken with pains which pierce deeply my intestines; now these intervals are so near each other, and the intensity of my suffering is so atrocious, that especially when I ascend the altar steps, I must use extraordinary efforts to keep myself from fainting. Do me the favor of examining me and prescribing, if possible, some remedy that will relieve me and permit me to continue in the fulfillment of my sacerdotal duties.'

"Performing a close examination, I found a voluminous hernia in the region of the right groin, rendered irreducible from extended adhesions, between the herniated viscera and the wall of the hernia sac. In which, perhaps from the wearing of a hernia brace that was too stiff and tight, there set in adhesive peritonitis which from the wall of the sac extended up toward the parietal peritoneum, also from the opposite side of the abdomen there was a sense of sharp sensitiveness that was painful, nauseating, and easily disposing him to vomit.

"The functions of the heart, of the kidneys, and the respiratory tracts appeared also now very normal, as they were more or less found several years before by me and Dr. Bignami.

"Moreover, considering the notable frequency of his pulse and the slight rise in temperature which accompanies such conditions, I knew that the best step was to suggest an operation. The good Padre, without being upset, welcomed my conclusion, observing simply:

"'It is too bad that I did not think of having you examine me before. Perhaps I would have begged that you operate upon me.'

"After a brief chat with the superior of the monastery it was decided, on that same evening, that the operation should take place as soon as possible."

And here it is worth the trouble to bring to light one particular which shows in all its greatness the righteous spirit by which this singular man even in the most difficult contingencies was always animated.

"'Padre,' with all simplicity and frankness I said to him the following morning, 'you who can with so much efficacy turn your mind to the Lord, beg Him now since it is the moment, that we wish to understand if really it is my hand that must perform the operation which you need, or if it be not better, for your greater security, to turn to another more competent colleague. The surgical undertaking which must be done on you certainly offers some difficulties, and I would not want really to be the one to bring graver harm to your health.'

"'No,' he answered without hesitating, 'prayers with this purpose I will never direct to the Lord.'

"'And why,' I insisted, 'is it not natural that in a moment of uncertainty one seek from the Lord the help of His light?'

"'No,' he repeated still once again, 'because with the request that you suggest I feel that I would offend Him.'

"'How?' I exclaimed then, surprised with his definite affirmation. 'Do you really think that it would be an offense to ask the Lord His help in an hour so decisive for your own health?'

"'Certainly,' he affirmed with emphasis and with the habitual smile on his lips; 'didn't Jesus teach us to love one another and bestow mutually the good which we need? And did He not add that, doing such, He would have blessed our actions? Why force Him to repeat that which He has already said once before? Is it not good works and love which you prepare to perform on me? Put then into execution your plan, be at ease, for the Lord will not fail to bless your hands.'

"In the evening of that day Giuseppe De Paoli of Balzano, who was a guest in the monastery, went at my request to my office in Rome to bring back the necessary surgical instruments and was to return in the early hours of October 5.

"A few days before this event two monastic cells were made into one fairly large room for conversing with visitors. When I saw a brother whitewashng the walls of this enlarged room the day after my arrival I remarked that it would make a good operating room, never dreaming that it had been prepared in time for Padre Pio's operation. This was the only room in the whole old monastery that could be used in this emergency. I prepared an operating table and all the materials were sterilized.

"October 5, Mr. De Paoli arrived with the instruments from Rome together with Dr. Angelo Merla of San Giovanni whom I chose as my assistant and also Padre Fortunato who, having done medical corps duty during the war, aided me efficiently in the preparation of necessary things. I waited for Padre Pio to return from celebrating Mass and hearing confessions even that very morning of the operation.

"Numerous confessions of strangers, celebrating a Requiem High Mass for deceased members of his community, and finally Benediction kept Padre Pio occupied until noon before he could return to the monastery cloister. We saw him approaching with a very slow gait, pallid from the sustained fatigue of the morning and from the physical pain which the hernia and his stigmata caused him. When he arrived in front of me he said:

"'Dear doctor, here I am in your hands, but please I do not want to be chloroformed.'

"My energetic opposition did not avail, nor did my arguments for technical reasons change his mind. He remained firm in his wishes, assuring me only that during the operation he would not move from the position we put him in. And added:

"'Would you know how to refrain, after you chloroformed me, from inspecting the side wound which you studied once before?'

"'No, Padre,' I answered in all sincerity, 'it would really be my first desire, to examine it again after all these years.'

"'You see then why I have a reason for refusing to take an anesthetic. Although I have received no instructions, I know that an order was given to my superiors by the Vatican, and it is my duty to see that it is respected. So, that is why even during the operation I intend to remain the master of my acts and my will.'

"Such was the temper of this man and priest that for the sake of obedience he cheerfully faced an ordeal that few would care to duplicate. He never made a single complaint, and only once I saw two tears roll down his cheeks while he moaned: 'Oh, Jesus, pardon me if I do not know how to suffer as I should!'

"The operation took about two hours at the end of which time we took Padre Pio back to his cell where he collapsed from exhaustion and remained unconscious for some time. I confess that during this period I took advantage of his condition and explored the wound over his heart which I had made a report on five years earlier. I was able to observe the same characteristics that I had made note of then.

"For the love of truth and exactness I must only add that the soft skin or scab which I found covering the wound on the left side two fingers from under the nipple in the preceding examination, was now fallen off, so that this wound appeared fresh and bright-red, in the form of a cross, and with brief, but evident *luminous radiations* which were released from the edges." (Many of the stigmatists have had this luminous radiation from the area of their respective stigmata—Author.)

"The post-operative course was satisfying. On the fourth day, after removing the medication, I did not observe any swelling or redness of the tissues around the incision; I took out some of the stitches. On the sixth day I removed the rest of the stitches and I considered him cured.

"After a brief convalescence he resumed his activities with greater vigor and without tiring himself as in the past."

OPERATION FOR A CYST

"Two years later about the middle of September 1927, having been informed by my colleagues and by friends of the town that there was a large progressively increasing tumor or cyst in the lateral region of the neck, I went to examine it and found it necessary to operate on him again. The day after my arrival, with the aid of Dr. Angelo Merla, who assisted me during the hernia operation, we began the surgery. Already knowing the disposition of his mind, I did not even think of insisting on any form of anesthesia. The cyst was about as big as a pigeon's egg and its removal and the stitching of the wound took about a half hour. During the operation there was not one word of reaction on the part of the patient, so much so that at the end of the operation I could not but ask him:

"Didn't you have any pain?"

"'Certainly I had it,' he answered.

"And then why no movement of the head, no complaint?" I replied.

"'For what benefit should I have moved myself or cried?' He observed, 'I would have embarrassed you and with this, your work would have been prolonged, and the more prolonged would be my pains. See, then,' he concluded smiling, 'that by not complaining I have simply worked for my own interest.'

"In spite of the suffering that he must undoubtedly have had for some time in the nape of his neck after the operation, he did not cease even one day to take care of the duties of his ministry, and on the following morning as though nothing had happened he was seen again in the confessional and at the foot of the altar.

"Within the fifth and sixth days, as it was also after the hernia operation, perfect healing took place and the stitches were removed. But the five wounds of the hands, the feet, and the side never healed. This fact is a riddle for the rationalists, the psychologists, and the exponents of hysteria to unfold."

GOLDEN RELIGIOUS JUBILEE OF FR. PIO

On January 22, 1953, Father Pio celebrated the fiftieth anniversary of his entrance into the Capuchin Order. According to the Ceremonial of the Order, the community assembled in the refectory and from there led Fr. Pio in procession to the church. On the way the *Psalm* 121 *"Laetatus sum"* was recited. Arriving at the altar Very Rev. Fr. Antonino da S. Elia in Pianisi, the Fr. Provincial, delivered a short, appropriate address and then received the renewal of vows of Fr. Pio. This was followed by a solemn High Mass celebrated by Fr. Pio. After the Mass, Fr. Pio sat on a chair in front of the altar and received the homage of his brethren. They kissed his hand, congratulated him and received the kiss of peace from him. The crowds were too large for the small church.

At dinner a number of lay people were present, besides friars from many Friaries. Most Rev. Fr. General, who had been at Foggia for a celebration, also honored the celebrant with his presence. Among the layfolk were relatives and friends of Fr. Pio.

In the afternoon there was a service of thanksgiving in the church at which the famous tenor, Bengiamino Gigli also sang. He with two fathers sang a three-voiced Litany of the Blessed Virgin. He also sang along with the Benediction hymns.

CHAPTER XII

Casa Sollievo Della Sofferenza

HOME FOR THE RELIEF OF SUFFERING
Dedication May 5, 1956

On the evening of January 9, 1940 in Father Pio's little Franciscan cell, the "Home for the Relief of Suffering" came into existence. With him were three of his friends. They were spiritual children of his, shipwrecked souls, who had peacefully reached the shores of faith from other, far different lands. The good Father had been talking for a long while. His words were, in their calm simplicity, a passionate elegy of the sufferings which afflict the human race, all the more terrible inasmuch as they represent the result of sin, the consequence of treachery by which man has tarnished his soul in the presence of God. At the same time they were a hymn of praise to the immense mercy of God and His boundless love for mankind! "One single act of love," he said, "on the part of man, one single act of charity is so great in God's eyes, that He could not repay it even with the immense gift of the entire Creation! Love is the spark of God in man's soul, it is the very essence of God personified in the Holy Spirit!" To God we owe *all* our love, to be adequate it ought to be infinite. But this cannot be, because God alone is infinite. But we must, at least, give our entire being to Love, to charity. Our *actions* must be such that Our Lord may say to us: "I was hungry, and you gave Me to eat; I was suffering and you cared for Me and comforted Me."

He who would carry out this ideal of Our Lord, must be self-forgetful, and, rising above his selfishness, bow down to the sufferings and the wounds of his fellowman, as to a brother. He makes them his own, knowing how to suffer with his brother for the love of God. He must know how to instill hope into his heart and bring back a smile on his lips, because he has restored a ray of light into his soul. Such a man offers up to God the most beautiful, the most noble of prayers, because such a prayer springs from sacrifice. It is the essence of love, of the unselfish gift of oneself, body and soul!

In every sick man there is Jesus in Person who is suffering, in every poor man it is Jesus Himself who is languishing; in every sick and poor Jesus is doubly visible.

Thus it was that the idea of a hospital sprang up and immediately became a reality. Padre Pio, after searching deep in the many pockets of his monastic habit, pulled out a small gold coin, which had been given to him for his charities. Handing this to his friends he said: "I wish to be the first to give a donation towards the Hospital." From that moment, many small contributions began to pour in. The very same evening two *lire* were given by a blind young man. Then other little offerings of one, two and five *lire*. Lists of subscribers came in, even from some Military Hospitals, sums of thirty or forty *lire,* made of small contributions of twenty and thirty *centimes.*

Then came a large donation of one million, three hundred thousand *lire* from a friend living abroad.

The sum of the small contributions reached the total of eighty thousand *lire*; all in prewar currency, of course.

The three friends, who saw the terrible scourge of war spreading even through their country, became deeply concerned about the Hospital. On the good Padre's advice they succeeded by investing the money so wonderfully acquired in the purchase of a landed estate. The dreadful storm of war seemed, almost, to extinguish all activity for the Hospital. Too great, too enormous was the extent of suffering throughout the entire world.

In the little Capuchin Church of San Giovanni Rotondo Padre Pio was praying with all his heart and soul. He took upon himself the sufferings of all and unceasingly implored God to grant relief. Our Lady of Divine Grace, in her picture above the main altar, seemed to have her countenance veiled in an expression of intense grief. All the tears of weeping humanity steeped in suffering seemed to stream down from her sorrowful eyes.

One could see people of all races and nationalities flocking to the little church up on the bare mountainside. For everyone Father Pio had a look, a gesture or a word of pity and comfort. At long last the dreadful scourge came to an end, with its aftermath of mourning, misery, hatred and ferocity. The poor human race was completely lost, dismayed, at the mere sight of its own gaping wounds and miseries.

The "Home for the Relief of Suffering" began to live again, and finally, on October 5, 1946, it received its full official status and legal constitution.

Its statute, among other purposes, declares that the

principal object of the Hospital is "to receive any person who appeals for assistance and love in the name
of Christ." This thought sums up the universal concept of love and brotherhood in God for all men.
And it is precisely in the name of this principle that
the managing board of the "Home for the Relief of
Suffering" inspired by Padre Pio with firm and un-
daunted faith, threw themselves with energy and zeal
into the realization of this great work.

But there were only four million *lire* at hand, in
greatly devalued, postwar currency. (Only about one
eightieth of the prewar rate.) It represented a big sum,
considering the miserable condition of the country
after the war. But it was far too scanty for a work
of such vast proportions as the one planned.

Yet the board placed all their unshakeable faith in
Divine Providence. On April 16, work on the building site was begun. The enterprise was attacked practically with tooth and nail, amid incredible obstacles
and against all kinds of difficulties and misunderstand-
ings. Some who gazed upon the steep and rocky
mountain slope, taken by storm by a few miserable
men, shook their heads. They thought them crazy,
megalomaniacs, and mocked and jeered them. The
little Friary, in its simplicity, seemed to look on in
astonishment, but it seemed also to extend, with the
wing of the Third Order hall, a benevolent hand towards the "crazy" enterprise.

The mountain began to open to the sun its reddish
wounds and its rock, broken and shaken by the explosions. The whole countryside was filled with the
roar of the blastings. (Peaceful ones at last, after so
many explosions of war and destruction.) It trembled

with the hammerings of picks and drills. The work now beginning to take shape was immense. The workers, alas, were too few. But much greater still, nay infinite, is God's Providence.

The plan for the building of the Hospital also included the principle of not asking anything of anybody, but seeking only God's help.

In the autumn of 1947, Divine Providence paid an unexpected visit. The foundation of the main edifice had been started and was still at the level of the soil. Miss Barbara Ward, from London, came to San Giovanni Rotondo, urged by spiritual motives, but also, perhaps, to some extent, by her vivid practical sense as an outstanding writer for the "Economist." As the result of her visit and without any request being made, 250 million *lire* of U.N.R.R.A. funds were assigned to the Hospital.

It is quite superfluous to relate what an incredible mass of trouble, often causing painful anguish, had to be met in the endeavor to obtain the 250 million *lire*, which according to the original request to Washington, ought to have been 400. But it revealed in no small measure, the amount of patient toil and suffering the members of the Hospital Board had to undergo.

With the aid of this unexpected and unhoped for assistance, the work took a more lively pace. There were still countless difficulties in the paying by installment of the 250 million *lire*, which consequently caused frequent interruptions in the work, lasting up to five months. But finally, towards the end of 1949, the last beams of the edifice were put into place. At the end of 1950 the entire walled structure of the main building, with about one-half of the general installations, and a few special units (radiology, physiotherapy, operating rooms, surgical units, chapel, etc.) were completed.

The organization of the whole enterprise was perhaps one of the strangest conceivable, and is possibly unique in the world! The entire enterprise is situated at about 1800 feet above sea level, on a barren, rocky mountain slope. It is about 25 miles from the nearest industrial center of any importance, and a very modest one at that, namely, Foggia. Since the situation was far distant from any supply depots, it became imperative to establish the principle of the greatest possible autonomy. Hence all the necessary workshops were provided, a kiln was built for making lime from stone dug out of the mountain side; a machine for producing slag of different dimensions as well as sand had to be purchased. Complete workshops were installed for the manufacture of the cement slabs, of artificial stone and marble. These were used on a large scale for external facing and internal decoration. Then there were the shops for the making of tiles of all kinds and dimensions (thousands of square feet) for floors and wainscotting. Complete and up-to-date machinery took care of the iron and wood work. This was installed for the manufacture of light alloy metal window frames and doors, metal and wooden furniture with accessories. When the building was completed all this machinery was installed in the rehabilitation center for young patients recovering from infantile paralysis. A special section, adjoining the Hospital was built for these cases.

One big problem which confronted the management was the complete absence of water on the site. To remedy this great need, connections were made with a branch of the Apulia aqueduct. Furthermore very large cisterns were constructed to collect the rainwater from the terrace of the building. For the supply of electricity a power plant with a diesel engine was erected. The installation of all the general services (hot and cold water, baths, radio, telephone and signals) has been completed. In order to practice the greatest possible economy, all the work both of building and installation, was centered within the hospital. Outside firms only supplied that material which could not be made on the premises. In other words, the hospital acted as its own building contractor and equipment installer. The whole plan was possible thanks to the genius and the great technical ability, as well as the complete devotion of the designer and director of works, Signor Angelo Lupi. The great economy realized through such a plan became evident. It can be verified and evaluated by consulting the account books and by the statements of a large number of technical experts and foreign visitors. Among these were the group which came with Leon Dayton, E.C.A. administrator, to inspect the work on Dec. 8, 1949.

The main structure of the edifice was completed, having accommodations for 350 beds and room for about 60 nurses. This hospital is not only the most beautiful that I have ever seen around the world but it is the most unique in that the main ambulance entrance is up on the roof where the patients are brought in by helicopters.

For the complete functioning of the hospital,

however, it is indispensable that the locality, which offered no possibility of accommodation be equipped with suitable dwellings for the doctors who are to dedicate their activity exclusively to this great work, without applying themselves to any other kind of professional service. It was therefore absolutely necessary that they have decent, comfortable living quarters for themselves and their families. The same applied, of course, to all the personnel and those permanently employed in the hospital (mechanics, electricians, chauffeurs, doorkeepers, gardeners, etc.).

Furthermore it was necessary that, from the day the hospital opened its doors, a department for the reception of incurables be functioning, so as to avoid overcrowding of the hospital wards. These latter were meant to provide exclusively for acute cases, because it was foreseen that, at least in the beginning, many patients suffering from chronic diseases are sure to seek aid and shelter from the charitable assistance of the institution. For this department a large house was donated with about 35 acres of land adjoining. The building, however, was in need of complete renovation and adaptation for the purpose intended.

In the plan, under pressure, not of a disputable pride of performing works of charity, but of an absolute necessity, provision was made for an isolation unit for contagious diseases. Likewise a section for cases of infantile paralysis was urgent. In a word, it was a question of actually realizing a vast plan. The technical operation of the hospital center is outstanding for its best and most up-to-date equipment, for its scrupulous accuracy and completeness. The dominating idea is that one must devote the best and most modern resources that God has placed at the disposal of man to the service of charity.

The entire personnel were carefully selected, taking into account first of all the moral qualifications as well as technical abilities, without, of course, neglecting the spiritual formation of each person, in strict conformity with the essential spirit with which of necessity, the whole institution is permeated. The entire nursing staff, without exception, was obliged to present all those certificates and diplomas required by law in their profession.

The institution has a particular ideal in mind concerning its employees. The Board trusts that Divine Providence will assist in its realization. The greater part of the staff is expected to tender their services in the spirit of true Christian brotherly love, *without salary*. The purpose of this is to decrease the immense burden of expense. These members of the staff are given appropriate accommodation conveniences and board. Their compensation consists in the material and spiritual advantages which the institution generously places at their disposal.

Nevertheless, everyone requesting membership on the hospital staff must absolutely possess the best moral and physical fitness. The latter will be ascertained by a scrupulous medical examination.

Spirit and Plan for the Functioning of the Institution

The spirit of this great charitable work consists above all in Christian charity practiced in its truest and broadest sense. But before proceeding it is necessary to point out that it is quite untrue, as some writers have erroneously stated, that in the "Home for the Relief of Suffering" no sick person will have to pay anything at all. This would be neither just nor possible. It would not be just because those who can afford it are required to pay their fees. If they demand special accommodation they will have to pay extra.

Those who enjoy some special assistance from mutual and insurance societies (municipal, sickness loans, accident benefits, social aid and the like) are accepted and their bill paid by the society of which they are members.

Those who, on the other hand, neither possess means of their own nor belong to any of the above mentioned aid or insurance societies (and in each case exact and complete proof have to be presented by the applicant), in other words, those who are really poor will be accepted and treated gratuitously.

In the hospital there is no distinction of class or difference of treatment. If there is chicken for the rich there is chicken for the poor. The only difference that is recognized will be the requirements of health or special diets prescribed by the doctor. The rooms fitted with private bathrooms are placed at the disposal of any patients who may need them, regardless whether they be rich or poor. Christian charity obliges all to have the greatest respect and delicate regard for the poor in particular. Therefore they must never be submitted to a feeling of humiliation by being received and treated gratuitously in the hospital.

At the time of their dismissal, therefore, they are accompanied to the office administration where an employee, in charge of the "Gambino Fund" settles their bill with money expressly provided for by this fund. He hands them a regular receipt just as any other patients leaving the hospital.

All have attempted and also in the future will try their level best to give the Institution the most inviting, cordial and serene atmosphere of hospitality possible. Everyone on the staff is expected to do his work happily and joyfully, to show forth the true Christian spirit of which the human soul is capable.

SERVITE DOMINO IN LAETITIA! (Ps. 99:1).
"Serve ye the Lord with gladness!"

One asks, why build such a majestic medical center in such a town and high in the Gargano mountains alongside the monastery? Is it not clear that the annexed church, which is four hundred years old, is dedicated to Our Lady of Grace, and that it is a garden where various graces bloom in every season of the year with wondrous abundance and variety of conversions and miraculous cures? For that reason the hospital was placed under the guard of the Madonna delle Grazie, who is today more generous with miracles than ever.

Padre Pio was the man of piety and charity; true

son of St. Francis, he wished all for others and nothing for himself. Donations go entirely for the benefit of the poor who also contribute their widow's mite with their humble offerings. Many small bank notes were bathed with the tears of the poor and suffering creatures, and these offerings were the most precious and dearest to the heart of the servant of God. And for the little that I have done through my lectures for the benefit of his glorious project, Padre Pio personally sent his kind thanks and blessings to me and to all the members of my audiences around this nation for their spontaneous and generous contributions.

The architect and engineer of this very attractive up-to-the-minute building employed in its construction the best ideas of Italian and foreign modern hospital architecture. He instructed the workers personally every day and I made note of the fact that, at the request of Padre Pio, ex-convicts were given employment with his smiles and benediction. He planned a park in front of the hospital. It is filled with thousands of plants which are cultivated in appropriate nurseries. And above these, on the hilltop is erected a very high cross to remind one of the constant presence of Christ, while a statue of St. Francis with outstretched arms, as a symbol of charity, is on the facade of the building.

Does not all this clearly give testimony to the incredulous, to the blind, to the denier of the omnipotence, mercy, and infinite love of God for His creatures? There will still be someone who will not succeed in discovering in Padre Pio the awe-inspiring conduit wire of innumerable graces. Certainly it is not easy to comprehend the souls chosen by Divine

Providence to be His own instruments, but it is rather easy to fall into judgments which are superficial, too earthly and above all, erratic.

In truth, Padre Pio, son of the Cross, was a great servant of the Lord, with a greatness that did not overshadow his humility which was so conspicuous and profound as to give the impression that he longed to be unrecognized as an attraction for those motley throngs which came from the most distant provinces and nations to crowd the church for his morning Mass at 5 a.m.

In the footsteps of St. John Bosco, of Cottolengo and of Don Orione, he learned to realize the universal dream of justice, of brotherhood, and of open-hearted charity. Without the bombastic discourses of those friends of the people who, pressed to the test, do not know how to strip themselves of their egoism, with very visible and tangible deeds, Padre Pio put into practice that command of love for your neighbor which Christ alone has told to the world.

ADDENDUM

Padre Pio's Death and Funeral
by Father Armand Dasseville, O.F.M., Cap.
Autumn, 1968

"That night he went home. He went to God. At
4:00 a.m. (of the 23rd), as we were making our way
to church for Mass, we heard about his death in the
morning, which had occurred at two o'clock. We were
stunned. We didn't want to believe it. But the large
number of police and soldiers stationed all over the
piazza of the church and friary confirmed our fears.
We waited from 4:30 to 6:30 a.m. for the church doors
to open, but they didn't. We spent the time in prayer,
especially the Rosary. Later that day the doors of the
church were opened to the public. The body of Padre
Pio was in an open casket in full view of everyone.
It lay just outside the sanctuary, below the Communion railing. Busloads of people kept streaming into
church day and night till the funeral on Thursday,
September 26th. Thousands of pilgrims from all over
the world, rich and poor, crippled and healthy, Italians
and non-Italians, came to pay their last respects and
to unite in sorrow over the loss of their common
father, Padre Pio.

"September 26, 1968 was a beautiful, sunny day
in San Giovanni Rotondo...about 100,000 people
witnessed the burial of Padre Pio. By 3:00 p.m. the
piazza of the church and the one in front of the

hospital nearby were filled to capacity. Thousands of people, mostly Italians, but many from the four corners of the world, had come to pay their respects. The funeral procession was made up of representatives of other orders and the secular priesthood. Slowly the funeral cortege wended its way down the hill from the church to the town of San Giovanni Rotondo, about a mile and a half away. The open casket with the body of Padre Pio was resting in an open hearse in full view of everyone. The Most Reverend Father Clementine of Vlissingen, the Minister General of the Capuchin Order, presided and walked in front of the hearse. The friars who had lived with Padre Pio served as honorary guards around the casket. Both sides of the street leading to San Giovanni Rotondo were lined with thousands of people. From windows, porches, or even the rooftops, men and women had gathered to get a better, last glimpse of Padre Pio. Slowly and solemnly the procession made its way through the narrow streets of the little town, which Padre Pio had made famous by his presence for more than fifty years. Amazingly enough, there was no hysteria. Only a few cries or outbursts from some women of San Giovanni Rotondo, who had known and loved Padre Pio for so many years, broke the silence of the procession. I saw men and women, priests and religious, unashamedly and in public, wipe away tears. From windowsills people had hung either their best bedspread, or their best tablecloth, or sometimes even a Persian carpet, and in its center there hung a framed picture of Padre Pio, surrounded by black cloth. Everybody was wearing his Sunday best. Flowers were strewn from many windows, and at times even from a helicopter that followed the whole funeral march.

"The procession took more than three hours through the streets of San Giovanni Rotondo. Many a Rosary and Litany of Our Lady were begun and finished before the procession returned to the church piazza for the outdoor funeral Mass. Father General and twenty-six other friars concelebrated this Mass. A magnificent eulogy was preached. It was all so beautiful and all so fitting for the man who for fifty long years had born the wounds of Our Lord on his body. As I walked in the procession and observed the people, I was reminded of a similar procession I had often read about. In 1226 the body of St. Francis of Assisi was also carried in procession. He too was a stigmatist. He too was very much loved by his town's people. When he died near the little chapel of Our Lady of the Angels, the Portiuncula, the friars had to bring him for the funeral services to Assisi. It was also a distance of a mile and a half. I can well imagine the thousands of people that must have lined the streets of Assisi or hung from their windows to get a last glimpse of this saint. The similarity of the processions was amazing. Neither Assisi nor San Giovanni Rotondo was a town rich in material things, but both were honored with a stigmatist, a holy man of God."

If you have enjoyed this book, consider making your next selection from among the following . . .

Moments Divine—Before the Blessed Sacrament. *Reuter* 8.50
Miraculous Images of Our Lady. *Cruz* 20.00
Miraculous Images of Our Lord. *Cruz* 13.50
Raised from the Dead. *Fr. Hebert*................................ 16.50
Love and Service of God, Infinite Love. *Mother Louise Margaret* 12.50
Life and Work of Mother Louise Margaret. *Fr. O'Connell* 12.50
Autobiography of St. Margaret Mary.......................... 6.00
Thoughts and Sayings of St. Margaret Mary....................... 5.00
The Voice of the Saints. *Comp. by Francis Johnston* 7.00
The 12 Steps to Holiness and Salvation. *St. Alphonsus*................. 7.50
The Rosary and the Crisis of Faith. *Cirrincione & Nelson* 2.00
Sin and Its Consequences. *Cardinal Manning* 7.00
St. Francis of Paola. *Simi & Segreti* 8.00
Dialogue of St. Catherine of Siena. *Transl. Algar Thorold* 10.00
Catholic Answer to Jehovah's Witnesses. *D'Angelo* 12.00
Twelve Promises of the Sacred Heart. (100 cards).................... 5.00
Life of St. Aloysius Gonzaga. *Fr. Meschler* 12.00
The Love of Mary. *D. Roberto*................................. 8.00
Begone Satan. *Fr. Vogl*....................................... 3.00
The Prophets and Our Times. *Fr. R. G. Culleton*.................... 13.50
St. Therese, The Little Flower. *John Beevers* 6.00
St. Joseph of Copertino. *Fr. Angelo Pastrovicchi*.................... 6.00
Mary, The Second Eve. *Cardinal Newman*........................ 3.00
Devotion to Infant Jesus of Prague. *Booklet*....................... .75
Reign of Christ the King in Public & Private Life. *Davies* 1.25
The Wonder of Guadalupe. *Francis Johnston*...................... 7.50
Apologetics. *Msgr. Paul Glenn*................................ 10.00
Baltimore Catechism No. 1..................................... 3.50
Baltimore Catechism No. 2..................................... 4.50
Baltimore Catechism No. 3..................................... 8.00
An Explanation of the Baltimore Catechism. *Fr. Kinkead*.............. 16.50
Bethlehem. *Fr. Faber*.. 18.00
Bible History. *Schuster*...................................... 13.50
Blessed Eucharist. *Fr. Mueller* 9.00
Catholic Catechism. *Fr. Faerber*................................ 7.00
The Devil. *Fr. Delaporte*...................................... 6.00
Dogmatic Theology for the Laity. *Fr. Premm*...................... 20.00
Evidence of Satan in the Modern World. *Cristiani* 10.00
Fifteen Promises of Mary. (100 cards)............................ 5.00
Life of Anne Catherine Emmerich. 2 vols. *Schmoeger* 37.50
Life of the Blessed Virgin Mary. *Emmerich* 16.50
Manual of Practical Devotion to St. Joseph. *Patrignani* 15.00
Prayer to St. Michael. (100 leaflets) 5.00
Prayerbook of Favorite Litanies. *Fr. Hebert* 10.00
Preparation for Death. (Abridged). *St. Alphonsus*................... 8.00
Purgatory Explained. *Schouppe* 13.50
Purgatory Explained. (pocket, unabr.). *Schouppe* 9.00
Fundamentals of Catholic Dogma. *Ludwig Ott*..................... 21.00
Spiritual Conferences. *Faber* 15.00
Trustful Surrender to Divine Providence. *Bl. Claude* 5.00
Wife, Mother and Mystic. *Bessieres*............................. 8.00
The Agony of Jesus. *Padre Pio*................................. 2.00

Prices subject to change.

Sermons of the Curé of Ars. *Vianney* 12.50
St. Antony of the Desert. *St. Athanasius* 5.00
Is It a Saint's Name? *Fr. William Dunne* 2.50
St. Pius V—His Life, Times, Miracles. *Anderson* 5.00
Who Is Therese Neumann? *Fr. Charles Carty.* 2.00
Martyrs of the Coliseum. *Fr. O'Reilly.* 18.50
Way of the Cross. *St. Alphonsus Liguori* 1.00
Way of the Cross. *Franciscan version* 1.00
How Christ Said the First Mass. *Fr. Meagher* 18.50
Too Busy for God? Think Again! *D'Angelo* 5.00
St. Bernadette Soubirous. *Trochu* 18.50
Passion and Death of Jesus Christ. *Liguori.* 10.00
Treatise on the Love of God. 1 Vol. *St. Francis de Sales* 24.00
Confession Quizzes. *Radio Replies Press* 1.50
St. Philip Neri. *Fr. V. J. Matthews.* 5.50
St. Louise de Marillac. *Sr. Vincent Regnault* 6.00
The Old World and America. *Rev. Philip Furlong* 18.00
Prophecy for Today. *Edward Connor* 5.50
The Book of Infinite Love. *Mother de la Touche* 5.00
Chats with Converts. *Fr. M. D. Forrest.* 10.00
The Church Teaches. *Church Documents* 16.50
Conversation with Christ. *Peter T. Rohrbach* 10.00
Purgatory and Heaven. *J. P. Arendzen.* 5.00
Liberalism Is a Sin. *Sarda y Salvany* 7.50
Spiritual Legacy of Sr. Mary of the Trinity. *van den Broek* 10.00
The Creator and the Creature. *Fr. Frederick Faber* 16.50
Radio Replies. 3 Vols. *Frs. Rumble and Carty* 42.00
Convert's Catechism of Catholic Doctrine. *Fr. Geiermann* 3.00
Incarnation, Birth, Infancy of Jesus Christ. *St. Alphonsus* 10.00
Light and Peace. *Fr. R. P. Quadrupani* 7.00
Dogmatic Canons & Decrees of Trent, Vat. I. *Documents.* 9.50
The Evolution Hoax Exposed. *A. N. Field* 7.50
The Primitive Church. *Fr. D. I. Lanslots.* 10.00
The Priest, the Man of God. *St. Joseph Cafasso* 13.50
Blessed Sacrament. *Fr. Frederick Faber* 18.50
Christ Denied. *Fr. Paul Wickens* 2.50
New Regulations on Indulgences. *Fr. Winfrid Herbst* 2.50
A Tour of the Summa. *Msgr. Paul Glenn* 18.00
Spiritual Conferences. *Fr. Frederick Faber* 15.00
Latin Grammar. *Scanlon and Scanlon* 16.50
A Brief Life of Christ. *Fr. Rumble* 2.00
Marriage Quizzes. *Radio Replies Press* 1.50
True Church Quizzes. *Radio Replies Press.* 1.50
The Secret of the Rosary. *St. Louis De Montfort.* 5.00
Mary, Mother of the Church. *Church Documents* 4.00
The Sacred Heart and the Priesthood. *de la Touche* 9.00
Revelations of St. Bridget. *St. Bridget of Sweden* 3.00
Magnificent Prayers. *St. Bridget of Sweden* 2.00
The Happiness of Heaven. *Fr. J. Boudreau.* 8.00
St. Catherine Labouré of the Miraculous Medal. *Dirvin* 13.50
The Glories of Mary. *St. Alphonsus Liguori* 16.50
The Three Ways of the Spiritual Life. *Garrigou-Lagrange, O.P.* 6.00

Prices subject to change.

Freemasonry: Mankind's Hidden Enemy. *Bro. C. Madden* 5.00
Fourteen Holy Helpers. *Hammer* 5.00
All About the Angels. *Fr. Paul O'Sullivan* 6.00
AA-1025: Memoirs of an Anti-Apostle. *Marie Carré.* 6.00
All for Jesus. *Fr. Frederick Faber.* 15.00
Growth in Holiness. *Fr. Frederick Faber.* 16.50
Behind the Lodge Door. *Paul Fisher.* 18.00
Chief Truths of the Faith. (Book I). *Fr. John Laux* 10.00
Mass and the Sacraments. (Book II). *Fr. John Laux* 10.00
Catholic Morality. (Book III). *Fr. John Laux.* 10.00
Catholic Apologetics. (Book IV). *Fr. John Laux* 10.00
Introduction to the Bible. *Fr. John Laux* 16.50
Church History. *Fr. John Laux* 24.00
Devotion for the Dying. *Mother Mary Potter* 9.00
Devotion to the Sacred Heart. *Fr. Jean Croiset* 15.00
An Easy Way to Become a Saint. *Fr. Paul O'Sullivan* 5.00
The Golden Arrow. *Sr. Mary of St. Peter.* 12.50
The Holy Man of Tours. *Dorothy Scallan.* 10.00
Hell—Plus How to Avoid Hell. *Fr. Schouppe/Nelson* 10.00
History of Protestant Ref. in England & Ireland. *Cobbett.* 18.00
Holy Will of God. *Fr. Leo Pyzalski.* 6.00
How Christ Changed the World. *Msgr. Luigi Civardi* 8.00
How to Be Happy, How to Be Holy. *Fr. Paul O'Sullivan* 8.00
Imitation of Christ. *Thomas à Kempis. (Challoner transl.)* 10.00
Life & Message of Sr. Mary of the Trinity. *Rev. Dubois* 10.00
Life Everlasting. *Fr. Garrigou-Lagrange, O.P.* 13.50
Life of Mary as Seen by the Mystics. *Compiled by Raphael Brown* 12.50
Life of St. Dominic. *Mother Augusta Drane.* 12.00
Life of St. Francis of Assisi. *St. Bonaventure* 10.00
Life of St. Ignatius Loyola. *Fr. Genelli.* 16.50
Life of St. Margaret Mary Alacoque. *Rt. Rev. Emile Bougaud* 13.50
Mexican Martyrdom. *Fr. Wilfrid Parsons* 10.00
Children of Fatima. *Windeatt.* (Age 10 & up). 8.00
Cure of Ars. *Windeatt.* (Age 10 & up) 12.00
The Little Flower. *Windeatt.* (Age 10 & up) 8.00
Patron of First Communicants. (Bl. Imelda). *Windeatt.* (Age 10 & up) 6.00
Miraculous Medal. *Windeatt.* (Age 10 & up) 7.00
St. Louis De Montfort. *Windeatt.* (Age 10 & up) 12.00
St. Thomas Aquinas. *Windeatt.* (Age 10 & up). 6.00
St. Catherine of Siena. *Windeatt.* (Age 10 & up) 5.00
St. Rose of Lima. *Windeatt.* (Age 10 & up) 8.00
St. Hyacinth of Poland. *Windeatt.* (Age 10 & up). 11.00
St. Martin de Porres. *Windeatt.* (Age 10 & up). 7.00
Pauline Jaricot. *Windeatt.* (Age 10 & up) 13.00
Douay-Rheims New Testament. *Paperbound* 15.00
Prayers and Heavenly Promises. *Compiled by Joan Carroll Cruz.* 5.00
Preparation for Death. (Unabr., pocket). *St. Alphonsus* 10.00
Rebuilding a Lost Faith. *John Stoddard* 15.00
The Spiritual Combat. *Dom Lorenzo Scupoli* 9.00
Retreat Companion for Priests. *Fr. Francis Havey* 7.50
Spiritual Doctrine of St. Cath. of Genoa. *Marabotto/St. Catherine* 12.50
The Soul of the Apostolate. *Dom Chautard* 10.00

Prices subject to change.

At your Bookdealer or direct from the Publisher.
Call Toll-Free 1-800-437-5876.

Prices subject to change.

ABOUT THE AUTHOR

For twenty-four years Father Carty worked with Father Leslie Rumble of Sydney, Australia in the apostolate of the radio and press. Radio Replies Press of St. Paul, Minnesota was founded by these two courageous priests, and hundreds of thousands of Catholic books and pamphlets were distributed by them through this outlet. To gather information for the present account, Father Carty went to San Giovanni Rotondo to visit Padre Pio, living right in the Monastery, where he wrote much of the book. Upon publication, Father Carty toured the United States, giving sermons in Catholic parishes on the subject of Padre Pio, promoting knowledge of this saintly stigmatist. On May 22, 1964, Father Charles Mortimer Carty died in Erie, Pennsylvania, while on such a tour.